THE END OF PRISONS

VIBS

Volume 261

a volume in
Social Philosophy
SP
Edited by Andrew Fitz-Gibbon

THE END OF PRISONS

Reflections from the Decarceration Movement

Edited by
Mechthild E. Nagel and Anthony J. Nocella II

Rodopi

Amsterdam - New York, NY 2013

Cover photo: Metropolitan Correctional Center, Chicago (Dreamstime)

Cover Design: Studio Pollmann

The paper on which this book is printed meets the requirements of "ISO 9706:1994, Information and documentation - Paper for documents - Requirements for permanence".

ISBN: 978-90-420-3656-7
E-Book ISBN: 978-94-012-0923-6

Printed in the Netherlands

Social Philosophy
(SP)

Andrew Fitz-Gibbon
Editor

Other Titles in SP

Evgenia Cherkasova. *Dostoevsky and Kant: Dialogues on Ethics.* 2009. VIBS 206

Craig Hanson. *Thinking about Addiction: Hyperbolic Discounting and Responsible Agency.* 2009. VIBS 209

Sanya Osha. *Postethnophilosophy.* 2011. VIBS 227

This book is dedicated to all those that have been murdered, exploited, and extinguished in the name of greed, normalcy, and domination. This book is dedicated to all who dare to imagine a world free from systems of control and fear and who persevere in compassionate ways.

CONTENTS

EDITORIAL FOREWORD

In 1998, the philosophy department at the State University of New York College at Cortland created an innovative program focused on social philosophy. The key components of the program are social and political philosophy, ethics, and applied philosophy. In 2007, following the successful implementation of the program, the department formed the *Center for Ethics, Peace and Social Justice* to extend the outreach of the program through publications, conferences, and a summer ethics institute for faculty, all centered on practice and activism. As part of that outreach, we are delighted to co-sponsor the VIBS special series in Social Philosophy.

The way we view prisons has undergone constant change. Though popularly assumed that prisons have always been, few realize that the modern prison grew out of the workhouse movement in the early nineteenth century. Jails were holding places before punishment was enacted. Prisons have been considered as the place of penitence and reform (hence "penitentiaries" from a religious root), or punishment and correction. The current understanding of the prison is a conglomeration of all these ideas.

The issues surrounding prisons are many and complex: from the moderate Howard League for Penal Reform in the United Kingdom, whose aims are "less crime, safer communities and fewer people in prison," and The Pennsylvania Prison Society that aims to provide a more humane and restorative correctional system, to more radical calls for total prison abolition. If the aim of prisons is to prevent further harm to society, then neuroscience may yet trump all reformatory movements if it can lead us to discover which parts of the human brain may need modification through drugs or surgery to decrease criminal activities. But such solutions are fraught with moral ambiguity.

Important questions this volume asks include: Why the United States has the highest rate of incarceration of all the developed nations? Is the present prison system effective in rehabilitating inmates? What ought to be our perspective on punishment, retribution, restitution and rehabilitation? Why is a disproportionate number of the poor and people of color in prison?

The End of Prisons moves beyond abolition of literal prisons to call for the end of all forms of incarceration, including non-human animals and nature. As such, it is a controversial book. Few will agree with everything herein, but a key element of a free society is free discourse and exchange of ideas.

Thanks are due to Provost Mark Prus and Amy Henderson-Harr of the Research and Sponsored Programs Office, SUNY Cortland for support and funding for the Social Philosophy series. Thanks, too, to EDB, copyeditor of choice with whom I have worked happily on many projects.

Andrew Fitz-Gibbon, VIBS Social Philosophy Special Series Editor, Associate Professor, Chair of Philosophy, and Director, Center for Ethics, Peace and Social Justice, State University of New York College at Cortland.

ACKNOWLEDGMENTS

An earlier version of the section 7 of Chapter Eleven, "Patriarchal Ideologies and Women's Domestication" was published in *Peace Review: A Journal of Social Justice,* July–September, 2011. We acknowledge gratefully that Cathy Marston granted us permission for using part of her poem "Justice is a Woman" (2012).

We would like to thank first and for most our friend and colleague Andrew Fitz-Gibbon who believed in this project and agreed to publish it in his series on Social Philosophy in Rodopi's Value Inquiry Book Series (VIBS). We would also like to thank everyone at Rodopi for their editing assistance in publicizing the volume. This book would not be possible if not for all the truly dedicated contributors—David Gabbard, Amy Fitzgerald, Jenna McDavid, Ernesto Aguilar, Melissa Chiprin, Ute Ritz-Deutch, Liat Ben-Moshe, Dennis J. Stevens, Amit Taneja, and Tiyo Attallah Salah-El. Thanks to Lois Ahrens, coordinator of the Real Cost of Prisons Project, who assisted us greatly by transcribing, editing, and providing research for Tiyo Salah-El's chapter. We greatly appreciate the endorsements from Kim Socha and Peter McLaren. We would also like to thank our many centers, institutes and programs with which we are involved. These include the Center for Gender and Intercultural Studies and Center for Ethics, Peace, and Social Justice at SUNY Cortland, Center for Excellence in Urban Teaching at Hamline University's School of Education, SUNY Cortland's Philosophy Department, Social and Cultural Studies Department, Fulda University of Applied Sciences, Institute for Critical Animal Studies, Save the Kids, American Friends Service Committees, Central New York Peace Studies Consortium, Peace Studies Journal, and the Journal for Critical Urban Education. We would also like to thank our families and friends.

Introduction

IMPRISONING THE NINETY-NINE PERCENT

Mechthild Nagel and Anthony J. Nocella II

You were put here to protect us
But who protects us from you?
Or should I say, who are you protecting?
The rich? The poor? Who?
- Boogie Down Productions, "Who Protects Us from You"

In September 2011, a grassroots movement, Occupy Wall Street, began in New York and quickly spread in the United States and around the world. It was a protest against the "one percent elites." As the movement grew, activists were beaten by night sticks, sprayed with pepper spray, clouded by tear gas, arrested and jailed by police who seem to be—as the protesters' posters noted cleverly—protecting corporate interests rather than people of the United States or even the government. In only a few weeks, the movement became international and there were more than a thousand arrests of protestors and dozens of arrests of journalists leading to a sizeable drop in the global index of the government's protection of freedom of the press (Mirkinson, 2011). One sarcastic slogan by the movement "The Government—Protecting and Serving the Shit Out of You," informs how law enforcement, who are actually part of the ninety-nine percent, has repeatedly assaulted nonviolent protesters.

A perfect example of these violent assaults took place at University of California Davis on 18 November 2011. A group of university students protested on a campus sidewalk by peacefully sitting down with their arms attached. They were surrounded by fellow students, staff, faculty, and media to bear witness to the oncoming police force in riot gear that was called onto campus by UC Davis Chancellor Linda Katehi. What was intended to be a peaceful day became one of the most blatant violent actions against the Occupy Wall Street movement when Lt. John Pike walked casually in front of the sitting protesters and sprayed them directly in the face with pepper spray.

This event attracted worldwide attention, and Pike was shamed and ridiculed by people writing on Facebook, bloggers, and, most powerfully, by artists who have airbrushed the image of him pepper spraying protesters into famous photographs, paintings, and other iconic media images. The images show him pepper spraying a starving child in a desert, Thumper from the Disney's *Bambi*, Spiderman, George Washington in Emanuel Gottlieb Leutze's

Washington Crossing the Delaware, a baby seal, Snoopy, Gandhi, the Smurfs, and ponies from *My Little Pony*. These artistic expressions express that anyone, even the most nonviolent and innocent among us, can become a victim of aggressive state repression.

The incident at UC Davis is not isolated, as violent force was recently used at Seattle's Occupy Wall Street when police pepper sprayed 84-year old Dorli Rainey. Her picture "went viral" on the internet, and she was interviewed by numerous newspapers and media sources including Democracy Now! and Keith Olbermann. Seattle police spokesman Jeff Kapel, evidently ignorant of how painful pepper spray can be, noted that pepper spray "is not age specific. No more dangerous to someone who is ten or someone who is 80 . . . These protesters are well organized, they're using homemade remedies to counter pepper spray" (CBS NEWS, 2011). However, spraying vulnerable people such as children, the sick, and the elderly is not without risks (Pinney, 2007). Someone with visual disabilities could also be extremely harmed. Kapel justifies the violent actions by arguing that the protests are "well organized" to make them appear more threatening. He goes on to say that the protesters have "homemade remedies," suggesting that spraying them is justifiable because they can easily "counter" the pain. With this same logic, can a police officer shoot protesters if they have a first aid kit?

Kapel states, "Pepper spray was deployed only against subjects who were either refusing a lawful order to disperse or engaging in assaultive behavior toward officers." This, of course, was not true in the case of Rainey, a retired school teacher, who complied with officers' orders.

A another example of police brutality toward the protesters occurred in Seattle. Nineteen-year-old Jennifer Fox was three months pregnant when she attended an Occupy Wall Street protest in Seattle. She was pepper-sprayed by police and struck twice in the stomach. Five days later, she suffered a miscarriage. News reports suggest that she told police that she was pregnant and that she was trying to leave the protest when police kicked her in the stomach.

Arguably, this now world-wide movement against corporate elites would not have won much traction if it weren't for civilian videotaped interactions between the police and unarmed protesters as described above. The police (and military's) impunity to brutalize peaceful persons shows us an aspect of state violence that has long been the raison d'etre of the establishment of the policing apparatus. It buttresses slave owners and corporate stakeholders as well as the authoritarian government of a nation-state which seeks to protect itself from the democratic will of the people (Linebaugh and Rediker, 2001; Linebaugh, 2006). Moreover, with the history of illegal political repression such as the assassination of political leaders, infiltration of organizations, framing activists with drugs, and illegal wiretapping of phones by law enforcement within the United States and aboard, it is no wonder that activists fight back using video cameras, social networks, and illegal undercover strategies to gather information that they then leak to the media and public (cf. Churchill and Wall, 2001a; 2001b).

Occupy Wall Street exposes and opposes the unjust gap between the very rich (dubbed the one percent) and the poor and middle class (the 99 percent). Anarchism, which is the driving force in this movement, argues that this movement is indicative of a class war. Having learned from the mistakes of earlier anarcho-globalization protests such as the Battle in Seattle 1999, this encampment strategy won over a sizeable segment of the non-politicized population, who sent cookies, books, and pizzas to the rapidly growing occupiers of Liberty Plaza, in New York City.

One major lesson Occupy movement activists have learned from prior mass demonstrations is how to handle police infiltration and police acting as activists and destroying property to stigmatize activists (Fernandez 2008). The middle class has understood some basic ideas of the capitalist logic of profit and exploitation since the government sponsored bail-outs of big banks. It remains to be seen if they will be drawn to anarchist or libertarian views of the state.

Much like the intents and purposes of Occupy Wall Street, this volume is about the wide-scale imprisonment the poor; about those in the LGBTQ community; about people of color; women; youth; and people with disabilities; about native Americans; about criminalized sexual offenders; and non-United States citizens; and about attitudes and actions regarding non-human animals and plants. It challenges domination and oppression by the one percent over the ninety-nine percent.

The original working title for this volume was *Prison Abolition*. After discussion among the contributors however, we changed the title to *The End of Prisons*. First, we wish to raise discussions about the telos of prisons—what purpose do they have? Second, prison abolition is strongly related to a particular movement to end the prison industrial complex. Following Michel Foucault (1977), we argue that prisons are also institutions such as schools, nursing homes, jails, daycare centers, parks, zoos, reservations, and marriage, to name a few.

Prisons are all around us and constructed by those in dominant oppressive authoritarian positions. There are many types of prisons—religious prisons, social prisons, political prisons, economic prisons, educational prisons, and, of course, criminal prisons. Individuals leave one prison only to enter another. From daycare to school to a nursing home, we are a nation of institutionalized prisons. Criminal prisons in the United States are not officially referred to as such, but rather as correctional facilities. A prison, as we define it in this volume, is an institution or system that oppresses and does not allow freedom for a particular group. Within this definition, we include the imprisonment of non-human animals and plants, which are too often overlooked.

Michel Foucault (1977) famously said, "Is it surprising that prisons resemble factories, schools, barracks, hospitals, which all resemble prisons?" (p. 228). We believe that this volume is one of the first to extend Foucault's logic, by making a connection between coercive institutions and all systems of domination as forms of prisons. We argue that the concept of the prison is far reaching, always changing and adapting to the times and the socio-political environment. We expand the concept of prison from concrete walls, barbed wire, gates, and fences to many of the institutions and systems throughout society such as schools, mental hospitals, reservations for indigenous Americans, zoos for non-human animals, and national parks and urban cultivated green spaces for the ecological community. United States imperialism, which promotes global domination and capitalism, not only imprisons convicted criminals, but its people, land, non-human animals, those that surround it (non-United States citizens) and those trapped within it (American Indians and immigrants).

When United States imperialism fails to control people through imprisonment, it has acted out its fascist agenda. Imperialism has enacted mass violence which includes genocide and slavery of people of color and has replaced viable ecosystems with shopping malls and factory farms (Best and Nocella, 2006). American Indians, Latinos, African-Americans, women, non-human animals, nature, and many others have fought back through self defense in-order to avoid being assassinated, becoming extinct as a species or group of humans, enslaved, or raped. Too often those of privilege and dominant positions, such as able-bodied heterosexual formally educated white Christian males, frown on these acts of self defense and identify them as violence and terrorism. Moreover, those in positions of privilege who work at or benefit from imperialist based institutions are often willfully ignorant of the mass violence directed towards oppressed people. Instead of resisting in solidarity with the oppressed, or calling out the corruption, they demand these oppressed people to act peacefully, while they sit on the sidelines. Such was the case when white citizens observed dogs biting African Americans in Alabama during the 1960s and Indians' heads being bashed in India by British law enforcement during Indian's independence movement.

Those in privileged and dominant positions often claim to be allies, but end up dictating what strategies and tactics the oppressed movement adopts. They claim to strive for peace and for everyone to look to make a new future before engaging in social justice and addressing the injustices of the past.

This volume speaks to the need for activists to engage in social justice before we can be in a place and space of peace. Without addressing and ending racism, sexism, homophobia, ageism, elitism, stateism, ableism, classism, and speciesism, we will never have peace. Moreover, those who are privileged and dominant are not in a struggle as those who are oppressed. Thus, those who are privileged and dominant must be willing to risk resistance and fight more for social justice than the oppressed, because they, not the oppressed, are part of the problem (Nocella, 2012). This volume argues that instead, those who are privileged and dominant should follow the lead of, and work *with*, instead of *for*, those who are oppressed.

While the title of the volume has changed, it is still dedicated to the abolition of all forms of prisons and has three significant purposes: (1) to redefine the concept of the carceral in a way that is rooted in lived experience within conditions of institutionalization, the mass industrial complex, and various systems of domination; (2) to examine prisons from an interdisciplinary academic-activist approach; (3) to stress that prisons of *all* kinds must end, including reservations that oppress native peoples, zoos that confine non-human animals, and parks that manicure, cultivate and, in essence, control nature. The abolition of prisons will be difficult and challenging. It might include self defense against acts of murder, torture, and rape. Those who are privileged and dominant might not adopt these tactics of self defense because no one is attacking them, but they cannot dictate the struggle or they will perpetuate the oppression.

All told, abolition encompasses many aspects of society. Rather than being satisfied with mere reform of systems of oppression, we argue for the complete eradication of systems that have not well served humanity and other sentient and non-sentient beings that have been subjected to human forms of domination. In other words, to be a true prison abolitionist, one must understand the complexities of how society has manipulated and dominated people, non-human animals, and plants to be exploited in different systems and institutions. While some in prisons find mental escapes, the vast majority of prisoners are unable to remove themselves from what has been called "total institutions," from walls, bars, and barbed wire prisons, which establish the "3 Bs" of the carceral regime—barriers, borders, and boundaries. We extend this logic of incarceration to those who live under systems of oppression such as the violence of poverty, racism, sexism, internalized colonialism, ableism, trans- and homophobia.

This volume is dedicated to abolishing all systems and institutions that act like prisons and dominate and oppress groups of people. Each chapter in this volume is dedicated to an examination of different forms of marginalization. Each investigates the unique prisons in which different oppressed groups exist. While many of these prisons are physical, such as an institution or industry, others are laws, theories, and philosophies such as marriage, social stigmatization, and domestication.

All of the contributions in this text tackle social, symbolic, or real imprisonment in the country that prides itself to be the freest of the so-called free world. Angela Y. Davis notes that whenever George W. Bush said the word "free," for example, "bringing freedom to Iraq and Afghanistan," his message was actually brought into relief when one substituted freedom for "capitalism" (2007). As this nation-state continues to unwelcome some immigrants from near and distant shores, it guarantees those with capital can freely roam the world over. Capitalism is unfettered by local, state, federal, and tribal laws, yet people are not free to move across borders of nation-states or across railroad tracks to the wrong side of town. For a number of authors, people marked as deviant or "Other," non-human animals, or nature, Michel Foucault's analysis about prisons and the asylum helps to frame their critique of imprisonment.

Anthony Nocella's article takes on the government's concerted repression of political dissent in a post-9/11 world. Animal rights activists and environmentalists have faced some of the harshest forms of punishment and have been deemed "terrorists" for disturbing exploitative factory farming or nonhuman animal laboratory work (most recently with the repressive 2006 Animal Enterprise Terrorism Act (AETA)). Others who have been singled out are Muslims in an Islamophobic United States, where today dozens of municipalities have enacted anti-Shar'ia laws, as a precautionary device, lest the local Muslim population decides to take the law into their own hands.

Nocella argues that that the much celebrated first amendment "freedom of expression" is a myth, oddly surviving throughout the mainstream's tales of American history. The myth forgets conveniently that this nation-state is built on the foundations of genocide and slavery. Drawing on Brian Glick's analysis of tactics of repression, he examines stigmatization of dissent not as criminalization, but post 9/11 as terrorization. Terrorization begins with surveilling and stigmatizing a group of dissenters that challenge authority. In the climate of the "war on terror" those so stigmatized are perceived as terrorists. He ends with a discussion of five responses to political repression: canceling, concluding, coping, confronting, and combating.

Foucault's abolitionist critique of imprisonment is relevant to David Gabbard's realization of the parallels between the regime of compulsory education and the carceral. He chronicles a personal story of a distraught father's journey through his (white) son's trials and tribulations with the punitive side of private Catholic schooling. While cognizant of the prestige and privileges that such schooling entails in the United States, he notes that his son drew attention for "misbehaving," enjoying rapping, baggy pants, and black Hip Hop artists, as well as engaging with black history and being politically active—in short becoming a "race traitor."

Gabbard's critical analysis draws on his own experience with schooling—as a young boy, he had already come to perceive that schools resemble prisons. But it wasn't until his own teenage son's run-in with school authorities for "trafficking" marijuana and being charged with a felony that he realized the implications of the much touted "school-to-prison pipeline." He notes that since the differences between compulsory schooling and jailhouses are only differences in degree, he prefers to recharacterize the pipeline as school-as-prisons. As long as we simply tinker with education reform but do not break out of the model of forcing every child into twelve or thirteen years of schooling, we will not have really freed children for a life-long exploration of truly meaningful education.

Ernesto Aguilar and Melissa Chiprin further elucidate the point Nocella makes, that some people are surveilled and stigmatized. The criminal justice system, or, as some say, the criminal injustice system, has a longstanding interest in policing a certain segment of the population on the basis of an "unrelenting paranoia related to blackness." With the end of chattel slavery, the planter class quickly resorted to other ways to target freed men and women:

the Thirteenth Amendment, which codifies slavery despite that it was meant to set them free, Black Codes, Jim Crow laws.

Various state and federal policies to date have ensured that the Civil Rights Movement would not achieve its dream of complete equality. Ironically, more black men are incarcerated today than were chattel slaves before 1865, a condition that Michelle Alexander (2010) has tellingly labeled "the new Jim Crow."

Aguilar and Chiprin also note the acute surveillance of other people of color and their subsequent over-incarceration. However, capitalist apologists are quick to exploit racial tensions between different groups of people of color. The newly energized immigration movement driven by Latinos is threatened to be hijacked by those who all of the sudden come to the rescue of the forgotten underemployed black person.

Immigration politics in the twenty-first century mark a challenge for a nation-state that prides itself to have built itself (*ex nihilo*) from immigrant labor. Ute Ritz-Deutch outlines the state's legal framework of policing North America's borders in an era of a war on terror. Coming to similar conclusions about the current legal climate as Nocella, Aguilar and Chiprin, she reasons, "if the Bill of Rights and United States Constitution no longer matter and if the principles upon which the country were founded can be suspended indefinitely and revoked without a semblance of public debate, then it could be argued that the United States is no longer a viable democracy with checks and balances." Moreover, the United States has criticized other nations for using military tribunals to prosecute civilians on the grounds that it severely curtails defendants' rights. Yet it has done exactly that with impunity, as in the case of the prisoners at Guantánamo Bay, Cuba. Furthermore, while torture is inexcusable in a viable democracy, the United States has instituted re-labeled torture as "enhanced interrogation techniques" and engaged in it to extract information from suspected terrorists. On the mainland, programs such as "Secure Communities" enhance federal surveillance in every locale of those who are undocumented, all the in the name of fighting the war on terror.

Ritz-Deutch also chronicles the history of anti-immigrant legislation and notes the disparate impact for women who are battered and denied effective protection from their abusers. The egregious human rights violation committed by United States' state actors against immigrants has severe ramification the world over.

Ben Carnes provides an important historical corrective from an indigenous American perspective on immigration discourse. Who, in fact, is an immigrant? He writes: "The imperialistic belief in Manifest Destiny justified the actions of immigrants, who later renamed themselves pioneers/settlers, in the dominance and subjugation of the native people of their lands and resources, including their culture and spirituality." The "Marshall Trilogy" rulings set into motion the dispossession of Indigenous peoples and a paternalism that deemed the dispossessed as mere guardians overseen by his ward—in short, those condemned to be driven into "reservations" are a captive population thanks to the legal philosophy of the federal government.

Unquestionably, reservations were meant to function as prisons. Another strategy of containment and, arguably, cultural genocide, was the boarding school experiment, where thousands of native children were forcibly sent and kept in prison-like deplorable environment. Barnes notes that during a 1993 congressional committee hearing on the religious rights of native prisoners, he testified about the negative effects of assimilation on a native's identity and self-worth: "We were never Americans and this land was never theirs, that is a myth used to confiscate our natural identity and the reality of our circumstances; we have always been sovereign peoples of this land."

Where Barnes highlights the harms of institutionalization of native peoples in order to "kill the Indian," Liat Ben-Moshe reviews the history of institutionalizing people with psychiatric and developmental disabilities in the United States. She characterizes mental hospitals as repressive institutions. She argues that merely closing these institutions along with prisons is insufficient; much more needs to be done to ensure safe community-living for all people with disabilities.

Taking her cue from W. E. B. DuBois's call for abolition democracy, Ben-Moshe argues that deinstitutionalization means to create new democratic institutions. Furthermore, following anti-psychiatry activist Bonnie Burstow and others, the movement of anti-psychiatry can greatly benefit from the penal abolitionist discussions of negative and positive reforms and whether any of them lead to the road of a meaningful "decarceration" of criminalized people. What should be done about "severe" cases? Drawing on Crip theory, Ben-Moshe notes that rereading "severe" as "defiant" helps to reposition center versus margins. Radical inclusionists believe that belonging is a human right for all, and that no individuals should be singled out to be pushed into repressive institutions.

Dennis J. Stevens picks up where Ben-Moshe's analysis of the merits of abolitionism leaves off, namely, what to do with those who are considered dangerous, or in Stevens' words, "the worst of the worst." Among today's "mad denizens" (sent off on a ship of fools in pre-modern times) are sexual violators, regardless of their age. Incredibly, sex offenses range from the banal—urinating in public—to the serious such as rape. Sexual offenses are considered scandalous and prosecutions against offenders feed a media frenzy unlike any other violent crime. They also raise the prosecutor's likelihood of reelection. Given the politicization of this office, many innocent are prosecuted, incarcerated, and even executed.

As Angela Y. Davis (1981) points out in "The Myth of the Black Rapist," when the courts sanctioned execution for rape (where the victim was not murdered), black men were disproportionately condemned to die for the rape of white women. Stevens' research bears out that the recidivism rates for sex offenses are no higher than for other violent offenders, yet they incur heftier prison sentences with higher sentences reserved for black men. If they survive prison rapes, often committed in complicity of correctional personnel, they may face civil confinement after their sentence ends and a hostile set of institutions "welcoming" them back.

Women prosecuted for sex offenses are at higher risk of being raped by staff or others and loss of "privileges" such as work and other meaningful programs. Prison programs designed for those with sex offender status increase the stigmatization and subsequent violence by other prisoners. Stevens joins Ben-Moshe and other penal abolitionists in arguing for an end to incarceration for these offenders. They lobby for decarceration and welcoming, safe communities where programs for sex violators are much more suitable than those offered within a total institution such as prisons.

With a focus on queer sexualities and identities, Amit Taneja furthers the unifying thread of this volume, namely, to center issues that otherwise face marginalization in institutional settings. Importantly, he notes that there is no homogeneous queer community. Instead, there are "sub-communities" such as LGBTQ people of color and LGBTQ people with disabilities, who self-identify using other labels than what has come to be known as the "gay" community, such as "same gender loving" and "queer crips."

Taneja points out how politicians have opportunistically singled out the queer community for moral condemnation, which has resulted in the destruction of patriotic (patriarchal) family values and the American moral fabric. This argument can be extended to despotic leadership in other areas, from Eastern Europe's right wing parties to President Mugabe's declaration that "homosexuality" is a Western practice and anathema to Zimbabwean's practices or identities.

Following the lead of the United States Southern Baptists, Uganda's leadership has gone farther by declaring any acts of "sodomy" worthy of capital punishment. In this climate of backlash and homophobia, Taneja worries that by focusing singularly on gaining access to "gay marriage" with all the issues associated with the patriarchal vestige of such an institution, other urgent concerns central to queer people's lives are muted. These include elder abuse, racism, youth homelessness and school violence, transphobia, and employment protections among others. It remains to be seen whether a queer liberation movement can find unity in struggling against homophobia and transphobia.

Social and cultural conventions directly impact how our natural environment is adapted to human's selfish needs. Amy Fitzgerald challenges the misguided culture/nature dualism that brings about a destructive anthropocentrism at the expense of non-human animals and nature. She explores nature's confinement to fit humans' aesthetic, economic, political, and symbolic needs and desires. Using the analytic tools of green criminology and ecofeminism, she notes a subtle linguistic shift in characterizing nature as environment in need to be managed, naturally, by human animals, especially vis-à-vis the challenges of environmental degradation and resource overuse. Such "management" has hidden roots in the drive to capitalist domination of wild areas in need to be "enclosed" and "protected." Poor people who use common areas for subsistence are uprooted. While green criminology helps us understand the construction of criminality beyond the familiar "criminal," ecofeminism invites comparisons of experiences of oppression between nature and the feminine.

Jenna McDavid critiques anthropocentrism. Her analysis of non-human animals' imprisonment makes a suggestive comparison with the grim spectacle of a man condemned to death in Foucault's opening lines of *Discipline and Punishment* (1977). She argues that this is what is in store on a daily basis for the nine billion animals annually tortured and slaughtered for human consumption. Factory farms in the Global North, particularly in the United States, produce daily horrors of wounded, sick, and dying animals. McKenna uses the term "trafficking," usually reserved for the illicit transport of humans, to characterize the fate of cows who are illegally moved through various states in India, destined for the slaughterhouse and the leather industry.

Are there humane practices of humans' engagement with non-human animals? McKenna alerts us that pet holding—in places such as zoos, circuses, and aquariums—is an unethical practice that enslaves non-human animals for human companionship and entertainment. Those who claim to be vegetarians but consume cow's milk and eggs have to come to terms with hypocrisy, as cows face enforced pregnancy and male chicks are routinely killed after birth. She encourages prison abolitionists to understand the parallels about the imprisoning of non-human animals as not a humane approach to learn about other species, but rather as a destruction of understanding and protecting, while confining and repressing non-human animals.

With her classic *The Death of Nature: Women, Ecology, and the Scientific Revolution* (1980), Carolyn Merchant shows that a scientific and capitalist justification of a dominion over nature also has detrimental consequences for the status of women in such societies. In that vein, Mechthild Nagel focuses on how patriarchal forms of imprisonment of women intersect with other forms of oppression discussed by several authors in this volume. She reviews prevailing ideologies that have limited girls' and women's mobility and choices within the private and public spheres. Ideologies such as the cult of true womanhood or cult of domesticity have had profound effects on women vis-à-vis American jurisprudence. In addition, colonial practices of impunity, curtailing reproductive rights of racialized othered women, ensured a fractured solidarity of women across racial boundaries. Along with Liat Ben-Moshe, Nagel questions whether measures of reform such as protecting imprisoned women from rape (PREA, 2003) or making prisons generally friendlier to women are reforms that abolitionists ought to embrace.

Long before the slogan "we are the ninety-nine percent!" was fashionable, Tiyo Attallah Salah-El, a decorated Korean War veteran who later became a prison abolitionist while serving a life sentence in prison for murder, opines that the United States' version of democracy is a sham, since only "the one percent are the ones who control the economy and have large and loud voices in Congress." Now a prominent voice in the penal abolitionist movement, Salah-El asks us to start organizing for a grander vision akin to mass movements in the past that have made a lasting impact. He joins Taneja in calling for an end to infighting or parochial visions for one's group progress over others and lists a number of ways to start the process of decarceration.

Since Salah-El suggested that California might have to start this process, after a decade of an ill-conceived "three strikes" law, it is indeed the case that the state was ordered to begin, in the words of Liat Ben-Moshe, "negative reform": emptying out the prison cells because of dangerous, life-threatening overcrowding conditions, which even the courts have called constituting a violation of the Eighth Amendment (i.e. cruel and unusual punishment).

While thinking about coalition building and alliances, Salah-El discusses contradictory interests involved in keeping the prison industrial complex alive. These include evangelical Christians who have been nicely rewarded with "faith-based" programs, and guards' unions who reap salaries and retirement benefits that they are fiercely protecting. Nowhere is that more apparent than in New York State, where several prisons were slated for closure thanks to the reform of the punitive Rockefeller Drug laws that has much curtailed new convictions.

What if there were no more prisons of any sort? Mechthild Nagel joins Salah-El's call for reducing the grip of the penal industries that pervade our lives. Excarceration, as the ultimate modality of post-punishment, is meant to free us from all forms of imprisonment that the neoliberal, patriarchal, racist state enforces. Nagel probes the possibility that the South African Ubuntu ethic might be a way to understand "positive peace." At the very least, this would require a radical revisioning of intersubjectivity, namely, not one adhering to the monological, autonomous Western Enlightenment project of the subject, but one bound by sociability not well known in the global North. If one subscribes to the belief that all human beings should be irreducibly interconnected with the Other in order to have a human and humane experience, then it would be much more difficult to dole out harsh judgment and act in ways that separation us from the Other. This is well documented with respect to ecological concerns—where we see the human animal's supremacy over non-human animals.

All the authors attempt to probe coercive or repressive institutional control and point to other forms of democratic and, where possible, non-hierarchical ways of living among human beings, non-human animals, and nature. Recent global developments in holding governments, global capitalist financial centers, and university boards of trustees accountable for their actions is the result of our imagining a world focused on a public good and public commons accessible to all. The contributions encourage us to think more deeply about people's power to unite and envision change. While abolitionists have long lived with the charge of being utopian visionaries, it appears to us that now is the time to act upon those dreams.

This is a critical, radical, interdisciplinary, transformative, revolutionary, and intersectional volume by activists and academics writing in a variety of styles, approaches, and forms from different political perspectives, philosophies, and positions. But all the contributions emerge from the de-institutional social justice movement that seeks to break down all systems of domination that promote and foster oppression, social control, and discipline. These institutions include, but are not limited to what we term the "5Cs of Conquest"—Colonialism, Capitalism, Civilization, Corporatization, and Commodification.

This volume is a hammer to all prisons small and larger, visible and invisible, national and international, walled and fenced, gated and barred. It is a call for the liberation of all from our many prisons we live in. It is calls for a total justice movement by the ninety-nine percent against the greed, exploitation, and selfishness of the one percent who promote a humancentric, able-bodied, white, male, heterosexual, neoconservative Western-colonial and capitalist agenda.

In hope of transforming one hundred percent of our society and ending exploitation, separation, and fear, we boldly envision a world based on respect, inclusion, peace, and justice. This volume will not be offer any panacea to transform or end these prisons, but it is one nail of the many that are needed to seal the coffin of all systems of domination.

One

THE RISE OF THE TERRORIZATION OF DISSENT

Anthony J. Nocella II

1. Introduction

We are all imprisoned, but discovering what institution is imprisoning us and how and why they do so are key research questions. The critical research of social imprisoning is grounded in the work of Michel Foucault and others who argue that the most powerful method to control a group of people is not by imprisoning them behind cement walls, barbed wire fences, and steel bars, but by instilling fear in them. A powerful method to instill fear is by stigmatizing a group of people as a threat and an enemy.

Activist and deputy chairman of the Illinois chapter of the Black Panther Party Fred Hampton, who was murdered by Chicago police on 4 December 1969 while sleeping in his bed, stated frequently in his speeches: "You can kill a revolutionary but you can't kill a revolution" (cited in Millies, 2008). Cesar Chavez, stated,

> Once social change begins, it cannot be reversed. You cannot uneducate the person who has learned to read. You cannot humiliate the person who feels pride. You cannot oppress the people who are not afraid anymore. We have seen the future, and the future is ours. (United Farm Workers of America 1993, p. 2)

Chavez, like Hampton and many others, knew that ideas, theories, and philosophies were the engines to every revolution and social movement. Theory without action is reactionary and akin to random, non-strategic and unorganized events with no goal or mission in mind. Many dictators and fascists knew this, and it is for this reason that propaganda and media control were the most powerful tools of social control. To this day most publishers and media outlets are owned and controlled by very few corporations and individuals, and they are most often run by wealthy, formally educated, white, able-bodied, Christian males.

This chapter examines the terrorization of dissent, which is a form of political repression. Brian Glick (1989) identifies four tactics of political repression, which I have simplified here as the "Four 'I's of Political Repression": (1) incrimination; (2) infiltration; (3) interrogation; and (4) incarceration. While all of these tactics merit study and should be identified together, this chapter only examines the first step of repression: incrimination. I suggest that after 11 September 2001, the repression of dissent has become the terrorization of dissent. By that I mean that many forms of dissent are now labeled by the media, law enforcement, politicians, corporations, and institutions as terrorist action.

The concept of incrimination falls under the theory of stigmatization commonly studied in the fields of sociology, psychology, and criminology. Stigmatization through labeling is one of the most powerful forms of repression. Stigmatization can be carried out with multiple methods. For example, a government may sponsor a propaganda campaign supported by oppressive scholarly work such as eugenics that supports white supremacy. The chapter begins by introducing critical criminology, a field that studies political repression. Next, I define social control, with emphasis on disability studies, and then political repression, setting the groundwork for discussion of terrorization. Finally, this chapter argues for positive strategic responses to responding to political repression.

2. A Critical Criminological Perspective

Critical perspectives on social control and political repression are studied within the field of critical criminology—a subfield of and challenge to mainstream criminology. Criminology's roots go back to the mid-seventeenth-century, most notably to Cesare Beccaria, an Italian jurist and author of *On Crimes and Punishments* (2009). Further, Jeremy Bentham, with assistance from his cousin, designed the architectural blueprint of the panopticon, a powerful method of surveilling prison populations (Foucault, 1995), models of which were used from the beginning of the modern imprisonment experiment in the United States. In 1958, conflict criminologist George B. Vold held in *Theoretical Criminology* that crime is an outcome of political conflict between groups with power and those that are powerless and disenfranchised (Bernard, Vold, Snipes, and Gerould, 2009). He argued that those with power create laws to defend their interests. Conflict criminologists, entrenched in a critique of class from a Marxist perspective, understood that conflict was a universal form of interaction amongst everyone. Therefore, conflict is not to be avoided or denied, but rather embraced. They viewed relationships as fused by unavoidable conflict.

Vold forged critical criminology (now regarded as a subfield in the discipline) out of conflict criminology (DeKeseredy and Perry, 2006). Beginning in the late 1960s and early 1970s, at the same time as the prison reform movement, critical criminology was founded on a Marxist critical theory critique of social order and power (DeKeseredy and Perry, 2006). It also has roots in the critical theory school of thought of the Frankfurt School. Critical criminology has become an umbrella field for many social justice-based subfields such as transformative justice (Morris, 2000), restorative justice (Zehr, 1995; Van Ness and Strong, 1997; Claassen and Claassen, 2008), feminist criminology (Renzetti, 2008), green criminology (Beirne and South, 2007), anarchist criminology (Ferrell and Clinton, 1995), radical criminology (Lynch, Michalowski, and Groves, 2006), and most recently, queer criminology (Ferrell and Clinton, 1995).

Critical criminology argues that crime is socially located and contingent on particular historical, cultural, and political norms. Further, critical criminology argues against punitive or retributive based justice systems in favor of restorative and transformative ones.

Critical criminology challenges domination and control of any sort, and therefore concentrates on issues of control and discipline (Fernandez, 2008). The first wave of critical criminology focused more on challenging and reacting than being proactive and establishing an alternative.

As the field matured in the late-1970s, so did the time to transition from reactive critiques and criticisms of retributive- and punishment-based criminal justice tactics and systems, to more inclusionary and rehabilitative alternatives. However, in Ronald Reagan's presidency, the war on drugs— modeled on the 1973 New York's Rockefeller drug laws—replaced rehabilitation efforts with mass arrests and incarceration, (Hartnett, 2010). The United States began the 1980s with approximately 500,000 adults in prison and ended the decade with more than a million (Justice Policy Institute, 2000). In the 1990s, most of the educational programs were taken out of the prisons by the government, as they were viewed as too costly.

While education has proven to be more effective then punishment, education has been replaced with factory jobs that profit corporations that have contracts with prisons across the United States (Burton-Rose and Wright, 1998; Davis, 2003). The substitution of jobs for education became a form of incarcerated slavery, which is defended by the 13th Amendment. This Amendment argues for the end of slavery except in the case of individuals who are convicted of a crime. The rise of the prison population in the 1980s, which was shaped into labor in the 1990s by corporations, gave way to the development of the prison industrial complex (Davis, 2003). This overpopulation within prisons was due to an unmanageable criminal justice system—too many cases dumped onto too few lawyers, judges, juries, and court rooms (Magnani and Wray, 2006). During the same time that the prison industrial complex emerged in the 1990s, so did many legal cases, which directly aided in the construction of the criminal industrial complex, making thousands of jobs for lawyers, police, probation officers, clerks, and legal aids. Concurrently, President Bill Clinton expanded neoliberal trade policies.

The 2000s were marked sadly by George W. Bush as an age of terrorism (Chomsky, 2002). This led to mass violence and an economic crisis by United States forces and corporations (Kahn, 2010). In 2002, the United States prison population grew for the first time to more than two million, overextending its bed limit (i.e., rooms for prisoners) (Davis, 2003). The United States' criminal justice system, grounded in a retributive punitive process, employs everything from ankle bracelets and the death penalty (in many states) for the purpose of controlling and putting fear in people.

When marginalized individuals cannot be imprisoned, the power of surveillance (Foucault, 1995; Parenti, 2003) and stigmatizing are used by media, law enforcement, governments, corporations, and institutions for social control to reinforce normalcy. If a group or individual threatens to jeopardize the profits, reputation, or power of the dominant social order, they are commonly first surveilled, then questioned, and finally, if they do not align with the common social and political norms, they are punished. The punishment can be as minimal as a fine or as severe as assassination such as occurred to Fred Hampton and Malcolm X. This process of promoting a dominant social order, or norm, is known in the fields of criminology and sociology as social control.

3. Defining Social Control

One of the most commonly examined topics by critical criminologists is social control. Social control regulates behaviors, identities, and ideas by constructing norms to establish boundaries of compliancy and conformity with the cultural status quo. Groups and individuals with behaviors, identities, or ideas that fall outside these boundaries are labeled deviant and abnormal and must be punished and disciplined by those in dominant positions who reinforce normalcy and social constructions (Pfohl, 2009). These systems and regulations that provide order and discipline provide social, political, economic, and religious power over the public. When these systems and regulations are broken, the institutions and state actions of punishing those who broke them are identified as political repression. Therefore, social control and political repression work together for the goal of protecting hegemony and domination. In *Policing Dissent* (2008), Luis Fernandez, a critical criminologist, argues that if one only looks at repression, s/he will be ignorant of a larger social context. He writes:

> In my view, the concept of repression, limited to overt tactics such as harassment, intimidation, assault, detainment, and murder, is too narrowly constructed and leaves out multiple spheres of contention and domination. In contrast, social control of dissent opens up the theoretical possibilities for broader studies of protest and control. (p. 9)

Fernandez views social control and domination as larger fields of study comparable to that of political repression and punishment. Political repression and punishment, while using tactics such as the death penalty, infiltration, wire-tapping, and home-raids, are all forms of social control. One specific form of this control method is *labeling*. Fernandez writes:

Labeling theory offers a more contemporary sociological approach to social control and deviance (Becker 1963; Pfohl 1994). Closely associated to symbolic interactionism, this approach argues that human behavior is relative, interpretive, and best understood in human interactions. In other words, meaning is a negotiated process: it is created rather than absolute and independent. In turn, deviant behavior is also an interpretive process. Therefore, what society holds as deviant behavior depends on the meaning and interpretation given to an act rather than the act itself. (Ibid. p. 21)

In labeling theory, it is important to ask these questions: Who is labeling? What is deviant? How do these deviant actions change? How and why are they accepted as normal within a constantly changing world? This construction is pivotal in the examination of dissent for two specific reasons. First, it asks why the particular movement's cause is viewed as deviant, abnormal, and not accepted; and second, it asks how institutions of power identify activists as deviant. Therefore, not only must the tactics and strategies of the dissenters be observed, but the cause as well. I must stress that not all labels are negative, but when labels are stigmatized, such as "abnormal," they marginalize and silence individuals, such as those who have disabilities. At this point, the label becomes a tool of political repression.

In *Stigma: Notes on Management of Spoiled Identity* (1963), Erving Goffman notes that stigmatization, unlike labeling, is always used negatively to discredit an individual or group. Labeling, on the other hand, does not always need to hold to a repressive or negative characteristic. For example, "Great" was not Alexander III of Macedon's last name. Yes, he was a king, the highest rank within the nation, but king does not equate to the subjective value of "great." Goffman, in describing a person who has been stigmatized, writes, "He possesses a stigma, an undesired differentness from what we had anticipated. We and those who do not depart negatively from the particular expectations at issue I shall call the normals" (p. 5). In relation to disability studies' critique of labels and stigmatization, he writes:

> We use specific stigma terms such as cripple, bastard, moron in our daily discourse as a source of metaphor and imagery, typically without giving thought to the original meaning. We tend to impute a wide range of imperfections on the basis of the original one, and at the same time to impute some desirable but undesirable attributes, often of a supernatural cast, such as "sixth sense," or "understanding." (Ibid.)

The majority of Goffman's work on stigma is related to the negative identity of people with disabilities or people who, as noted above, are referred to with a disability term to insult an individual, group, event, object, action, or idea. Labels are a form of social control and are reinforced by forms of punishment to those that conduct positive acts outside of the negative stereotype.

For example, as someone with disabilities, I have published a number of books and completed a doctoral degree. However, because of these accomplishments, others have argued that I either do not have a disability or someone is doing my work for me. In contrast, if I get a low grade on a paper, forget something at home, or yell at someone, people accept and justify my actions as normal because I have disabilities.

Furthermore, stigmatization was part of the reason I hesitated to come out as part of the LGBTQQIA community because Western science, specifically eugenics, argues that the only reason people are gay is because they have a disability. Further, Goffman quotes a person with physical disabilities on breaking-out of his/her disability identity, noting that

> people do not only expect you to play your part; they also expect you to know your place. I remember for instance a man at an open-air restaurant in Oslo. He was much disabled, and he had left his wheel-chair to ascend a rather steep staircase up to the terrace where the tables were. Because he could not use his legs he had to crawl on his knees, and as he began to ascend the stairs in this unconventional way, the waiters rushed to meet him, not to help, but to tell him that they could not serve a man like him at that restaurant, as people visited it to enjoy themselves and have a good time, not to be depressed by the sight of cripples. (Ibid., p. 120)

Goffman goes on to provide many other examples from people with disabilities speaking about breaking-out of their labels. For example, people with physically disabilities are not thought to be able to dance; on the contrary, people with any type of disability can dance, for even if they are in comas, they might be dancing in their minds. Another example of misunderstanding those with disabilities is when people question why the blind would go to a movie or buy a television since they cannot see to enjoy the entertainment; this assumption ignores the other sensory capabilities of persons who are blind.

The most powerful purpose and effect of labeling and stigmatization is the establishment of moral panic, which promotes social fear. Moral panic was first introduced by Stanley Cohen in his book *Folk Devils and Moral Panics* (1980) to describe the feeling expressed when social order, interests, and values are threatened. A few examples of moral panic include the War on Drugs launched in the early 1980s (Churchill 2002a); the generalization that all Muslims are terrorists post-September 11, 2001 (Odartey-Wellington 2009); and, most recently, anti-capitalist activists such as anarchists, environmentalists, and animal rights activists have called a "new class of folk devil" and as violent and terrorists (Fiona Donson, Graeme Chesters, Ian Welsh and Andrew Tickle, 2004). Therefore, a common reason that governments and other institutions of power often construct enemies, such as in the war on terrorism, is because they want to establish social fear, which will allow them the ability to control society and reinforce their conception of "normality" that also keeps them in power.

4. Defining Political Repression

Literature on political repression centers on the relationship between the state and dissent. Most of the literature ranges from government strategy, behavioral shifts of dissidents and authorities, political-historical analyses (Davenport, 2000), documentation of repression and the results of repression. According to Conway D. Henderson (1991, p. 121), "Political repression is the use or threat of coercion in varying degrees applied by government against opponents or potential opponents to weaken their resistance to the will of the authorities" (Stohl and Lopez, 1984, p. 7). This definition is compatible with the broad spanning literature in the field of political repression (Goldstein 1978; Stohl and Lopez, 1984; 986; Reiter, Zunzunegui, and Quiroga, 1986; Rodley, 1986; de Neufville, 1986; Goldstein 1986; Jones, 1988; Michell et. al. Moreover, as Henderson notes, the general concept of this definition "is also widely recognized by governments, international organizations, and professional groups" (1991 p. 121).

My only criticism of this definition is that from an activist's perspective, it downplays the violent actions of governments, characterizing repression as merely "coercive." This overlooks the specific actions, including illegal tactics (e.g., COINTELPRO, see below) often employed by a government to limit or destroy necessary public dissent. In some cases, such actions include physical violence, torture, and murder. This is not to suggest that the state, the United States and beyond, is a monolithic entity. The government is a complex, continuously changing, and, at times, self-critiquing institution. Further, because of private security (e.g., Wackenhut), correctional facilities, and the military (e.g., Blackwater), along with illegal militias and paramilitaries working covertly for world governments (e.g., the Janjaweed in Darfur region of the western Sudan), political repression is not limited only to formal governmental institutions. Therefore, I define *political repression* as the specific legal and illegal targeting, covert or overt, of political activists to control, eliminate, and/or weaken their ability to create political change.

Recent literature suggests a growing interest regarding response to repression by dissidents (Lichbach, 1987). Some theorists argue that an increase in repression will cause increased dissent (Gurr, 1970; Snyder and Tilly, 1972; Becker, 1976; Denardo, 1985; Cameron, 1988). Others believe the extent of dissent largely depends on economic shifts (Buss, 1961; Lichbach 1987; Gupta, Singh, and Sprague, 1993).

When the economy is unstable, dissent is likely to be high; and when it is strong, dissent is likely to be low. Of course this pattern also reflects the dissidents' own budgets and resource mobilities. Another pattern of response is that dissent will likely increase along with repression until a certain point when it decreases due to the dissidents' cost-benefit analysis centered on the relationship between repression and dissent (Gurr 1969; Gupta and Venieris, 1981; Davenport, 2000;). A significant amount of research goes beyond issues of repression on a domestic level, to examining civil war, revolution, international war, tyranny, and dictatorships as part of the larger scope of repression.

Political repression "has become institutionalized in American life, an unwelcome legacy from the sometimes brutal, sometimes hysterical attacks on political dissidents. Every branch and every level of government has participated in suppressing free expression" (Schultz and Schultz, 1989, p. xi). Beginning with the genocide of Indigenous Americans to the present day, with the limiting of animal rights activists' freedom of speech through the Animal Enterprise Terrorism Act (AETA) signed in 2006, political repression is woven in the historical fiber of United States history. States are always hierarchical entities that depend on repression as well as cultural hegemony to maintain control (Bodley, 2005). America's form of repression reflects the country's origins in the British Empire, though it has unfolded through the centuries in its own distinct manner.

A review of the literature on this topic reveals three major characteristics of political repression in the United States. First, repression tends to be legalistic and subtle (Levin, 1971; Grossman, 1976). Second, it is constrained by norms and procedures (Balbus, 1973). Third, it is administered by multiple levels of government (Kopkind and Lang, 1970; Jones, 1988). Today, political hegemony of corporate media acts less as a social information center and more as a think-tank for supporting a particular state policy; therefore, the media has become a corporate propaganda-promoting machine and spin-artist justifying political repression (Chomsky, 2002).

Further, the United States' political repression might tend to look sparse because the government often does not recognize other countries' and non-government organizations (NGOs) to carry out investigations of it. Consequently, compared with other countries worldwide, the United States appears to be much less repressive. Overall, democratic regimes appear less likely to use large-scale repressive tactics as authoritarian regimes (Henderson, 1991; Poe and Tate, 1994; Rummel, 1996; Blanton, 1999) because democracies offer more peaceful avenues for expressing one's grievances, including public protest, boycotting, petitions, voting, lobbying, and running in an election (Rummel, 1996; Blanton 1999). However, even in democracies, political repression occurs selectively.

5. Overview of United States Political Repression

Robert Justin Goldstein's *Political Repression in Modern America: From 1870 to 1976* (2001) shows in vivid detail that political repression has a long history in the United States. From the Sedition Act of 1798 to the Red Scare during WWI, from McCarthyism to COINTELPRO (Counter Intelligence Program), the government has systematically and repeatedly violated the rights and liberties of its citizens. Furthermore, many indigenous American, black liberation, peace studies, and social justice scholars argue that the United States was founded on political repression such as the horrifying unjustified violent genocide of indigenous Americans and enslavement of black Africans, which is hard not to agree with. These scholars, in addition to many other social justice scholars, claim the genocide of Indigenous Americans and Latinos (from Mexico and South and Central America), the enslavement of people of color (the majority from Africa), servitude of those from Asia, the institutionalization of people with disabilities, and the domestication of women are strategic forms of political repression that were used within the development of United States political social, and financial institutions. Those repressed and silenced throughout United States history have not been forgotten (Schultz and Schultz, 1989; 2001).

In the United States, one organization more than any other has implemented strategic repression: the Federal Bureau of Investigation (FBI) (Swearingen, 1995; Jones, 1988; Buck, 2000; Churchill and Wall, 2002a, 2002b; Cunningham, 2003). Between 1956 and 1971, the FBI operated a secret counter-intelligence program known as COINTELPRO, the purpose of which was to "expose, disrupt, and neutralize" (Buck, 2000) their targets, specifically radical left-wing organizations that caused a "domestic security threat" (Jones, 1988; Earl, Soule, and McCarthy, 2003) such as the American Indian Movement and the Black Panther Party (Jones, 1988; Jones 1998; Peltier, 1999; Carson, 2002; Churchill and Wall 2002a, 2002b), along with even more moderate groups such as the American Friends Service Committee (Glick, 1989). The FBI also targeted individuals perceived as connected ("associated") to so-called radical groups or whose individual political beliefs were perceived as too leftist (Price, 2004).

The FBI used repressive (and in some cases illegal) tactics that included phone taps, infiltration of organizations, framing of dissenters, excessive prison sentences, constant surveillance of individuals and groups, creation of rumors and lies within social movements, and even assassination attempts (Schultz and Schultz, 1989; Churchill and Wall, 2002a, 2002b). Despite the condemnations of such tactics by the Church Committee Report in 1976, they continued such operations in the 1980s, harassing groups supporting Central American peoples under attack by the United States, such as CISPES (Committee in Solidarity with the People of El Salvador) (Blum, 2004; Cunningham, 2004). Throughout the 1980s and 1990s, the FBI appeared to have a free hand in political repression, such as with the LGBT and AIDS activist communities and organizations like ACT UP (Stockdill, 2002).

6. Strategy of Political Repression

When studying repression, one must not only look at the methods (punishment) and reasoning (discipline), but also at the entity employing it (Davis, 2003; James, 1996). Repression is carried out in a variety of methods, ranging from the private sector controlling work schedule and conditions of employment, to the government controlling social behaviors and political expression through open and hegemonic means. The state acts as a form of authority in multiple spheres such as reinforcing social norms that construct the infrastructure of society (Marx, 1959; Gramsci, 1989). As Friedrich Engels writes: "Authority, in the sense in which the word is used here, means: the imposition of the will of another upon ours; on the other hand, authority presupposes subordination" (qtd. in Tucker, 1978, p. 730).

While it is critical to "draw lines between right and wrong uses of governmental authority to seize and damage persons and property" (Tilly, 2003, p. 27), I am limiting my scope to the wrongful and illegitimate use of government authority to repress the legitimate exercise of civil liberties and dissent, viz., political repression. In the discussion of right and wrong uses of governmental authority, Charles Tilly defines the two categories as force (legitimate/ legal) and violence (not legitimate/illegal). He states that there are "three insuperable objections" in distinguishing the two (2003, p. 27). First, what is legitimate force? Because this is a contentious issue, "demonstrators and police are almost always contesting the boundary between legitimate and illegitimate uses of coercive means" (Ibid.). Second, Tilly claims that a continuum exists between legitimate and illegitimate authority. I disagree with him on this point because raiding a home or imprisoning someone is always illegitimate from an anarchist perspective because punitive and coercive actions are never justifiable. And he does not answer the underlying question: who determines what is and is not legitimate? If it is the law, then political repression is a form of legal procedure, but if it is founded in social morality and social justice, then it is based on a larger debate over ethics. Law, throughout time, has always been challenged by social ethics, while social ethics, which are more fluid and less dogmatic, are developed through constructive communal dialogue.

Tilly discusses a third objection, involving the relativity of legitimate force and violence. *When repression occurs, who gets to tell the story of the event?* Does it depend merely on who is in control at a given moment? "If the rebels had won, would their violent acts have converted retroactively to legitimate force?" (Ibid., p. 28) Therefore, these questions center on the fact that political repression is hard to determine, and that even the claims to define the concept are problematic. Basically, he offers a variation on the cliché, "One man's terrorist is another man's freedom fighter." This is a very problematic relativist position that renders all uses of force and violence equally good or bad, but impossible to discern without some kind of criteria, which Tilly doesn't adequately provide.

Similarly, Tilly identifies the two acts—*repression* and *facilitation*—differently in earlier writings (1978). He claims the middle-ground between repression and facilitation is *toleration*:

> Governments respond selectively to different sorts of groups, and to different sorts of actions. Sometimes the discriminations are fine indeed: the same government which smiles on church services bringing together a thousand people assembled to pray for salvation shoots without hesitation into a crowd of a thousand workers assembled to pray for justice (Ibid., p. 106).

In the eyes of the government and, more importantly, corporations, dissidents (or people engaged in dissident acts) are not mere criminals but a threat to national security and corporate profits. Toleration similar to that of acceptance from a social justice education perspective is not to respect, but rather to control and allow a group of outsiders ("Others") to enter the dominate identity's place. In the action of toleration and acceptance, those identified as "normal" are the dominators while the "abnormal" are the dominated.

7. Defining Terrorization

From the perspective of critical criminology, the "war on terrorism," was established by the Bush Administration to attack those who where a threat to the United States' post 9/11 policies and corporate interests. It was this propaganda strategy, known as the "war on terrorism," which was actually the terrorization of dissent. The "war on terrorism" provided the perfect cover for *a war on democracy* in the form of government, corporate, and law enforcement attacks on civil liberties, free speech, and domestic dissent of virtually all kinds (Chomsky, 2005). Clearly, "terrorism" is not just a word; it is a weapon. The definition is politically motivated by the user to target certain individuals or groups.

As state and local United States law enforcement becomes militarized with a heightened level of attention on domestic terrorism and an increase in high power weaponry, the local vandal, robber, murderer, and even dissenter is constructed into a terrorist. *Terrorization*, with its foundation in criminalization, stigmatizes through labeling or branding one's adversaries as terrorists. This labeling maligns the dissidents' causes/goals, demonizes and portrays them as deviant while, conversely, legitimating the oppressor's cause and taking any means necessary to secure it. This dynamic is similar to that of stigmatizing people with disabilities with labels such as retard, lame, crippled, blind, fools, idiots, and morons, which establish them as abnormal and those in elite power through the institutions of science, medicine, government and education as normal.

Terrorization is a form of political repression and social control that has existed for as long as dissent has existed. As the militarization of United States law enforcement becomes a reality, so does, by default, the terrorization of dissent and common criminals (i.e., military on one side and terrorists on the other). Terrorization, a new concept within label theory, falls within two bodies of literature: social control and political repression, which I will view through the lens of a critical criminologist. Although such labeling has long existed in the United States, the scope and magnitude of its use greatly expanded after 11 September 2001. Specifically, I will use a case study to illustrate how actions on behalf of the animal advocacy movement became stigmatized by being labeled as terrorism post-9/11 and during globalization of capitalism and mass ecological crises such as the oil spill in the Gulf Coast of Mexico and the extinction of thousands of species.

It is another means of terrorization.

8. Guilt by Association

As we were told by parents and teachers when we were children, and as is reiterated by law enforcement and politicians when we become adults, our friends are a reflection of us. In a legal context, this means that if your friends are criminals, then you are most likely a criminal. *Guilt by association*, a weapon to convict, imprison, and silence dissent, has been used throughout all political history, most notably in the United States during the 1950's Red Scare which repressed communists, anarchists, and those who related themselves in any way with them (Goldstein, 2001). If you knew or associated with communists during the McCarthyian period of mass witch-hunts, you, too, were guilty of conspiracy and seen as a threat against the United States (Chang, 2002).

Another example of guilt by association is the massive arrests of Muslims that followed the terrorist attacks of 9/11. National security policies legally allowed racial profiling of Muslims as possible terrorists or supporters of terrorists simply because of their race (Akram and Johnson, 2002). Seven years later, in 2008, an article was published by Juan Cole on Salon.com explaining that "[a] person's travel and occupation, as well as race or ethnicity, could be grounds for opening a national security investigation" (para, 1). Most recently in 2008, President Barack Obama experienced guilt by association firsthand during his presidential campaign. First, he was associated with Reverend Jeremiah Wright, who had been very critical of the Bush Administration (Ross and El-buri, 2008). Next, he was associated with Professor William Ayers, a retired Distinguished Professor of Education and Senior University Scholar at the University of Illinois at Chicago and co-founder of the radical 1970s Weather Underground, an anti-US government student movement associated with a bombing campaign decades ago. One time, Obama, along with others, had held a meeting with Ayers on the topic of national education (Shane, 2008). This one meeting was enough to cause Obama's opponents to malign him as having terrorist connections. Thus, when defining an associate, it is important to stress the difference between friends, professional colleagues, membership within an organization, and those within the same cause.

9. Responding to Political Repression

Historically, the act of dissent has been labeled and demonized as *deviant behavior*, and often thought to be a mental illness, rather than a rational and emotional response to repressive political and economic forces, especially in the context of social change. Currently, there is little analysis or research available on how people, groups, and movements respond to political repression. When I examined whether they respond in thoughtful or reactionary ways, I concluded that activists respond in both ways.

It was thought that individuals who could not conform to social change became deviants, mentally ill, or insane (Pfohl, 1994). Today, law enforcement, with the assistance of psychologists and psychiatrists, still believe individuals who conduct acts of social justice can be profiled based on *motivation* alone, commonly suggesting that people who carry out acts of social justice do so based on emotions rather than intellectual understanding. This opposition of rational versus irrational serves as an analytical construct to diminish the legitimacy of dissent. It is another means of terrorization. To understand any action from an individual, one must understand the complexity of motivations, as well as the specifics of the context.

Along with so many others in academia and in activism, I have too often interchanged the terms motivation and reason, overlooking and not valuing differences between the terms and the cause of one's action. This interchanging of the terms needs to be challenged and addressed for two major reasons: 1) motivation and reason have two completely different definitions; and 2) when wrongfully using motivation as the cause of one's actions, activists are often dismissed as having mental disabilities. On the other hand, those who conduct acts out of reason are dismissed as not being passionate or dedicated to their cause.

To start, the wrongful labeling insults the disability community because it implies that activists identified as "terrorists" and "extremists" have no legitimate rationale and only act out of motivation (i.e., emotion). Therefore, activists, revolutionaries, and lone wolfs who are labeled terrorists and extremists are stigmatized as illogical, irrational, and are labeled as insane and mentally disturbed or disabled. Consequently, that construction demonizes people who have mental disabilities as deviant, who, with that argument, should be institutionalized because those individuals labeled as terrorists who have mental disabilities are all violent threats to society. This construction also insults the activist community because their political and social beliefs can be brushed off as "mentally disturbed" and deviant, with no logical or theoretical understanding of their cause. Motivation is based on emotional and psychological characteristics, which drive a deeper understanding of how individuals take a path toward social justice, while reasoning is based largely on logic and intellect, which acknowledges that individuals have agency.

Through my experience in activism and in conducting an extensive literature review, I have developed five general responses to political repression by activists and socio-political groups. They are: *canceling*, *concluding*, *coping*, *confronting*, and *combating*. I call these the *5Cs of Responding to Repression*. The following describe each of the 5Cs of responding by activists or groups to political repression (see Figure 1):

Canceling is the abrupt elimination of all dissent activity.

Concluding is the gradual closure of all dissent activity, though not cancellation because people are still in jail, processing court cases, paying fees, or conducting counter-suits.

Coping is to keep constant, but not retreat or lose sight of one's overall goals; hence, it is a form of managing repression.

Confronting is to publicize the fact that (an) individual(s) or group(s) is/are being repressed, but not take aggressive legal or illegal steps to eliminate the repression, usually due to a lack of resources or public support. In some cases, publicity eliminates the repression and may even advance the cause. Dissidents in this form of response are concerned with the overall goals of the group or movement.

Combating is to advance the goals of the group/movement, to take legal or illegal measures to eliminate repression, and to achieve justice for already implemented repression against them. For instance, this may involve a counter-suit against the city police or the FBI. Not only are activists aggressively advancing their cause, they are seeking to achieve legitimacy through their legal and/or illegal actions.

Each of the responses is potentially in the repertoire of the activist or group and can be used either to address a particular event, campaign, group, or complete social movement. Further, these responses could be used to explain a diversity of actions. For instance, while an event could be cancelled at a university, and the student group could be coping with academic repression (Nocella, Best, and McLaren, 2010), the overall movement could become more organized and confrontational to State power.

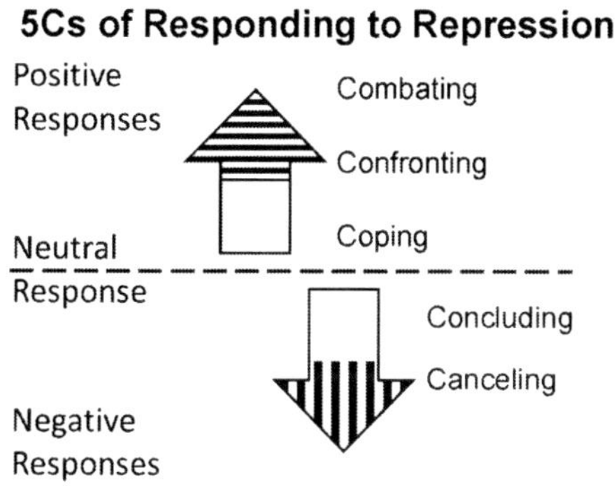

Figure 1. 5Cs of Responding to Repression

Activists' use of the 5Cs depends on many factors, particularly the goal and strategy of political repression by the government toward them. Activists or groups, except in the case of imprisonment and assassination, always have agency in deciding how to respond to political repression. In the case of an informant in an activist group/movement, it is very important to stress how activists have agency and that the state does not entirely determine or eliminate choice from the individual. This is not to say that the United States government and its law enforcement officers conduct their acts legally; they do not. Officials admit that, willingly or not. A case-in-point is COINTELPRO, which aided in the assassination, torture, framing, and division of activists and groups between mid-1950s to the early 1970s (Churchill and Wall, 2002a; 2002b).

Sometimes it is impossible to win one's freedom or political campaign in the face of intense political repression where the government is not "playing fair." But one must never deny that s/he has agency, which is defined here as the power to determine one's own choice. This does not mean one always has the power to determine the outcome, but people have the choice to decide how to believe and act. Activists and groups throughout time have stressed their agency in many forms, including the use of powerful rhetoric.

Prior to his execution by the state of Texas, Shaka Sankofa, a poor, black, male prisoner defended his innocence. Sankofa gave his last statement, which was witnessed by Reverend Jesse Jackson, Al Sharpton, Bianca Jagger, and others, with thousands of supporters from around the world gathered outside the walls. He spoke brilliantly about the horrors of racism and classism in the United States. He then restated Fred Hampton's famous lines, "You can kill a revolutionary, but you cannot stop the revolution" (qtd. in Mathúna, 2000). Even knowing he would soon be strapped to a cold metal table with his arm pulled tight to accommodate the lethal injection, Sankofa eloquently and strongly proclaimed that he, and every revolutionary, has agency.

Each response by an activist group or activist depends on the political climate, available resources, perceived possible consequences (e.g., collapse of organization, imprisonment, or fines), and, most importantly, the tactics used by authorities. Practice Theorists, such as French sociologist Pierre Bourdieu, argue that actions are not independent from systematic and individual motivations and practices (1977). Further, the concept of cultural capital refers to the ability of an individual to move in and out of societies, groups, and communities that s/he affects and is influenced by not because of financial value, but because of the value s/he offer others, such as his/her knowledge, experience, or social relationships on a particular topic.

The 5Cs of political repression are not the final determinate to study one's response to political repression, but a beginning point for developing a general framework of identifying how one responds. Furthermore, each response, while dependent on the strategy and tactic of political repression employed by the state or private agency, is determined by the activist or group. Therefore, someone's agency cannot be entirely taken away or manipulated by external forces, even while one's physical body can be imprisoned or killed. This framework for response will help show how the members of a movement respond to terrorization.

Although there exist many responses to repression in books, articles, videos, and online, these are not analyzed in an organized way in a field of study. In this chapter, I have organized a specific sub-field of study on responding to political repression, *political repression response*. As repression becomes more advanced in the United States and abroad, social movements must become more sophisticated and systematic about their actions toward law enforcement and other agencies. The only way to fight and exist in a continuously repressive society—advocated for the most part by corporations and carried out by governments—is logically and, more importantly, cohesively in a collaborative and respectful way.

Information on political repression from one organization or group is shared to another and then another, until that information on that event is spread throughout the world to every social justice activist. This information gives activists possible solutions on how to respond to similar situations. How does a movement respond to a grand jury? Do we speak to cops? Do we call the media when our house is raided? Do we have a press release if we are framed for a crime? To understand these questions, we must understand the type of repression, how the victim responded to the repression, and the result of this response. From these factors we can determine what actions are best to take in the future. It is only through activists sharing their experiences that this information can be analyzed, written about, and then applied to social justice movements as a whole.

10. Conclusion

This chapter has explained how stigmatization is a form of imprisonment from a critical criminologist perspective. It has expanded on the study of the terrorization of dissent and has helped establish the field of political repression response literature. In closing, the questions for social justice activists are not "Will you experience repression?," or "How will you work for social justice?," but rather "What type of repression will be employed against you and when will it be served?" While there are many forms of repression toward dissenters, this chapter is dedicated to examining stigmatization. The saying goes, "sticks and stones may break my bones, but words will never hurt me." The person who made that rhyme up never went to middle school, where children use words to make others cry or feel ashamed. This adolescent abusive word-calling tradition does not cease as children become adults; rather, it becomes more sophisticated and known as stigmatization.

My interest in responding to the imprisoning and repression of stigmatization gains inspiration from a statement by Martin L. King Jr. in his "Letter from a Birmingham Jail": "So the question is not whether we will be extremists, but what kind of extremists we will be. Will we be extremists for hate or for love? Will we be extremists for the preservation of injustice or for the extension of justice?" (1964, p. 88). This quote stresses that society will label activists, but the activists' power lies in what they will they do with this label. Will activists respond against being marginalized by labels through stigmatization or will they not resist? Will activist reclaim a negative label like queer and make it a proud and powerful identity, theory, and field of study, which challenges the construction of gender? Activists cannot control what type of repression will be served, but they can control how to respond to it. This response is best articulated by James Farmer Jr., played by Denzel Whitaker in the *Great Debaters* (2007). He states in a debate on racism at Harvard University that those that are repressed have a "duty to resist. With violence or civil disobedience. You [people that are white] should pray I choose the latter." Further, to be in solidarity and an ally with the oppressed, one must risk and challenge those systems that were constructed to dominate and destroy. This will mean losing friends, jobs, family, and possibly being arrested and imprisoned. Moreover, I believe those individuals such as myself, in places of privilege and domination, have an obligation to fight day in a day out to dismantle all systems of domination, which oppress people, plants, and nonhuman animals.

Two

RETHINKING THE "SCHOOL TO PRISON PIPELINE"

David Gabbard

1. Introduction

One Tuesday, I had to go to the high school to pick up my oldest son at 9:00 a.m. He had stayed up through the night until 4:00 a.m. working on a report for his English class that was due that day and wanted me to pick him up early, as soon as he turned in the report. I wasn't happy that he'd procrastinated so badly, but I understood where he was coming from. He was exhausted; I saw no sense in making him sleepwalk through the rest of his classes that day since he had more work to get done on his Senior Project, which was due the following day. I agreed that he needed to come home and get some sleep.

As I drove down the long road leading through the student parking lot to the front of the school and the visitor's lot, a tall middle-aged African-American man with a mouthful of chewing tobacco stepped out of a red pick-up truck and waved for me to stop. "I need to know who you are and why you're here," he said.

Cursing under my breath, I thought, "They pay this guy to play parking lot gestapo?" But I refrained from giving him a hard time, even if he was spraying tobacco juice into my Saturn with every syllable. He might be gross and remarkably inconsiderate, but he didn't make the policy to harass everyone who tried entering the school from this direction. He was just a tool of the school. He was probably happy to be getting paid for mostly sitting, chewing his chaw, and exercising what authority had been delegated to him when the situation called for him to do so.

"I'm here to pick up my son for a doctor's appointment," I lied.

"Well, you can't go this way. You have to go back out, turn right, and take the entrance up by the tennis courts."

That's when I noticed the barricades that been installed a little further up the road. I wondered how much money those had cost, and why it mattered so much to control traffic flow. I already knew that the principal ran the school like a high security prison. Harassing students with a strictly enforced dress code wasn't enough. Each of his first three years at Conley, my son had received in-school suspension for the hideous crime of being caught twice with his shirt not tucked in, and each time she sent a letter to our home address informing us that one more violation that year would result in his being suspended from school for three days. Now, she had apparently decided that it was judicious to place a guard in the parking lot to enforce her policy dictating which entrance parents and other visitors had to use.

"You can turn around up there," he spat at me. I just did as I was told.

When I went into the Student Services Office to have Jackson called out of class, the Assistant Principal was there completing paperwork.

"How are you doing?" he asked.

"Fine, I'm just here to pick up my son for a doctor's appointment."

"Yeah," Barbour said, "I saw him this morning, running around trying to get something done in the media center. I was going to give him a 'tardy,' but he gets one 'free pass' each semester. I warned him that he'd get a 'tardy' next time."

I had had confrontations with the Assistant Principal before. He was a decent enough guy, but the Principal micro-managed his actions. He understood that *the Principal* was boss. The *Assistant* Principal had no discretion in enforcing *the Principal's* policies. During the previous academic year, the assistant had acted as if he hated the situation. Evidently, things had changed this year. Now, I was a little miffed at the tone of glee I perceived in his voice—as if I was supposed to be grateful for the school's lenience, or that the assistant's benevolence.

It took great effort for me to conceal my contempt for the school administration and the entire school system that seemed so committed to the enterprise of making students and their parents hate school.

"Yeah, we ran out of printer paper at home last night and the bus must not have gotten him here in time to go to the media center to print out his report for his first period English class. I'd have been pretty upset had you given him a tardy under those circumstances since he was trying to do the right thing."

"Well, like it or not, students are required to be in their first period class by 8:20 a.m., and he wasn't. Rules are rules."

"Regardless of circumstance?" I asked him.

"Yes, sir."

2. From "School *to* Prison" to "School *as* Prison"

"*Corruptio optimi quae est pessima*" ("The corruption of the best is the worst"). How perfectly this early Christian adage captures the essence of compulsory schooling. The prison-like culture that I described of my son's high school has become the norm in schools all across the United States. This trend has not gone unnoticed, as we see a growing body of literature on what is being called "the school to prison pipeline" (SPP).

The American Civil Liberties Union (ACLU) has challenged the SPP issue as a major component of its Racial Justice Program, and characterizing it as a disturbing national trend wherein children are funneled out of public schools and into the juvenile and criminal justice systems. Many of the children who land in the juvenile justice system have learning disabilities or histories of poverty, abuse, or neglect, and would benefit from additional educational and counseling services. Instead, they are isolated, punished, and pushed out. "Zero-tolerance" policies criminalize minor infractions of school rules, while high-stakes testing programs encourage educators to push out low-performing students to improve their schools' overall test scores. Students of color are especially vulnerable to push-out trends and the discriminatory application of discipline.

The ACLU has also launched SchooltoPrison.org, a password-protected forum for impact litigators, direct services attorneys, and other legal advocates across the nation to share ideas and strategies for stemming the flow of children from schools into the juvenile and criminal justice systems. With the common goal of challenging the SPP, members of this online community exchange litigation strategies and resources among allies.

SPP has also attracted the attention of The Advancement Project, an innovative civil rights law, policy, and communications "action tank" that advances universal opportunity and a just democracy for those left behind in America. In their 2010 report, *Test, Punish, and Push Out*, The Advancement Project argues the following points:

While zero tolerance policies and high-stakes testing are usually considered separately, these two policies are actually closely related, sharing the same ideological roots. Together they have combined to seriously damage the relationship between schools and the communities they serve.

These two policies have turned schools into hostile, alienating environments, effectively treating many of our youth as "drop-outs-in-waiting." The devastating end result of these intertwined punitive policies is a "school-to-prison pipeline," in which huge numbers of students throughout the country are treated as if they are disposable, and are being routinely pushed out of school and toward the juvenile and criminal justice systems (Ibid., p. 3).

While I cannot stress enough the importance of The Advancement Project's report, we must recognize more than the shared ideological roots of high stakes testing and zero tolerance policies. We also need to recognize the shared historical roots of prisons and schools. Understanding those shared roots might help us learn to temper our expectations of schools and school reform. More significantly, it might help us recognize that we ought to prioritize the abolition of compulsory schooling even ahead of prison abolition.

Long before I ever encountered Michel Foucault's classic *Discipline and Punish* (1977), I vividly recall as a young child already making an intuitive connection between school and prison. Two of my "classmates" and I were sitting on the short flight of concrete steps leading down from the side exit of the gymnasium to the asphalt schoolyard. Although I cannot remember the precise words that I used, I recall asking them whether either had ever recognized the similarities between schools and jails. We, the students were analogous to prisoners, condemned to serve out a thirteen-year sentence. The teachers functioned as the guards, assigned to pace us through our daily drills. The principal, of course, was the warden, charged with maintaining the good order of the entire institution. My peers immediately recognized these parallels and we had great fun during the remainder of our recess plotting our "school break."

Even my elementary school principal must have had some awareness of these parallels. Despite being a genuinely amiable man who loved bringing a laugh or smile to others, he fabricated a makeshift "electric paddle" that he kept in his office as a sort of joke that rapidly took on certain mythical qualities among the students. In reality, the "electric paddle" was nothing more than a ping-pong paddle wrapped in aluminum foil with a telephone cord duct-taped to the handle. Ingeniously, the principal had duct-taped the other end of the long telephone cord to the giant metallic instrument panel of the intercom system with its large knobs, dials, and gauges. Few of us ever actually laid eyes on this contraption, but it was precisely the mystique of the thing that lent such power to its legend as a deterrent against serious violations of school discipline. Although no student ever heard of the paddle ever being used on someone, none of us wanted to become the first.

Since I'd worked out this rudimentary connection between schools and prisons, one question lingered in my mind and festered there until it spawned within me a mild form of passive-aggressive resistance to school. I understood why prisoners were forced to be incarcerated. They had committed some crime, and I presumed—quite incorrectly as it turns out—that they had been sentenced to denial of their freedom as a form of punishment. I could not understand, however, what I had done to deserve school. At that time, I had no concept of the word "compulsory." Nevertheless, for me, to be a student was to be a prisoner. The classroom was a jail cell, and I had been pressed into labor against my will.

With the exception of the one day at recess during my second grade, I don't remember ever sharing my thoughts and feelings on these matters with my peers at any great length. Had I done so, maybe I would have discovered that I wasn't alone. From outward appearances, however, no one else seemed to have any awareness of these ideas.

I was never the kind of child to openly challenge adult authority or attempt to organize a serious resistance movement. I fell somewhere between those who just seemed to uncritically follow, if not embrace, the rules in pursuit of the highest grades and the greatest recognition and rewards, and those who just refused to play the game at all. In retrospect, I would describe the first group as those who had already been *disciplined* into the values, norms, and standards of behavior demanded of children by schools and who had those values, norms, and standards enforced and reinforced at home. Members of the second group, on the other hand, most certainly had *not*! They arrived at school *undisciplined*, and, to varying degrees, they resisted discipline once they arrived, regardless how many times they were punished by the guards and warden for their disobedience and refusal to go along with the program. Very few of these in the second group were really "bad children" who seemed to enjoy picking on and bullying other children or blatantly causing trouble. Most of them approached resistance much more passively. Either they didn't have the background for school learning at home and just felt confused and frustrated by school, which resulted in them stopping trying, or they were totally unchallenged and bored by the whole process and didn't want to bother.

Looking back, I feel a real empathy for those children, now fifty-year-olds like me. The only thing that separated me from them was our "choice" of curriculum track. Though I chose the college-prep over the general education track, I, like my son, was still an under-achieving resister who either failed or passively refused to recognize the benevolence of the institution. School, for us, was less an "opportunity" to be taken advantage of and more a "sentence"—an infringement of freedom—to be endured until liberation (graduation).

Only one flaw, though it was a massive one, characterized my original thoughts on the connections between schools and prisons. I had assumed that schools were modeled after prisons. Upon reading Foucault, I was shocked to learn that just the opposite was true. Prisons since the nineteenth century were modeled after schools. If schools failed to adequately discipline docile bodies into becoming productive workers and obedient citizens, prisons could offer remedial discipline.

In his controversial *God Is Not Great* (2007), Christopher Hitchens draws a sharp distinction between atheism and anti-theism. Whereas an atheist does not believe in the existence of a deity or deities, an anti-theist rejects the desirability of any such belief:

> Some people I know who are atheists will say they wish they could believe it. Some people I know who are former believers say they wish they could have their old faith back; they miss it. I don't understand this at all. I think it's an excellent thing that there's no reason to believe in the absurd propositions of (theism). The main reason for this, I think, is that it is a totalitarian belief. It is the wish to be a slave. It is the desire that there be an unalterable, unchallengeable, tyrannical authority who can convict you of thought crime while you are asleep, who can subject you—who *must* indeed subject you—to a total surveillance around the clock, every waking and sleeping minute of your life (Hitchens, 2010).

Parallel to Hitchens's rejection of the very notion of an omnipotent, omnipresent, omniscient deity, I reject the right of the state to subject us to an institution that it attempts to afford those same powers.

I vividly recall a day my son came home from school when he was just in the first grade, complaining of a sore chin. "I get done with my work before everybody else," he told me. "And when I ask the teacher what to do next, she tells me to just sit there and put my head on my desk." Evidently, the weight of his head on his chin resting on his folded arms atop his desk caused the soreness. Then came the question I knew would one day come, "Why do I have to go to school, dad?"

What was I to tell my son, given all I believe to be the truthful answer to that question?

Of course, there are actually multiple truths that could be told in response to that question, and none of them, told honestly, are very gratifying. At the most basic level, children have to go to school because the government says they must—an often forgotten, overlooked, or regularly ignored fact that ought to make each of us nervous about the enterprise of compulsory schooling from the start. It certainly explains why so many children wind up hating school. Many, if not most, of them are not in school there because they want to be, but because they have to be.

According to the Alliance for Excellent Education (nd), 7,000 students drop out of school *every day*! Who knows how many more *tune* out because they don't see any relevance in the curriculum?

Of course, I wasn't going to tell my own child to drop out of first grade, but it's hard not to empathize with children who make that decision at some point in their school career. It's hard not to find sympathy for them, because we know what the consequences are for refusing the advertised beneficence of compulsory schooling. Or, at least, we used to.

One of the first lessons in most Foundations of American Education courses such as the one I teach entails sharing Thomas Jefferson's belief that America should become a meritocratic society rather than an aristocratic society (1779). In an aristocracy, one's position in a society stratified along economic and political lines was determined by one's birth. Economic and political power remained concentrated in the hands of just a few families and was passed on from generation to generation. The growth of the market and the rise of the new merchant class in the seventeenth and eighteenth centuries would challenge the aristocratic traditions of European feudalism. Eventually, that challenge would fuel the rhetoric of quasi-democratic revolutions such as ours in 1776 (Beard, 1913).

For Jefferson, a system of public schools would help ensure that one's position in the new American society, which had, of course, remained highly stratified, both politically and economically, would be based on *merit* rather than birthright. So, if you went to school, worked hard, and demonstrated sufficient talent and ability, you could aspire to and achieve whatever position in society you wanted, or at least a position high enough to guarantee yourself and your family some measure of economic security.

These ideas helped form the basis of what we've come to know as the American Dream Ideology. Horace Mann would later borrow from Jefferson in formulating his arguments favoring creation of a tax-supported system of compulsory schools in the state of Massachusetts. To strengthen the persuasiveness of his rhetoric, Mann "framed" his proposal, not as government-mandated schools, but as "Common Schools." They would be "common" in three important ways. They would impart a "common" political philosophy to weaken political strife at a time when America's working classes were at deep odds with the ownership classes. They would impart a common religious

(Christian) doctrine to ameliorate the ongoing conflict among the various Christian sects at the time. Finally, and most importantly for our purposes here, "common" in the sense that children from all walks of life would attend the same schools and, therefore, have the same opportunity to demonstrate their talents and abilities and justify their future position in America's stratified social order. In theory, this meant that children from wealthy families who "failed" at school would end up as poor adults, while poor children who excelled at school would end up as wealthy adults. According to Mann's promise, and in keeping with Jefferson meritocratic vision, common schools would function as a great social equalizer.

Mann's promise has yet to be fulfilled because it has always been a false promise. Children of the most elite classes have, with rare exception, never attended public schools. So, those schools have never been truly "common." The state of Massachusetts alone is home to forty private boarding schools such as Groton, where the price of tuition for "boarders" is $48,895 and $37,020 for "day students" (Forbes, 2010). Interestingly, when we research the dates those schools were founded, we find that most of them were established toward the end of the nineteenth century, just when larger numbers of children from lower class families began being pushed into the public schools created in accordance with Mann's vision.

Comparably, here in North Carolina, where Jim Crow laws once segregated children into black schools and white schools, we have numerous so-called "Christian academies." When we research the dates of their founding, we find they were created in the early 1970s, shortly after the 1964 Civil Rights Act put teeth into the 1954 *Brown v. Board of Education* decision and ushered in a period of government mandated desegregation.

Elite and privileged groups have always had the financial or political means to pass their advantages on to their children. So, it becomes hard to take someone like Bill Gates seriously when, in his teacher recruitment commercial for Teach.gov, he says, "My success came from how lucky I was to have some great teachers" (2010). Maybe so, but shouldn't he at least preface that with an acknowledgement that he was also "lucky" to have a father wealthy enough to pay $25,000 a year for his tuition at the Lakeside School, whose course catalog easily rivals most small private liberal arts colleges?

How many of us who attended public schools had the same opportunities available as afforded in private schools? Perhaps more people would demand such a curriculum, but few of us have any awareness of the existence of places like Lakeside or Groton, let alone any knowledge of their curricula.

Nevertheless, if only because employers, primarily since the 1950s, began requiring educational credentials from job candidates, the meritocratic argument for schooling did develop some measure of legitimacy over the years. A significant difference is observed between the unemployment rates in 2008 for college graduates and high school graduates, and a nearly identical difference (17.9 percent) between those who earn a high school diploma and those who do not (Center for Labor Market Studies, 2009).

Since the 1950s, then, most Americans learned to take the rules of the game for granted. If you work hard in school and graduate, you'll be able to find a job and establish some economic security for yourself. But that myth is quickly coming unraveled.

In the words of a New Jersey man who lost his job in 2010, "I did everything right, I played by the rules, I got skills, I excelled in my job, all to no avail . . . I don't know what I'm going to do," he continued. "All the years of both parties talking about free trade agreements and how we will retrain America was just a bunch of BS; it was easy to say all that when times were good" (Delaney, 2011). Barack Obama made these changes to what we used to take for granted as the "rules of the game" official, or at least publically acknowledgeable, in his 2011 State of the Union address:

> Many people watching tonight can probably remember a time when finding a good job meant showing up at a nearby factory or a business downtown. You didn't always need a degree, and your competition was pretty much limited to your neighbors. If you worked hard, chances are you'd have a job for life, with a decent paycheck and good benefits and the occasional promotion. Maybe you'd even have the pride of seeing your children work at the same company.
>
> That world has changed. And for many, the change has been painful. I've seen it in the shuttered windows of once booming factories, and the vacant storefronts on once busy Main Streets. I've heard it in the frustrations of Americans who've seen their paychecks dwindle or their jobs disappear—proud men and women who feel like the rules have been changed in the middle of the game.
>
> They're right. The rules have changed. In a single generation, revolutions in technology have transformed the way we live, work and do business. Steel mills that once needed 1,000 workers can now do the same work with 100. Today, just about any company can set up shop, hire workers, and sell their products wherever there's an Internet connection. (Obama, 2011)

Lest we be duped into renewing any faith in the "change" we were told we could "believe in," President Barack Obama has pledged to the United States Chamber of Commerce that he would pursue even more free trade agreements—this time with Panama, Colombia, and South Korea. With the North American Free Trade Agreement (NAFTA) having eliminated nearly 900,000 United States' jobs between 1991 and 2003 (Scott, 2003), it ought to strike us as highly unlikely that these pending new agreements will do anything but dim the economic prospects of America's youth, making it even harder for parents to point to a future economic payoff to motivate their children to stay in school.

According to an April 2011 report from the Economic Policy Institute, "the unemployment rate for workers age 16–24 was 18.4 percent—the worst on record in the sixty years that this data has been tracked" (Shierholz and Edwards, 2011 p. 1).

Even under the best of economic conditions, I could not honestly tell either of my sons that doing well in school and earning a four-year college degree would guarantee that they will be able to find a job in their chosen fields. In today's economy, however, a four-year degree is even less certain to secure employment, as the unemployment rate for college graduates in 2010 reached nearly ten percent. With eighty-five percent of college graduates reporting that they are moving back home with their parents, we can expect that number for 2011 to climb even higher (Ibid.).

I can tell my children that a college degree still improves their chances for satisfactory employment over merely graduating from high school. The jobless rate in 2008 for those with a four-year degree or higher was 13.3 percent, while it was 21.2 percent for those with 1–3 years of post-secondary education, 31.9 percent for high school graduates, and 54 percent for young high school dropouts. As well, the rate of incarceration for youth between sixteen and twenty-four years of age is six times higher for high school dropouts and than for college graduates. Thus, the number of years of formal schooling one completes strongly correlates to both risk of unemployment and risk of incarceration (Center for Labor Market Studies at Northeastern University, 2009).

3. Conclusion

At its core, the problem is this. The continued existence of compulsory schooling perpetuates the myth that people's success or failure hinges on their performance in school. While the labor market may demand increased levels of educational attainment, the flow of jobs leaving the country due to outsourcing can still undermine a person's best efforts. Our failure to challenge this myth allows the state to blame schools for the larger problems in the economy that result in shrinking opportunities for people to find work.

In 1983, the Reagan administration published its *A Nation at Risk: The Imperative For Educational Reform*, a report of the National Commission on Excellence in Education, which has been considered a landmark event in modern American educational history. Among other things, the report contributed to the ever-growing (and still present) sense that American schools are failing. It touched off a wave of local, state, and federal reform efforts.

Unfortunately, however, the only meaningful changes we have witnessed in schools over the past thirty years since publication of the propaganda campaign that blamed schools for the alleged inability of United States-based corporations to compete in the global economy have been the implementation of high stakes testing/accountability and zero tolerance policies. Neither of those policies has changed the nature of compulsory schooling, but have only served to intensify its effects; namely, disciplining docile bodies to accept monotonous work as an inevitable part of life while subjecting those who refuse to recognize the beneficence of this therapy to remedial discipline in prison.

The truth is that schools will never be reformed as long as they are made compulsory by the state.

The United States, which has less than 5 percent of the world's population, has 25 percent of the world's prisoners (Liptak, 2008). Figures range from between 2.3 and 2.5 million Americans living behind bars. As the market economy continues its collapse, we should expect to see these numbers escalate, as globalization and domestic neoliberal policies continue to create a larger surplus population of people whom the market cannot absorb. The National Association for the Advancement of Colored People points out in its April 2011 report, *Misplaced Priorities: Over Incarcerate, Under Educate*:

> Over the last two decades, as the criminal justice system came to assume a larger proportion of state discretionary dollars nationwide, state spending on prisons grew at six times the rate of state spending on higher education. In 2009, as the nation plummeted into the deepest recession in 30 years, funding for K–12 and higher education declined; however, in that same year, 33 states spent a larger proportion of their discretionary dollars on prisons than they had the year before (p. 1).

Corporations and Wall Street investment firms also recognize and seek to capitalize on this same trend. The prison industry complex is one of the fastest-growing industries in the United States. Even the federal government and its defense contractors exploit the situation. "According to the Left Business Observer, the federal prison industry produces 100 percent of all military helmets, ammunition belts, bullet-proof vests, ID tags, shirts, pants, tents, bags, and canteens" (Pelaez, 2008).

All of this leaves us to wonder just how much our dominant institutions and our culture actually value education as anything more than an investment opportunity for increasing corporate profits while simultaneously affording those same corporations increased opportunities to control the levers of social control. In this sense, we have to wonder if compulsory schooling is becoming increasingly part of the problem instead of the solution.

Three

CRIMINALIZATION OF CULTURE AND THE RISE OF DISSENT

Ernesto Aguilar and Melissa Chiprin

If we are to be honest with ourselves, we must admit that the "Negro" has been inviting whites, as well as civil society's junior partners, to the dance of social death for hundreds of years, but few have wanted to learn the steps. They have been, and remain today—even in the most anti-racist movement, like the prison abolition movement—invested elsewhere. This is not to say that all oppositional political desire today is pro-white, but it is usually anti-black, meaning it will not dance with death. - Frank B. Wilderson III (2007, pp. 31–32)

1. Introduction

The United States' criminal justice industrial complex has become a sprawling, massive enterprise. Policing and incarceration has evolved a sociopolitical mythology that applies regardless of law or method. Racial profiling, "stop and frisk" actions by law enforcement, and sentencing disparities are manifestations of such observations. Contemporary criminal justice engages racially oppressed groups in its matrix to maintain the social order. In its "Justice on Trial," the Leadership Conference on Civil and Human Rights traces challenges people of color face related to the judiciary, law enforcement, sentencing, and imprisonment. It notes:

There is a self-perpetuating, cyclical quality to the treatment of black and Hispanic Americans in the criminal justice system. Much of the unfairness visited upon these groups stems from the perceptions of criminal justice decision-makers that (1) most crimes are committed by minorities, and (2) most minorities commit crimes. Although empirically false, these perceptions cause a disproportionate share of law enforcement attention to be directed at minorities, which in turn leads to more arrests of blacks and Hispanics. Disproportionate arrests fuel prosecutorial and judicial decisions that disproportionately affect minorities and result in disproportionate incarceration rates for minorities. The accumulated effect is to create a prison population in which blacks and Hispanics increasingly predominate, which in turn lends credence to the misperceptions that justify racial profiling and "tough on crime" policies (2000).

The tensions of racism and the criminal justice system have been exhaustively researched and detailed. In 1990, the Sentencing Project famously observed how jails and prisons house men of color, primarily black, disproportionate to their numbers in the overall population. Sentencing Project Executive Director Marc Mauer noted one in three black men will find themselves incarcerated in their lifetime. In addition, institutional racism may have significant consequences on communities of color and on prisoners themselves. In oppressive systems of domination, exploitation, and abuse the power of choice is a false notion. Yet untold numbers of people are blamed for circumstances as if they chose to be in these situations. Upon further investigation choice was not a real option.

Since the end of slavery, the criminal justice system has been used by white populations to support power, debilitate communities of color, and force people of color into beliefs of their own inferiority.

Different suggestions for addressing racism in the United States criminal justice system have been devised. Many ideas miss the fundamental need of society to rectify institutional white privilege. Correcting inequities is often obscured by emerging ideologies obfuscating the role of race and power.

Amid the rapid growth of incarceration, concerns from the African American community have emerged about the impact of the criminal justice system on young people. As states have tended to move away from imprisonment as a state project and instead to award contracts to private industry, prisoners often receive pay rates much lower than what unincarcerated workers would earn (Wagner, 2003, p. 3). We might consider such a practice questionable. Byron Price, writing in December 2010 in the *Atlanta Post,* points out the 13th Amendment of the United States Constitution permits slavery and involuntary servitude as punishment for conviction of a crime. Price, who authored "The Motivation behind Black Imprisonment" remarks such wording has been the avenue for the state, via the prison-industrial complex, to use people of African descent for capitalist production. "Karl Marx characterizes the oppressed as the surplus population," Price says. "In this discussion it connotes the black male population" (2010).

North American society has an unrelenting paranoia related to blackness. The use of "people of color" by those who interchangeably want to say, but cannot, "not black," to efforts to erase all notion of race as a ploy to avoid accountability, to the attempts to associate whites and blacks with the same brush of racism when prejudice occurs, absent history, are just a few examples of this phenomenon. Structures of white supremacy are already well-equipped to explain law enforcement, judicial procedure, and application of penalties in a way intended to appear just. In the criminal justice realm, people of color, primarily those of African descent, face many challenges in achieving justice. Contending with such efforts is the notion that fairness to all is ensured and the days of prejudice are but relics of the past.

Until such conversations on race are raised broadly and openly in the context of criminal justice, matters of criminal justice will not be seen through a racial and class justice lens. As Becky Petit and Bruce Western note, such overlooked issues have tragic results:

> As for racial minorities, researchers [argue] that the poor are perceived as threatening to social order by criminal justice officials. ... The poor thus attract the disproportionate attention of authorities, either in the way criminal law is written or applied by police and the courts. Consistent with this view, time series of incarceration rates are correlated with unemployment rates and other measures of economic disadvantage, even after crime rates are controlled. (2004, p.156)

Such issues require the general public see the broader idea of racism and criminal justice as a facet of oppression.

2. Black History and Social Position

Understanding racism in the United States criminal justice system is essential in exploring the construction of white supremacy, capital, and power within the United States. Unjust sentencing, racial profiling, police brutality, and juvenile justice, among many subjects, are more than singular issues, but are symptoms of a larger issue: systemic disenfranchisement of people of color.

Many people do not get an adequate teaching of history. Our collective understanding of the African American experience is, for most, a vague image of enslavement and the Civil Rights Movement. The fortunate may get rudimentary primary-school instruction of Reconstruction. This may come as no surprise, given dominant groups could be assumed to compose these books and teachings. As a political and ideological choice, history books and the dominant, primarily white, society has excised the pain, indignity, and injustice people of color faced. Such texts further omit the benefits and impunity for crimes whites enjoyed. James Illingworth is one of scores of writers who try to give a glimpse at a world ruled by cruelty in pursuit of capital:

> The whip has come to represent the everyday violence of life under slavery, and rightly so. Few slaves went through their lives without experiencing this form of punishment at one time or another. The pervasiveness of violence hinged not on the personality of a given slaveholder but on the nature of the system itself. Even those planters who shied away from the most extreme forms of punishment used physical force to discipline their enslaved black workers. Bennett H. Barrow, for example, was a Louisiana planter who refused to employ an overseer due to their reputation for excessive cruelty toward the slaves. Nevertheless, even this "humane" master's diary was full of occasions when he indulged in a "general whipping frollick," beat "every hand in the field," or attacked a particular slave and "cut him with a club in three places." (2010)

Arguing for a new framework, a new means of discovery in which we consider at the root of oppression, domination, and exploitation is the philosophy, if you will, of the construct of a loveless human—defined as one who is deviant, less than human, and needed to be controlled, punished and destroyed. Scholar bell hooks writes:

> Early on in our nation's history, when white settlers colonized Africans through systems of indentured labor and slavery; they justified these acts of racial aggression by claiming that black people were not fully human. In particular it was in relation to matters of the heart, of care and love, that the colonizers drew examples to prove that black folk were dehumanized, that we lacked the range of emotions accepted as a norm among civilized folk. In the racist mindset the enslaved African was incapable of deep feeling and fine emotions. Since love was considered to be a finer sentiment, black folks were seen as lacking the capacity to love. (2001, p. xix)

Youth who face a dominant cultural narrative that considers them useless and incapable are more likely to face challenges. Children of color embody these biased interpretations of behaviors, and applied practices. By design their role is to fulfill the dominant culture's reasoning that serves to feed white supremacy and class superiority allowing for mass incarceration. hooks argues "[i]n the Diaspora, most black people's relationship to love has been shaped by the trauma of abandonment" (p. 18). Within this understanding, "there is a history of power, freedom and choice juxtaposed against the legacy of powerlessness, enslavement, and absence of choice, a complex emotional backdrop unfolds" (p. 19). The dominant narrative is a reductionist one of slavery. A means of control the oppressor utilizes in framing the discussion effectively eliminating a rich meaningful picture of black people's history as nuanced, layered, and textured.

Criminal justice has been a response to dilemmas the dominant society faced in the past. The Black Codes, Fugitive Slave Act, and formalized criminal justice system were intended as tactics for policing people of African descent in a different way than whites. The response of whites to such repression was justification and defense. Anthropologist Oscar Lewis documented what he called a culture of poverty, exemplified by impulse control, present-time orientation and an inability to defer gratification, as the cause of social inequality (Massey and Denton, 1993, p. 15). A judiciary that was initially used to maintain white power eventually changed the ways people could legally treat persons of color, racist white community mores and attitudes were passed down to this day, so that even now African American potential is discounted.

The popular narrative of these instances of racism and active efforts to deprive people of African descent of human rights might well be presented as reactionary or the work of bigoted malcontents. In truth, as Jason Morgan Ward (2011) points out, white resistance to equality is pervasive, spans decades, and is far more sophisticated than overt forms of discrimination. The defense of the color line gave way, as those approaches lost their appeal, to conservative Americanism in areas such as housing, fair employment and education (p. 82). With opportunity shorn away from the notion of the American Dream, desperation and feelings of mistreatment created an untenable situation for people of color. Just as vitally, criminal justice and its application had repercussions on individual African Americans. Examples of these repercussions included how African Americans saw prospects for justice, and how that shaped the behavior of people of color in ways that deferred out of trepidation, intimidation or plain expediency to white supremacy. Such deference extended further to the institutions and power-brokers of the moment. Although it is necessary to acknowledge such matters, my intention is not to merely recite a historical review many other volumes have already related such accounts of facts.

3. Racism Home to Roost: Black Criminalization

As a new layer to such issues, researchers Bobbie Boland and Melody Morton Ninomiya (2009) unearth a sometimes forgotten aspect of what criminalization reflects for communities of color: institutional neglect and the long-term stripping of resources and support. While sociologists long exposed how relative deprivation can affect people's minds, the hyper-criminalization of deviance has raised the stakes. Even one's failure to stay within the legal superstructure as a response to poverty and state hostility or indifference can create life-changing problems. Instances of this, as Boland and Ninomiya point out, are obvious in the disproportionate numbers of incarcerated women, and women engaged in the criminal justice system who have survived significant histories of sexual and physical abuse. Women with low self-esteem, few educational and vocational opportunities, who are dependent or face other problems, are overrepresented in the system as well (p. 122). States have cut down the safety nets created in the 1970s to help the economically disadvantaged, women, and people of color. The result has been several generations of women who had few resources. Without access to education, social services or institutional support, people, white or of color, face bleak prospects. A condition of white supremacy is that such criminalization is expected for people of color.

To understand the nature of criminalization and incarceration, it is essential that we look at the underlying systems of oppression embedded within almost every institution. The media repeatedly present scenes, so that when the public is exposed to any aberration, it neatly fits into a narrow view of awful incidents. The statistics are as plentiful as they are heartbreaking. Graham Boyd points out that 1,981,395 males of African descent were subjects of chattel slavery in 1860, juxtaposed to 2017, when the state will incarcerate an estimated 1,999,916 African American males. (2001, p. 6)

Policing of young people of color has created a dynamic where the majority of youth regard *themselves* as problems in the eyes of law enforcement. A 2007 project by the Center for Crime and Justice Policy Research at Suffolk University revealed teens would not seek help from the police when they were being mistreated by peers.

What is the deeper story behind what the media reports of predominantly young African American men and women in chains, against walls or being beaten up and shot by law enforcement. More critically, how is such treatment normalized, even accepted, by white society. The expectation of run-ins with police has had a powerful effect on how African Americans see themselves, their lives and hopes, how they interact with the world, and how whites perceive those lives. More tellingly, University of California, Los Angeles researchers Yesilernis L. Peña, Christopher Federico, and Jim Sidanius found white/African American asymmetry when it came to distrust of the criminal justice system. Contrary to media imagery, such opinions decreased as African Americans ascended the class structure. Such could likely be credited to the fact that, even as their economic fortunes rose, African Americans did not witness a commensurate change in treatment by authorities.

In the most practical sense, the idea of speaking up is a part of North American political and popular culture, from the Boston Tea Party to a plethora of activist slogans that have permeated the mainstream, such as "silence=death," "speaking truth to power," "your silence will not protect you," and so forth. The Youth Justice Coalition argues:

> unfortunately, in the United States, where consumer culture collides with the rights of individualism, almost all our talking is focused on blaming or exposing the individual person, and on fixing you—instead of on exposing unjust conditions and the inhumane treatment of people and fixing the system. So, the whole industry of psychology, psychiatry, and talk shows dominates voice in America. Having a voice in this context doesn't often lead to a conversation about oppressive conditions or on the race, gender, class and other inequities that sustain this oppression. In other words, having a voice doesn't guarantee that a person will fight for personal or community liberation. (2007)

The evolution of the suspicion state varies from crude abuse to a sophisticated web of control. Relating back to the idea of having a voice and believing one is speaking out, such control and silencing prove often to be the same. As communities experience and witness aggressive expansion of the criminalization of youth within all institutions, juvenile detention centers, the incubators for adult prisons, continue to grow. In August 2011, *The Washington Post* reported on Texas trends of ticketing children for run-of-the-mill schoolyard misbehavior (St. George). According to Texas Southern University's Earl Carl Institute for Legal and Social Policy, 62 percent of those ticketed in Dallas schools are African American. Houston Municipal Court Judge David Fraga told the *Post* he sees about 150 juvenile ticketing cases a day during the school year, about half of them school-related. What does this mean for young people of color? While such issues as criminal records, which may be expunged in some states, and engagement with the court system are day-to-day worries, a more insidious problem is how young people of color see their stake in society.

Without a doubt, the assimilation impulse, especially for the young, has a thoroughly North American tenor. Youth, inherently insecure and yearning for acceptance, and people of color who desire a part of the American Dream, are often too eager to prove their loyalty. But within cages where youth are held, "being yelled at" is a constant—juvenile prisoners wake up to the voice of anger and end their nights by the voice of anger. Survivors of the juvenile detention centers when asked, what are the conditions inside, repeatedly, they would say we were yelled at, as though the yelling permeated their being and terrorized their spirits. For youth to have a voice in this context can be dangerous, for that yell means much more than the words or sounds uttered Disobedience may mean an extra month locked up. With or without a medical diagnosis it would mean also prescription of drugs like Seroquel. Interviewed for this book chapter, community organizer Jesse Bliss who has worked for the past decade in juvenile detention centers says she believes medication has become the "go to" as a means of addressing behavior issues with juvenile inmates. In its report, "Betraying the Young," Amnesty International corroborates that observation, noting the use of what is referred to as chemical restraints to be widespread in juvenile detention facilities, both state and private. Patricia J. Williams reminds us that moral complacency may not be moved until catastrophic events take place. Her essay, "Obstacle Illusions: The Cult of Racial Appearance," gives us a glimpse of the self-doubt on which law enforcement and other authorities have long preyed:

> [W]e are afflicted with the class-jumping hyper-vigilance of the embarrassed former peasant, trying to suppress the truth of exuberant family origins when what is at stake is not a broken rule of etiquette, but an entire sense of belonging in a yearned-for world. . . . The ritual dismissal of those "beneath" on the social ladder (however defined) too frequently mirrors the internalized admonishment of the anxious newly arrived—right-fork anxiety, left foot-in-mouth, the merciless rush to judge others because one's own humiliation is pre-ordained. The self betrays itself when trying hardest. For the real rules are so silent, so thoughtless, small as a detail—an earring? An inflection?—yet a matter of birthright, imparted in the nursery, hoarded until the grave. (2000, p. 153)

In the case of youth incarceration, failing to obey can bear a heavy cost for young inmates. Despite that there is virtually no research to support the use of psychotropics on children for such conditions as "acute aggression." Many are routinely administered psychotropic drugs to restrain or punish as an alternative to effective treatment (National Mental Health Association, 2004; Burton, 2010).

The state's reliance on silence and invisibility allows the mass incarceration of children, disproportionate numbers of which are black, and brown-skinned youth and children living in poverty. Most notably, youth incarceration creates the illusion of a society that does not deprive its youth of housing, education, and health care. Throughout these abuses, how children must feel in this situation is almost unfathomable. Such scenarios make children hyper-visible to the state as criminals but invisible to the state as youth worthy, like all other children, of a warm environment, home, love, education, health care, and nutrition. California is still one of the few states in which the police are given extraordinary power over youth's lives. Police were empowered through gang injunctions to stop people because of appearance, including being bald and looking "gang related." Such happens on top of laws that already make it illegal to be a gang member.

Kim McGill of the Youth Justice Coalition (2007) discusses youth policing in the context of the daily routine of being approached, known as "common law right to inquire." In this scenario, questions will be asked by uniformed police officers such as: Do you have identification? Then, police are permitted to require detailed information. The idea that someone is suspected of criminal activity as justification for infringement on personal rights is not questioned.

Another intrusion occurs when police to stop and frisk people without asking any questions. This is a direct attack without any warnings, all of it legal. Suppose for a moment, if these are experiences readers do not regularly endure, that it was your neighborhood deemed bad, and your child's every move seen as suspicious. Consider the impact of police in full uniform, armed and positioned to greet your child throughout the day, at school, while playing with friends. The truth is that just about anything can be considered suspicious because the laws are so vague. Many are suspicious because the color of their skin marks them as dangerousness or deviant.

4. Racial Justifications for Black Disempowerment

Re-imagining history in a way that erases or obscures the truth of such crimes must also be seen for another outcome: communicating that memory is no longer crucial. We cannot honestly look at a societal problem without understanding the broader landscape of interpersonal violence, violence within the home, state violence, and so forth. Often, the public orientation toward process fails to acknowledge that not everyone is subject to the same rules within the system in which said processes are applied. In criminal justice and the issue of black criminalization, how race is discussed and redefined to shape understanding should be a noteworthy moment of conversation.

Michelle Alexander calls the current United States criminal justice conundrum an extension of a generations-old inability to confront the country's racist past. Much has been written about the historical use of racist terror, but scholars like Alexander strongly imply knowledge of that past demonstrates we must focus on the present. Such attention is necessary, unless we want to continue to leave history to sort out what could be changed and eradicated. Examples of society's collective failure to understand personal and social history abound. For instance, violence in the home up until the 1970s was considered a private matter. Society has only recently come to popularly understand the impact of violence of fear on the psyche. On January 1, 2002, Penal Code §1473.5 became law, making California the first state in the nation to permit battered women convicted of killing their batterers to file a writ of habeas corpus with evidence demonstrating how the battering and its effects led to the killing. A vast labyrinth of inequalities, well contained by patriarchy, imperialism, racism and class inequity, are in no small part informed by a past's applications in the present. In *The New Jim Crow: Mass Incarceration in the Age of Colorblindness*, Alexander writes:

> What has changed since the collapse of Jim Crow has less to do with the basic structure of our society than the language we use to justify it. In the era of colorblindness, it is no longer socially permissible to use race, explicitly, as a justification for discrimination, exclusion and social contempt. So we don't. Rather than rely on race, we use our criminal justice system to label people of color, "criminals" and then engage in all the practices we supposedly left behind. Today, it is perfectly legal to discriminate against criminals in nearly all the ways it was once legal to discriminate against African Americans. Once you are labeled a felon, the old forms of discrimination, housing discrimination, denial of the right to vote, and exclusion from jury service are suddenly legal. As a criminal, you have scarcely more rights, and arguably less respect, than a black man living in Alabama at the height of Jim Crow. We have not ended racial caste in America; we have merely redesigned it. (2010, p. 2)

In short, where extralegal force against people of color ruled the day as a means to destabilize communities and cow individuals into submission, a new legal infrastructure enforces old racism and white urges to reign in non-white challenges to hegemony. Far from being random, isolated occurrences, or deviations from policy, abuse, and acceptance of the same is given the weight of appearing systematic and directed. Actions appear calculated to terrorize particular groups of people and designed to maintain social control. (Williams, 2006, p. 250)

In *American Methods: Torture and the Logic of Domination*, Kristian Williams writes about torture of war detainees in the American military prison at Abu Ghraib: "Torture is not incidental to state power; it is characteristic of that power. Torture doesn't represent a system failure; it is the system." (Ibid., p.3). He continues:

> There are three dimensions to the nexus of torture and state power. First, there is the instrumental aspect. States use torture for specific identifia-

> ble ends, whether to coerce individual people or to intimidate. Second, torture serves as an expression of status. It represents the power of the state, making it manifest on the body of its victims. It also communicates the elevated status of the torturer and the degraded position of the prisoner. Third, and perhaps most troubling, torture can arise as a function of the position of power itself—not in response to opposition, but as an exultant tribute to the state's own ascendancy. It is the nature of power to expand, to search out its limits. Graphic abuses become a predicable consequence of unchecked power, especially within institutions within institutions that are by their nature coercive, or in settings that are already degrading to those who endure them. Just as invading armies, zero-tolerance police campaigns, supermax prisons, juvenile detention facilities and more, without extraordinary measures taken to insure otherwise, sublime machines will continue to generate atrocities. (Ibid, p. 250)

How whites define themselves and racial minorities has been the subject of extensive scholarship, but in the area of criminalization, these definitions appear to take on a new weight. How did it get this way? While this chapter explored earlier how blackness is framed as deviant, the reappraisal of whiteness and race in general bear consideration. The Pennsylvania experience is fascinating in this regard, for it was the state that was the seat of United States antislavery activism and historically a place that found much success in building the foundation for what would become American cultural identity (Tomek, 2011, p. 82). That identity, based in ideas of unity and opportunity, was also couched in the worry that persistent discrimination and lower-class status would only serve to breed resentment and revolution. In the late 1700s, ideas of blacks and "depraved condition," or that slavery left people of African descent with lowered moral faculties and hatred of whites, endured. By negotiating a complex politic, where convincing whites of the problems national disunity and breakdowns in commerce (typified in Southern conflicts over industry of the period) could have on their own ambitions, black uplift could be seen as helpful in the capitalist project.

Where white society found explicitly naming African Americans as criminals a century or more ago, such terming today is untenable. Wording is a matter of process and verbiage that enforces the legitimacy of the system of law. One of the myriad complexities of such an acknowledgment is understanding how such racialization is predicated on the agreement with the abstract notion of equality within the system, regardless of race. The Civil Rights Movement successfully ended segregation and many federal and state protections were created. Reasonably, one could argue that these concessions and victories resulted in a society that saw new opportunities for people of color. By the end of the twentieth century, states such as California, considered a liberal stronghold by most, seek an end to Affirmative Action and other programs to rectify institutional racism. Such political offensives appeal to those who want to believe centuries-old racial disparities have been eliminated by the successes of the Civil Rights Movement. But organized, institutional racial advantages for whites, often unacknowledged or invisible yet persistent, have abetted the gulf for which racism in criminal justice is but a bellweather for a society that has yet to come to terms with race.

5. Capital's Failure and the Revolt

In 2011, the Occupy Wall Street movement and allied local Occupy endeavors became an international political incident to discuss class and economic inequality. Most popularly, Occupy demands focused on corporate corruption and the gulf between rich and poor. Public demonstrations in Oakland, New York City, Los Angeles, Houston, Portland, Denver and many other cities were met with arrests, dispersal tactics and other police activities. Amid a grinding financial crisis, it should be no secret why social unrest occurred. "Pain and humiliation, along with surveillance, confinement, and the more basic use of violence, are major elements of state power" (Williams, 2006, p. 250).

Capital's contractions inevitably become the foil for the snuffing of the social contract. The global economic recession has persisted for decades in communities of color. Unemployment, lack of educational resources, environmental racism, food injustice, and inadequate housing have become expected by the racial majority which holds power, and for people of color who have been forced to deal with lowered expectations. The Occupy Wall Street pickets became an outlet for the fury people felt. Ron Daniels states:

> Black folks who have lost their homes to foreclosure or are underwater because of the sub-prime mortgage scam, black students who are drowning in debt from student loans and the black joblessness should mount parallel but supportive "Occupy" marches and rallies all across the nation. (2011, p. 2)

Solving myriad social problems in a capitalist anatomy has proven almost impossible. North American white supremacy, supported by corporate interests, *comprador* politics, and an institutional failure to take suffering as a national emergency not a crisis of choice, has proven durable over decades. Yet where the majority sees discontent, its origins are not hard to discern just under the soil. The following studies illustrate examples:

In his study, "Excluding Blacks and Others from Housing: The Foundation of White Racism," Joe R. Feagin (1999) points out modern racism, itself the outcome of slavery and segregation, has insured people of color are unjustly treated in housing scenarios, from bold discrimination to mistreatment in insuring, lending, etc.—a situation Feagin terms residential apartheid. Most whites, he reminds readers, contend they are not responsible for segregation.

Economic dispossession has put food sovereignty and food justice out of reach for most people of color. Food First reports efforts in the Global South are aimed at sustainable agriculture, clean water, fair prices for goods, and freedom from GMO contamination. Many North American communities of color are not broadly considering such topics, or the effect of such self-determination on a community and hopes for a future (Food First, 2010).

Private prison construction has been termed by groups like Critical Resistance as environmental racism for their placement in poor communities and tax advantaging. "They suck up scarce local resources such as water; they require towns to pay for roads, sewers and utilities; they generate tens of thousands of miles of commuting pollution, often in the most polluted parts of the state; they take irreplaceable land out of any productive use, wasting valuable public resources for nothing but holding people in cages" (Braz et al., 2006, p. 96).

For years, politicians have manipulated class and racial inequalities as issues of choice or hard work. Choice becomes an unexamined judgment of others; an adjective easily cast upon others lives. A convenient way for the oppressor to continue to blame those they oppress, to be at peace with themselves and society. For those who choose "bad" behaviors, they should expect to be punished. Conversations fill dining room tables, history books and pop culture of those who make these bad choices. Compounding the concept of choice is a racist state that allows some choices to be overlooked when acted upon by one whose space is guaranteed as "good." Yet, for those deemed unacceptable because they exist, such individuals are guaranteed at best an unreasonable, unjust struggle to achieve. In a larger sense, that struggle may include avoiding state terror such as by the police, in schools, and in places of employment.

Victor Rios, writing in *Punished: Policing the Lives of Black and Latino Boys* (2011), reminds readers that prisons are regarded by some scholars as a socially accepted means for controlling and managing unemployed and "surplus" racial populations. Amid global austerity measures, rebellions accompany state drives to decimate public sector jobs, worker protections, and expectations of youth. Though North Americans believe rioting to be emblematic of the Third World, the fact so-called civilized nations like Greece, the United States, and the United Kingdom saw riots is significant. The need to control and direct the poor, the non-white and the unemployed in North America, international poster land for the bounty of the free market, is crucial in defense of an economic system that benefits the wealthy. Since the Reagan years, where America was held aloft in many a President Ronald Reagan oratory as the "shining city on the hill," and even before, the United States has been idealized. Inequity could, in any idealized scenario, are inconsequential. As the aforementioned Sentencing Project research notes, prison populations are growing.

In *Lockdown America: Police and Prisons in the Age of Crisis* (2000), Christian Parenti opines that reportedly errant populations fall outside the white supremacist capitalist framework. In brief, this framework works as: go to college and develop a skill of use to business/industry and go to work for said corporations, doing the work as specified, or become entrepreneurial and model the approach of opportunity and profit. We can either model such through circumstance or disenfranchisement, or incur the wrath of the powerful as a penalty for such. For many black youth, whose childhoods are shaped and informed by torture, to optimistically forecast what will become of you is difficult. Many of these adults and children considered errant in Parenti's assessment live an existence most of us could not survive for a day. Yet his remark is instructive in how we should understand black exploitation, both from a criminal justice standpoint and from a space of how the dominant culture seeks to control through resources.

In a framework Occupy Wall Street Movement conversations appear to be creating, a new means of discovery in which people consider the root of oppression, domination and exploitation is the philosophy that centers the black experience. We can also consider the construct of hooks' ideas mentioned earlier of a loveless human defined as one who is deviant, less than human, and needing to be controlled, punished, and destroyed. Economic challenge and subjugation of the self that white communities face is nothing new for people of African descent. Black parents, out of love, were compelled to break the spirits of children to prepare them for a society that would punish them for being themselves. There was a huge price to pay to be rebellious as most children are, and black children were denied so many natural states of child development so as to protect them from a racist world, a world that hated their black being. As many who are oppressed, abused, exploited they develop survival skills that do not serve them well in their private lives. Such as reliance on lies, and manipulation for one's survival of mind, body, and spirit are at stake. So we see how a racist culture not only dehumanizes one, but creates a false self, a self that may transgress boundaries and laws. This will make one appear suspect.

With economic conditions worsening, and attendant racism and criminalization on the upsurge, resistance is the only option. Growing sentiment appears to be in the direction of more people of color being involved in Occupy Wall Street and associated movements. Though anecdotes about diversity have been mixed (Patton, 2011), the Occupy Wall Street movement captured so much attention and energy in part because it represents the first popular United States movement to broadly tackle the economic inequality leading to incarceration and criminalization. One of its most provocative implications, unlike the Tea Party movement, is Occupy Wall Street's lack of emphasis on taxation to create economic justice. Many Occupy Wall Street organizers, movement observers note, grasp that, in the case of social programs, governments can take these items away and thus political ambitions much instead aim higher (Jarvis, 2011, p. 54). Scores of writings have emphasized the need for racial justice activism in this context.

Rinku Sen asks "How can a racial analysis, and its consequent agenda, be woven into the fabric of the movement?" and argues that "[w]e need to interrogate not just the symptoms of inequality—the disproportionate loss of jobs, housing, healthcare and more—but, more fundamentally, the systems of inequality, considering how and why corporations create and exploit hierarchies of race, gender and national status to enrich themselves and consolidate their power" (Sen, 2011, p. 12). Occupy Wall Street and its allied movements appear to be shifting the dynamics and pushing activists to change their organizational tactics. In New York City, Occupy Wall Street activists of color approached issues of inclusion strategically, working to be present in all Occupy Wall Street working groups, forging alliances with supportive whites, and leading outreach to communities of color (Alcindor, 2011). Such experiences could be a blueprint for others seeking to widen the discussion created by such spaces. Groups like Women Occupy and Occupy Patriarchy contend "institutions such as Wall Street are manifestations of the far deeper and greater problem of patriarchy which depends in large measure on the exploitation, disempowerment, and subjugation of women" (Marshall and Miriam, 2011). With the enduring financial downturn, the development of fresh activism, community engagement and political theory is sure to continue.

6. Conclusion

In *Are Prisons Obsolete?* Angela Y. Davis writes racism still influences contemporary structures, attitudes and behaviors, in spite of institutional claims of its irrelevancy today. "Nevertheless," Davis writes, "anyone who would dare call for the reintroduction of slavery, the organization of lynch mobs or the reestablishment of legal segregation would be summarily dismissed. But it should be remembered that the ancestors of many of today's most ardent liberals could not have imagined life without slavery, life without lynching or life without segregation" (2003, p. 23). And in this simple but direct idea, Davis captures the greatest monument to white supremacy and criminal justice: the ability of a society, especially its most fortunate members, to pretend one of history's most harsh factors in education, opportunity, and incarceration was somehow a relic of history.

Among North America's most prominent cultural wars is how such history is told. Amidst some of the more egregious efforts, Trymaine Lee writes, "Tennessean Tea Party activists are calling for removal of references to slavery and mention of the country's founders being slave owners. . . . In 2011, the Texas Board of Education approved more than 100 revisions to textbooks involving social studies, economics, and history for Texas's 4.8 million students." Lee criticized these revisions saying, "The Texas revisions include the exploration of the positive aspects of American Slavery, lifting the stature of Jefferson S. Davis to that of Abraham Lincoln. (2012)"

Much of United States history that has disappeared is critical to a complete and relevant analysis helpful in understanding sexism and racism. Davis (1990) writes, "If we are not afraid to adopt a revolutionary stance, then we must get to the root of our oppression. After all, radical means 'grasping the root'" (p. 14). A population's collective memory is fortified when it understands the actions its members are making are due to a violent history of trauma and annihilation of spirit and soul. From this acknowledgment can come the means to restore and rebuild a self not constructed by the perpetrator. No longer betraying and hating the self they see in each other, instead people of color challenge actions and underlying beliefs in themselves and their criminalization. Bell hooks writes of such pervasive deeply embedded roots rarely spoken.

> Even in the face of racism's most vicious institution, slavery, initially on all fronts enslaved black folks refused to embrace white notions of our inferiority, but that changed when white racists doled out privileges and rewards on the basis of skin color. (2001, p. 57)

A caste system based on skin color was imposed, in which black people internalized and upheld white supremacist hatred and violence. Hooks further exposes the roots of systems of oppression utilized not only to assault but to incarcerate:

> Just as the dehumanization via objectification of enslaved black women's bodies was spearheaded by patriarchal white males, enslaved black males who embraced patriarchal thinking (no doubt that women were inferior to men was already ingrained in their psyche before coming to the so-called New World, as women were subordinated by men in most archaic societies globally) began to value lighter skinned women over their darker counterparts. (Ibid.)

It was through the rape of black women by white masters that allowed for this color caste system to be an instrument of destruction, leading to much of the racism and sexism within the Civil Rights Movement without the white man's presence. Hooks illuminates key moments in time that helped create privileged or lack of privilege based on skin color:

> Annals of history show the lighter-skinned black male was often viewed with suspicion. The lighter skinned female was seen as more likely to affirm and uphold patriarchal white male power. As the object of white male desire, she was perceived as a creature the white male could subjugate at will. (Ibid.)

We can see the roots of racism and sexism stemming from sexual violence. We can see why so many do not want such teachings to be part of the story. Many institutions rely on the tenets of racism and sexism to prevail.

For the social justice-minded individual, examination of racism and sexism must also look at progressive forces in history. Exploring successes and failures is needed. For example, the women's movement of the 1960s and 1970s saw tensions, which are critical in understanding racism and sexism. Many scholars have documented the betrayal by white women of their "sister(s)" within the women's movement. Davis writes:

> White women who were then primarily involved in the consciousness raising process failed to comprehend the relationship between welfare rights movement and the larger battle of women's emancipation. Neither did they understand the importance of challenging the marginalization of black women as a struggle in which all women who identified with women's liberation ought to have participated. (1990, p. 27)

Such conflicts led to distrust and anger of white feminists. Davis (1990) locates some of the root causes of racism within feminism(s). "In order for the women's movement to meet the challenges of our times, the special problems of racially oppressed women must be given strategic priority. During the early phases of the contemporary women's movement, women's liberationist issues were so narrowly construed that most white women did not grasp the importance of defending black women from the material and ideological assaults emanating from the government." (Ibid.)

The statistics of African Americans ensnarement in the criminal justice system and betrayal by ostensible supporters are depressing. Yet the personal stories may be the most dispiriting. Juvenile detention centers educator Jesse Bliss describes the harsh conditions placed upon the lives of children locked up. Prisoners not being fed, deprived of sunlight, and violence sanctioned at all levels are common. In some institutions, pregnant girls allegedly may not receive adequate pre-natal care and are allowed 1-3 days with their children following birth. In California and other states, young girls while pregnant are relocated into units for children who are on suicide watch, considered a threat to the general population. As Victor Rios points out in *Punished*, generations of young men of color are changing the ways they think and act to compensate for the law enforcement connection they expect to have in their lives. How they see their masculinity in this context, and how young women define themselves conversely, is shaped by peers who share their subordination to juvenile justice. Beyond whatever debates the political class may have over assimilation versus self-determination, the existence of hope for futures that do not involve prison are seen by youth as dim at best. Faced with a majority in denial about their plight, youth of color face long odds.

Convenient scapegoats have been created as ways of deflecting issues of poverty, suffering, and torture. These scapegoats are further a means of neglecting and controlling real opportunities for advancement for people of color. Inevitably, assertions like these draw blistering anger from institutional powers and their supporters. Yet, if slavery could not destroy the spirit of black people, would that not give young black and brown children a history to draw from in order to not fall in to the traps and snares designed to incarcerate their bodies? If we challenge the obstacles with this powerful historical understanding, perhaps radical change may be realized.

Different movements over the decades have sought to challenge the ways society looks at prisons. Until the United States is ready to prioritize racial justice and account for its past and present, and for all beneficiaries to openly acknowledge their gains, criminal justice will remain a matter with which there will always be contention. Michel Foucault observed that prison reform's flaw was in its inextricable link to prison development; "improvements" to the system make the system itself "better" and not necessarily more just. Such refusal to even discuss the racist dimensions of how incarceration is conducted and how law is practiced in North America hint at the apprehension discussions of change enliven. Yet since prisons were invented in Western countries in the 1700s, one would be hard pressed to find instances in which criminal justice was not inequitably applied to people of color or the economically disadvantaged. In its post-apartheid period, South Africa may best be remembered for its Truth and Reconciliation Commission. The Commission hosted scores of witnesses to testify on the institutional racism of apartheid, its effects on black and white, and the apartheid regime's crimes against humanity. Those testimonies are preserved online, and represent but one means of addressing racial justice.

Excising racism from criminal justice is a struggle of challenging white racial omnipotence in North America and the world. If George Jackson, writing in *Soledad Brother* (1994), is to be believed, incarceration's aim of physical and psychological abuse is the elimination of deviance. Changing these dynamics, if change is even possible, will require radical approaches. Such approaches must in truth be positioned on a change in the society itself. As the globe saw in 2011 with the Occupy movement, people in many countries are concerned about austerity measures and stagnation. If these societies can force a more revolutionary change remains to be seen.

Four

IMPRISONING FOREIGN NATIONALS

Ute Ritz-Deutch

This chapter focuses on the detention of non-United States citizens, a diverse group that includes documented and undocumented immigrants, asylum seekers, torture survivors, victims of human trafficking, suspected terrorists and so-called unlawful enemy combatants, physically and mentally ill people, minors, and others. Since they are not United States citizens, they are especially vulnerable and many face additional challenges in the United States justice system, such as language barriers, limited access to translation services, lack of legal representation, and of habeas corpus—the longstanding right to be heard by a judge and to seek release from unlawful detention.

I will first examine the imprisonment of non-United States citizens who have been caught up in the war on terror. They are held in United States prisons, on United States military bases in other countries, in secret prisons or black sites around the world, and at the United States naval base at Guantánamo Bay, Cuba—a territory where the United States exercises complete jurisdiction and de facto sovereignty. After years of imprisonment and torture, most of prisoners held at Guantánamo Bay were found to have no ties to terrorism and have had to be released. While in custody, these prisoners were routinely tortured in direct violation of several Geneva Conventions that regulate conduct during war and the treatment of prisoners. Since the United States is a signatory to these conventions, it is legally bound to uphold them. As Barbara Olshansky (2007) and others have noted, by blatantly violating these international human rights norms the United States has also lost considerable moral ground in the eyes of the international community.

Tragically, legislation and funding intended to combat terrorism has also been used in the United States for the massive detention of immigrants (both documented and undocumented). Many detainees are imprisoned solely because of immigration-related violations, which fall under civil but not criminal law. They are victims of draconian legislation that mandates detention and deportation for minor, non-violent crimes. Granted, these prisoners generally do not face the torture and other grave abuses known to have occurred at Guantánamo; nonetheless both groups of prisoners have common grievances and their treatment is often in violation of the United States Constitution and international human rights law. Non-citizen prisoners are routinely subjected to human rights violations, which have been documented by governmental oversight offices and non-governmental organizations (NGOs), reported to the United Nations, and challenged in United States courts.

According to the World Prison Population List published by the International Centre for Prison Studies (Walmsley, 2009), the total reported world prison population in 2008 was 9.8 million prisoners, a rate of 145 per 100,000. The United States is the global leader in imprisonment, with more than 2.2 million people held in United States prisons, a rate of 756 per 100,000 (Ibid.). The United States has the largest total number of reported prisoners and the highest incarceration rate—five times the global average.

The current situation and the continuing growth of the prison industrial complex in the United States is a monumental crisis caused by our failure to constructively address human rights and social justice issues.

The United States State Department has consistently criticized other governments for using military tribunals to try civilians, because it eliminates due process rights and undermines the rights of individuals to a fair and public trial. Military tribunals are generally conducted in secret and often the prosecutor and judge is the same person, evaluating evidence that is held to different standards than it would be in a civilian court. The accused is likely to be defended by military personnel, who may not be given access to evidence that could render a verdict of non-guilty. For these reasons civil rights and human rights organizations have consistently argued that even terror suspects should be tried in civilian federal court. Regrettably, in the past decade some countries have justified their own abuses of prisoners on the grounds of expediency, citing United States actions as precedent. The magnitude of the damage caused across the world in regard to human rights can only be assessed in the long run, but the deterioration of rights during the first decade of the new millennium cannot be denied. It may take decades before the United States can rehabilitate its image as a country of law and justice.

The terrorist attacks of 9/11 were heinous and deserve condemnation. It is also understandable that the United States government felt compelled to use extraordinary measures to ensure the security of the nation. However, in the name of security many civil rights protections have been suspended, which poses the question of how far the government should be allowed to go before it violates its own raison-d'être. If the Bill of Rights and the United States Constitution no longer matter, and if the principles upon which the country were founded can be suspended indefinitely and revoked without a semblance of public debate, then it could be argued that the United States is no longer a democratic republic with viable checks and balances. It has become a state in which one branch of government (the executive and the military) has excessive control, in which the laws the United States Congress passes can be ignored, judicial oversight can be circumvented, and individuals can be oppressed even if they committed no crime or pose no threat. These are the hallmarks of dictatorial regimes, not the principles of a democracy.

Transparency and accountability are absolutely essential for a legitimate democracy. After 9/11 the actions of the Bush administration became shrouded in secrecy, and it took years of pressure and action from the Center for Constitutional Rights, the American Civil Liberties Union (ACLU), Amnesty

International, Human Rights Watch, and other groups before some measure of transparency was restored. A ghastly picture emerged from the limited information that initially became available to the public, although the International Committee of the Red Cross (ICRC), which has periodic access to detention sites around the world, had compiled information about human rights abuses at United States detention sites for years and had submitted reports to the United States government, which were ignored. According to the investigations of the Inspector General (Office of Inspector General, 2008) of the United States Department of Justice, interrogation techniques at some of these sites were egregious enough to make agents of the Federal Bureau of Investigations (FBI) uncomfortable and unwilling to participate.

In the months following the 9/11 attacks, the United States military offered financial rewards to civilians in Afghanistan and Pakistan for turning in persons with suspected terrorist ties. Thousands of people were caught in the dragnet and subsequently imprisoned. According to a report titled *Guantánamo and its Aftermath* (Fletcher & Stover, 2008), the United States military did not have effective screening processes to separate innocent suspects from actual terrorists. When the military belatedly instituted such measures, these were found to be in flagrant violation of the United States Constitution.

Consequently many innocent suspects were arrested on mere hearsay and detained in several facilities including Bagram in Afghanistan and Abu Ghraib in Iraq, and later at the United States military base at Guantánamo Bay in Cuba. These prisoners had no access to lawyers nor could they bring their case before a judge; they had no way to prove that they were innocent and unjustly imprisoned. During their imprisonment at Guantánamo detainees endured physical and psychological torture, including prolonged stress positions, temperature extremes, sleep deprivation, sensory deprivation and/or bombardment, beatings, sexual abuse, and interference with religious practice (such as desecration of the Koran); they were also terrorized by attack dogs (Olshansky, 2007; Meeropol, 2005; and Fletcher & Stover, 2008).

A series of high-level government directives coming from the Departments of Justice and Defense from September 2001 to April 2003 authorized these so-called "enhanced interrogation techniques." Torture and other cruel, inhumane, or degrading punishment is unconstitutional and in violation of the Geneva Conventions and the International Convention against Torture. Furthermore, torture is not allowed under the United States Army Field Manual, which prompted the military Judge Advocate General Corps to speak out against these techniques. The Bush administration argued that the Geneva Convention Relative to the Treatment of Prisoners of War did not apply to suspected members of terrorist organizations.

The official justification of the United States administration and the Department of Defense was that the United States was engaged in a war—the war on terrorism. There has been a longstanding debate among scholars and policy makers about the definition and nature of war and consensus has been elusive. However, based on international law, in particular the Geneva Conventions and their two protocols, war is defined as armed combat between two states and therefore does not apply to members of al Qaeda, who do not represent a government or a state. Furthermore, the United States Congress while authorizing military use after 9/11, never declared war. Based on the United States Constitution and International Law the so-called war on terror is therefore not legally recognized as a war. The question of legal definition has a bearing on whether or not terror suspects can be treated as prisoners of war or as civilians. Each group has specific rights and neither can be tortured.

According to the Geneva Conventions prisoners of war have to be assessed by a "competent tribunal" that can determine their status. Civilians likewise have to be assessed on an individual basis and if they are accused of crimes, they can be criminally prosecuted. The United States refused to grant POW status to prisoners taken in Afghanistan and elsewhere, but it also refused to treat them as civilians. In essence the government argued for the creation of a third and separate category for so-called unlawful enemy combatants, who have absolutely no legal protection. While the creation of a new category may make pragmatic sense in recognition of the new realities of international terrorism, it does not justify stripping suspects of rights that are recognized for the other groups.

This fallacious reasoning, which holds that some prisoners are outside the protection of international law and the United States Constitution, allowed the administration to arrest thousands of people without evidence, cause, or proper screening procedure, to transport them out of the country to places like Guantánamo, to torture them in an effort to obtain evidence, and to keep them in prison indefinitely without access to legal counsel or an independent court. According to the United States Supreme Court the administration's policies of indeterminate detention were clearly unconstitutional. In *Rasul v. Bush* (2004) the Supreme Court held that United States federal courts do have jurisdiction to hear habeas corpus cases brought by non-United States citizens held at Guantánamo Bay, since the United States has complete jurisdiction and control there. In *Boumedien v. Bush* (2008) the Supreme Court again held that non-United States citizens can file a writ for habeas corpus and furthermore that the Military Commissions Act of 2006 suspended this right in violation of the United States Constitution.

By 2010, after a year-long review, the United States government and advisors from the military and intelligence agencies estimated that only around fifty of the remaining prisoners at Guantánamo had ties to terrorist organizations and only thirty-five of these could be prosecuted. After years of interrogation, it appears that ninety-five percent of all the inmates held at Guantánamo could not be linked to terrorism.

Testimonies obtained under torture are not credible or admissible under international law, nor do they produce reliable intelligence. After being tortured, Asif Iqbal and Shafiq Rasul, two British citizens, signed confessions admitting to being present in a video of Osama bin Laden, even though they initially maintained and the British intelligence service M15 proved to the United

States that they were actually in Britain during the time in question (Meeropol, 2005, pp. 40-41). They were released in 2004 after years at Guantánamo. Had they been granted due process rights, access to a lawyer and an impartial court, they would have been able to prove their innocence much sooner.

Tragically but not surprisingly, former prisoners who have been released continue to suffer from the psychological effects of torture and have extreme difficulties reintegrating into civilian life. According to the Convention against Torture and Other Cruel, Inhuman, or Degrading Treatment or Punishment, people cannot be sent to countries where they will be tortured; consequently some of these former prisoners held at Guantánamo could not be returned to their country of origin and are now living in countries where they do not know anybody and have no family support. Among them were Muslim Uighurs, who had fled Western China from persecution and were consequently caught up in the dragnets in Afghanistan. Years after the courts had ordered their release from Guantánamo, they were finally able to leave and resettled to the Republic of Palau and elsewhere. To date the United States government has not offered an apology to any released prisoners, nor has it offered financial compensation to the victims (Fletcher & Stover, 2008). Some prisoners, even though cleared by the courts, are still held in United States custody because no country is willing to receive them.

The treatment of prisoners at Guantánamo has evidently not improved the national security of the United States, but instead has been utilized by terrorist organizations as a recruitment tool. The entire rationale for eroding civil rights and suspending due process apparently yielded no beneficial security results. Despite President Obama's promise to close Guantánamo, resistance from Congress has kept the facility open. In addition, the president signed the National Defense Authorization Act (NDAA) into law on December 31, 2011, thereby codifying the practices of the Bush Administration to apprehend persons of interest anywhere in the world (not just in combat zones) and to detain them indefinitely without having to officially charge them or give them a trial.

While most of the prisoners captured in the dragnets of the war on terror were originally detained in Afghanistan and Pakistan, immigrants of Middle Eastern descent were also targeted in the United States (Meeropol, pp. 145-148). Civil liberties activists estimated that immediately following the 9/11 attacks approximately two thousand immigrants were rounded up in the United States and placed in immigrant detention. The FBI placed these inmates into three categories depending on whether or not the agency considered them to be of interest, high interest, or undetermined interest. The latter category included all those individuals against whom the FBI had no evidence and who they could not link to terrorist activities.

According to Meeropol, the United States Justice Department ruled that suspects in all three categories must be detained until the FBI could prove that they had no terrorist ties (p. 148). These detainees were considered guilty until proven innocent; they were not granted due process rights as guaranteed by the Bill of Rights to all persons in the United States, they were not given access to lawyers, and indeed many of them were disappeared without their families being notified of their whereabouts. While in detention these prisoners, most of whom were never criminally charged, were placed in maximum security prisons under conditions generally reserved for the most violent prison population (Ibid., p. 148-157). Abuses at these facilities have been routinely reported.

In the weeks following the terrorist attacks the United States Congress with unprecedented speed and very little discussion passed the USA PATRIOT Act of 2001 (Uniting and Strengthening America by Providing Appropriate Tools Required to Intercept and Obstruct Terrorism Act) granting the executive branch the power to expand its surveillance and increase the information shared between criminal and intelligence agencies. In addition the PATRIOT Act limited or removed judicial oversight of the surveillance process, meaning the government could wire-tap telephones, monitor emails and gain access to medical and financial records of citizens and non-citizens alike without first acquiring a court order. As the acronym of the act implies, the government, especially the executive branch, considered people who opposed the legislation to be unpatriotic. In December 2001, Attorney General John Ashcroft even stated that activists opposing government policy were trying to scare the nation "with phantoms of lost liberty," thereby aiding terrorists and eroding national unity (Meeropol, p. 18). Since it went into effect, the PATRIOT Act has been used as a tool to target political and anti-war activists and dissidents who had nothing to do with 9/11 but could now be labeled terrorists for opposing the government, and be prosecuted by evidence that previously would have been considered inadmissible in a court of law.

Increased sharing of information among different branches of law enforcement also led to an increase in detention and deportation of undocumented immigrants, even if they had no connection to terrorism. Under special agreements such as 287g (section of the 1996 Illegal Immigration Reform and Immigrant Responsibility Act) local law enforcement agencies have been deputized to do the job of federal agents, while under the so-called "Secure Communities" program police departments are required to collect fingerprints on all persons processed and to share them with the Department of Homeland Security, in addition to the FBI which is already standard practice. A traffic ticket that results in the violator being taken to the police department (which is more likely to happen to persons of color) could therefore lead to deportation. According to civil rights groups, racial profiling is endemic in these methods. The tools initially designed to improve the government's capacity to apprehend and foil terrorists have consequently turned into a mechanism to target the weakest members of society: those who lack citizenship status. Indeed, the largest number of non-citizen prisoners in United States detention has nothing to do with the war on terror. Despite record funding, the Department of Homeland Security (DHS) and Immigration and Customs Enforcement (ICE) have not demonstrated that these funds are used to apprehend terrorists or persons who actually pose a threat to the nation.

While, as I show below, the detention of immigrants has skyrocketed since 9/11, the United States Congress had already considerably undermined legal safeguards for non-citizens prior to the attacks. The Antiterrorism and Effective Death Penalty Act (AEDA) and the Illegal Immigration Reform and Immigrant Responsibility Act (IIRIRA) of 1996 both curtailed habeas corpus and due process rights of non-citizens. As a result of this legislation, detention and deportation has become mandatory for a large number of immigrants, both documented and undocumented. The category of "aggravated felony" for which even documented immigrants can be deported, has been expanded to include many minor crimes, including shoplifting charges (Meeropol, p. 24). Amnesty International, which interviewed immigrants in detention, found among lawful permanent residents who were deported for minor crimes a native of Haiti, who was deported for "two convictions of possession of stolen bus transfer passes" and a native of Guyana, who was convicted of "signing traffic tickets using a false name" (Amnesty International, 2009, p. 19). Tragically, the personal element has been removed from the judicial process and judges no longer have the discretion to decide individual cases by considering all of the extenuating circumstances.

Since IIRIRA went into effect, the detention of immigrants has tripled. Whereas in 1996 immigration authorities had a daily detention capacity of fewer than 10,000 beds, by 2009 over 30,000 immigrants were in detention daily. Amnesty International reported that on average detainees were held for 37 days before being deported (AI, p. 6), although some have been in prison for months and even disappeared in the system for years without judicial review, without ever seeing a judge who could determine if their detention was even warranted in the first place. Frequently asylum seekers are detained even though the community in the United States where they hoped to resettle vouched for them and was willing to put up bond. This was the case of a Buddhist monk, who had escaped Tibet after being tortured because of his religious beliefs (p. 21). Despite affidavits from the American Tibetan community, who ensured the United States government that he would show up for his immigration hearings, he was imprisoned for ten months, after which his asylum request was finally granted.

According to the United Nations Working Group on Arbitrary Detention, governments should seek the least intrusive means and detention should only be used as a last resort and not as a first measure. It would be in keeping with international human rights norms to offer alternatives to detention whenever possible. Placing undocumented immigrants on a reporting system instead of incarcerating them could also mean considerable cost savings. On average the federal government spends $95 per prisoner a day, which totaled $1.8 billion in 2009; detention alternatives are projected to cost $12 per person a day (p. 4). Since many who have entered the United States illegally have lived in the United States for decades, have families and established businesses, they generally do not pose a flight risk. Over ninety percent of immigrants placed on a reporting system have complied with its requirements.

Since immigration falls under the jurisdiction of the federal government (and not state governments), immigrants are supposed to be in federally supervised detention facilities. Because of a shortage of prison space, the federal government contracts state and local jails as well as privately run prisons to house immigrants. In late 2009, immigrants were detained in a hodge-podge system of over 350 different facilities across the nation. This generates enormous profits for private corporations and county coffers, especially if they cut corners on the care of their inmates. According to a report submitted to the United Nations Special Rapporteur on the Rights of Migrants (Greene & Patel, 2007), the lucrative business of receiving federal contracts under Intergovernmental Service Agreements with ICE, has enabled counties to finance the construction of new jails and defray their operating costs. Some public jailers have gone on record boasting about their abilities to cut expenses below the per diem rate they receive from the federal government for housing immigrants (Ibid.). For the prison industry, immigrants have become the modern-day cash crop, and government officials in some impoverished rural areas herald the boom of immigrant detention as economic development that creates jobs for the community. This system, while generating revenues and profits, encourages substandard treatment of prisoners.

Undocumented immigrants in detention (as well as those who are documented but cannot immediately prove their status) are often denied access to telephones, translation services, or law libraries. Unlike suspected criminals they are considered guilty until proven innocent. While the United States Constitution protects due process rights of "all persons" in the United States and not just United States citizens, many of these rights have been undermined with the passage of IIRIRA and the policy changes enacted by the Department of Homeland Security. Even though immigration violations fall under civil law, undocumented immigrants have fewer rights than persons accused of a criminal offense. The government does not provide them with a free attorney if they cannot afford one and detainees have also complained that they were prevented from contacting legal aid societies or their embassies. Amnesty International (2009) found that the medical needs of detainees were routinely ignored and that over ninety people had died in immigrant detention from 2003 to 2009. Under the Bush administration it was nearly impossible to get official figures because DHS and ICE were shrouded under a cloak of secrecy.

The Obama administration promised greater transparency and after years of pressure ICE pledged to reform its system. In 2010 the agency finally released an official list of the detainees who died while in federal custody. It also made a detainee locator database available online, which makes it easier for families and attorneys to find out where prisoners are held. While far from perfect, greater transparency is at least a modest improvement. Nonetheless, the overall rate of detention and deportation has increased under the Obama administration, which has deported well over one million people to date. From September 2009 to September 2010 over 400,000 immigrants were detained and most of them were subsequently deported, at a daily rate of more than one thousand. The deportation cost for 2010 alone was more than $5 billion (over $12,000 per deportee). Despite of these expenditures the overall levels of immigration have only been moderately affected, since the flow of migrants is more controlled by labor demands in the United States than by restrictive laws and enforcement policies.

Among the people in immigrant detention are asylum seekers, torture survivors, and victims of human trafficking. Even though unlawful entry is a civil offense, people apprehended without documentation are often housed together with prisoners held for criminal offenses. The imprisonment of children has also been deplorable. The Hutto detention facility run privately by Corrections Corporation of America in Texas, for example, was sued for detaining families including children in substandard conditions. Amnesty International and Detention Watch Network reported violations throughout the detention system. Detainees were excessively restrained and Amnesty International (2009) reported that even expectant mothers were shackled on the way to the hospital and immediately after delivery. As one mother interviewed by Amnesty International lamented, "My baby was delivered while I was in prison . . . I missed the birth of my child and, I'll never get that back" (AI, p. 27).

Prisoners also complained that they were verbally, physically and sexually abused, deprived of food, medicine, physical exercise and their right to worship. Even the United States Government Accountability Office (GOA) reported to Congress that on many occasions ICE failed to comply with its own detention standards, although the GOA fell short of characterizing it as a "pervasive or persistent pattern of non-compliance" (GOA, 2008).

People can be deported for unlawful entry or overstaying their visas. However, long-term permanent legal residents and even United States citizens have also been detained, especially if they could not immediately prove that they had legal status. This includes United States citizens born abroad to United States parents, or persons born in the United States, who have no birth certificate because they were not born in a hospital (AI, pp. 20-21). Some United States citizens suffering from mental illness were deported because they had no representation and no capacity to navigate the bureaucracy and prove their status. Detainees have been transferred from mental health institutions to ICE facilities without their medications and without the knowledge of their doctors or families. In 2007, ICE deported a mentally disabled United States citizen to Mexico and it took his mother several months before she was able to locate him and return him to the United States (AI p. 22).

In the current system, non-citizens who are in the United States legally can be deported for relatively minor offenses, including driving while under the influence of alcohol. Judges no longer have the discretion to consider all of the extenuating circumstances, for example how long the person has been in the country, how long ago the crime was committed, or whether the person has a spouse or children who are United States citizens. These practices have also been deplored by the Organization of American States. When Human Rights Watch (2010) filed an amicus brief in the case of *Wayne Smith and Hugo Armendariz v. United States* before the Inter-American Commission on Human Rights, the commission ruled that mandatory deportation violates the American Declaration on the Rights and Duties of Man.

A report compiled by Human Rights Watch titled Forced Apart (HRW, 2009) shows that since AEDA and IIRIRA went into effect, 20 percent of all immigrants deported were documented and in the United States legally. Implementation has affected over one million United States citizens, whose families have been torn apart. The vast majority have been deported for minor, non-violent crimes, even though the United States government officially claims to focus its efforts on deporting violent non-citizen criminals (HRW, 2009). Tragically, every year approximately 10,000 United States citizen children lose one or both parents because of deportation and if they cannot be placed with family members they end up in foster care. While foster care may be an important alternative for children from families that abuse or neglect them, this is generally not the situation in deportation cases. Thousands of children who instead leave the country with their parents become de-facto deportees even though they are United States citizens.

Another particularly vulnerable group consists of undocumented immigrant women of color who are in abusive relationships, since abusers often use the immigration status of their partners as a means to further their control over the victims. While domestic violence affects women, children and (to a lesser degree) men of all ethnic groups and classes, those who experience multiple layers of subordination and oppression are most at risk. The existence of the Violence Against Women Act (VAWA) and the Victims of Trafficking and Violence Protection Act (VTVPA) is insufficient to address this crisis.

Roberta Villalón studied Latina immigrants, who left their native country to help their families survive and subsequently ended up in abusive relationships in the United States. Granted, VAWA and VTVPA have made it possible for a small percentage of battered women to obtain U-visas because they were victims of crime and to ultimately gain citizenship. However, not all survivors of gender violence are protected because the laws "prioritize certain survivors over others on the bases of their national origin, race, ethnicity, gender, sexual orientation, or class background" (Villalón, 2010, p. 37). The current immigration system thus replicates the institutionalized inequalities in the United States that are based on race, class, gender, and sexual orientation.

Many immigrant women are afraid to call the police or to seek assistance for fear of being deported—a fear that is not unfounded. There have also been many reports, involving the police departments in New York City and elsewhere, of police not providing translation services to immigrant women who do get the courage to complain about domestic violence, and of police officers failing to file reports or follow up. Needless to say, this distrust between immigrants and law enforcement has only increased in the last few years because any contact with police can lead to detention and deportation, even for people who are victims of crimes and have no criminal record themselves.

In the last decade, enforcement has become the primary mechanism by which the government seeks to curb immigration. Instead of addressing the structural inequalities and enacting comprehensive immigration reform, the government focuses on imprisoning the most vulnerable immigrant populations to deport them. Immigrants (both documented and undocumented), most of who come from Mexico and Central America, represent the fastest growing prison population in federal detention. According to a report the United States Bureau of Justice Statistics submitted to Congress (BJS, 2005), over one quarter of all detainees in federal prisons are immigrants; since the government has not kept consistent and comprehensive record of their immigration status it is hard to ascertain how many of them were in the country legally. Some prisoners are detained for violent criminal offenses, but most are only charged with immigration-related civil offenses and are waiting to be deported. It is even more difficult to establish statistics for state and local prisons, which hold more than ninety percent of all the detainees. Some non-citizens accused of violent crimes have been sentenced to death and executed by individual states such as Texas, which failed to notify the respective embassies. Since the federal government has obligations vis-à-vis foreign governments these executions of foreign nationals have created diplomatic strains and have had a negative impact on foreign relations.

The increasing detention of non-United States citizens also impacts United States citizens. According to Detention Watch Network, one out of every five families in the United States is of mixed status, comprised of citizens and non-citizens (including documented and undocumented persons). Non-citizens are one of the most vulnerable populations in the United States and make convenient scapegoats. Undocumented immigrants have been lumped into the same category as terrorists, both legally and in the popular imagination, and are also blamed for the country's economic woes. Some politicians appeal to their constituents by claiming to be tough on immigrants, deporting as many as possible and therefore supposedly securing the border.

This approach is not only simplistic but also dishonest. Immigrants have not caused the economic crisis that started in 2008, nor are they responsible for the terrorist attacks of September 2001. Moreover, border enforcement can never solve the problem of immigration since it fails to address the underlying causes of migration, which are deeply rooted in the consequences of free-trade agreements, foreign policy interventions, and structural global inequalities. The increasing incarceration of non-United States citizens may appease some people who are afraid of their own eroding economic status in society. However, it is not a viable solution to society's ills. Part of the solution has to be comprehensive immigration reform that also addresses pathways to legal status. In addition, free trade agreements like NAFTA should be reconsidered since they only allow free flow of capital and goods but inhibit free flow of labor. At the very least the question of open borders should be raised in the national discourse.

With the mid-term election in November 2010, the United States House of Representatives came under the control of the Republicans, which means that comprehensive reform will be shelved until after the next legislative cycle. Consequently advocates have shifted their focus from comprehensive reform to influencing the practice of immigration enforcement, urging the president and the Department of Homeland Security to protect the civil rights of all persons. On the state level advocates are challenging specific anti-immigrant laws and local ordinances.

The struggles on behalf of immigrants, including non-citizens, are likely to continue, especially in the aftermath of anti-immigrant legislation such as Arizona's SB 1070 and Alabama's HB 56, which many states are looking to copy. Such acts require local police to question anyone they "reasonably suspect" of being undocumented. Needless to say, racial profiling is endemic in this process and SB 1070 is being challenged in the courts. The United States Supreme Court has recently struck down most of the provisions in the Arizona law, but upheld the section that directs police officers to ask persons they encounter in the line of duty of their immigration status. The failure of the DREAM Act (Development, Relief and Education for Alien Minors Act) to pass the Senate in 2009 was a setback for young immigrants who were brought to this country as children, and who are now being punished for their parents' actions.

Anti-immigrant laws such as Arizona's SB 1070 and Alabama's HB 56 have gained attention in the media, but the "Secure Communities" program (S-Comm) has not. The program urges states to sign a Memorandum of Agreement (MOA) with ICE that requires local police to collect biometric data on all persons processed and to report this to the Department of Homeland Security, regardless of conviction status. Once ICE has received this data, it determines whether the person is deportable. This agreement does not require local police to be deputized as immigration enforcement agents. The goal of DHS is to have full implementation by 2013, thereby giving the federal government "a technological presence in every prison and jail."

Unfortunately these kinds of dragnet measures do not target violent criminals. Several reports by the Center for Constitutional Rights and other organizations show that the majority of immigrants deported by ICE had no criminal record or only minor offenses, some of them decades ago. Already thousands of people have been deported under S-Comm, among them victims of crime and other persons who sought help from the police. Despite its name, Secure Communities has the effect of making communities less secure because more people fear the police and hesitate to report crimes, which is why many police chiefs across the nation have spoken out against Secure Communities agreements and 287-g agreements. In May 2011 Illinois Governor Quinn announced that the Illinois State Police were withdrawing from S-Comm because the program had failed to meet its stated goal, namely to deport immigrants "who have been convicted of serious criminal offenses" (Julia Preston, "States Resisting Program Central to Obama's Immigration Strategy," *New York Times*, 5 May 2011). Illinois thus became the first state in the nation to pull out of the program after having signed an agreement with ICE.

Secure Communities agreements are routinely entered into without any public discussion and ICE only publishes the actual text of the MOAs after they have been signed by the governors. This lack of transparency and further erosion of civil rights ultimately affects all persons living in the United States, including United States citizens, since such a program cannot be implemented without racial profiling unless all persons are processed identically. Since public debate has been largely lacking about S-Comm, the public is mostly ignorant of these secret negotiations. Frequently, ICE has failed to accurately and truthfully inform local jurisdictions of the financial burden associated with the implementation of S-Comm, which will lead to greater labor and training costs for police and may also require the purchase of additional technology.

While the political discourse in the United States has become more polarized and the lack of meaningful action by the president and Congress has been deplorable, grassroots movements continue to grow, resisting current policies and advocating for change. The efforts by some members of Congress to revise the Fourteenth Amendment of the United States Constitution that grants citizenship to all persons born in the United States, and to revoke citizenship of people whose parents were undocumented, speak powerfully of the reactionary and exclusionary sentiment prevalent in much of the country.

At this time it is all the more crucial for immigrants and immigrant rights activists to keep this issue alive, to speak out about the injustices of the current immigration system and its devastating impact on families, the economy, and civil rights, and to seek change. Grassroots action and community mobilization can make a considerable difference in the lives of people. In New York State, hundreds of immigrant rights organizations offer assistance to immigrants or lobby for reform, although many face a serious budget crisis. There is an urgent need for change and coalition building since the current system affects millions of people a year.

Federal policy has arguably been a disaster; on the local level enforcement has been uneven and varies significantly among jurisdictions. As the report *Justice Derailed* (NYU School of Law, 2011) shows, New York's northern border has been subject to aggressive policing. In Rochester, New York, at Lake Ontario, the United States Customs and Border Patrol (CBP) has a strong presence and detains thousands of immigrants a year, among them international students and faculty, who have permission to be in the country but whose immigration status the agents may not understand. Border patrol agents have boarded domestic buses and trains, questioned people about their immigration status and then placed them into detention and deportation proceedings (Justice Derailed, 2011). Since CBP claims a jurisdiction of one hundred air-miles from the coast or an international border, two out of every three people residing in the continental United States live in what the

ACLU has called a de-facto constitution free zone. All persons in that zone, including United States citizens, are subject to questioning by the border patrol. In some areas, such as the Rochester-Buffalo corridor on New York's northern border, undocumented immigrants travel at particularly high risk, especially if they are people of color or have a noticeable accent.

In New York City, on the other hand, the city council and the mayor have directed police to not ask people about their immigration status unless it is part of a criminal investigation. Locality can make a big difference, as can advocacy on the local level. Similarly, reports have found that the economic exploitation of undocumented workers is "significantly lower in municipalities where established advocacy groups were fighting for the rights of low-wage and immigrant workers" (Semple, 2011).

Ensuring the constitutional protections and human rights of non-citizens is crucial for everybody in our communities across the country. Indeed, targeting minority groups and placing them into a separate legal category that deprives them of fundamental rights is a dangerous precedent that ultimately erodes the rights of all. Increased surveillance and data collection on everybody living in the United States creates a society less free and more Orwellian. It strengthens the state's exercise of disciplinary power while at the same time making it possible for government officials to avoid dealing with the root causes of immigration, especially the increasing disparity of wealth in the United States and across the globe. It also continues the process of criminalization and incarceration of millions of people in the United States, without offering alternatives that are more just, humane, and economically sound.

When it comes to the detention of non-United States citizens and the continuous erosion of civil rights in the United States what is at stake is not only the dignity of hundreds of thousands of prisoners and their families, but also the very nature of governmental authority and its justification in law. Ultimately, laws and the way they are enforced in the United States or elsewhere under United States jurisdiction have long-ranging repercussions for the international community; they impact human rights practices everywhere and have real consequences for millions of people all over the world.

Five

RESERVATIONS AS PRISONS

Ben Carnes

They made us many promises, more than I can remember, but they never kept but one; they promised to take our land, and they took it.

- Red Cloud, Oglala Lakota

Native peoples have always maintained a spiritual relationship with the land that is not one of ownership, but of a caretaker. We view the land as children view a mother who provides for their needs. The reverence is expressed in how we pray and through the values that are passed on through the generations. Without the land—the earth—we could not exist. However, when immigrants began arriving upon our shores, their concept of the land was in contradiction to our principles. In retrospect, humoring their idea of owning the land set into action a tragic chain of events that would constitute the longest ongoing act of terrorism in our homelands.

In spite of documented historical records to the contrary, history books, federal holidays, and judicial/political machinations have avoided those truths, creating an illusionary tale in the minds of people today. History is written by the colonizer. The imperialistic belief in Manifest Destiny justified the actions of immigrants, who later renamed themselves pioneers/settlers, in the dominance and subjugation of the Native people of their lands and resources, including their culture and spirituality.

When the word "reservation" is mentioned, some romantically envision Plains Indian on horseback, pow-wows, and tipis, while others disdainfully think of casino rich Indians enjoying government handouts! I doubt if this misperception would be foremost in their thoughts if they knew how we have arrived to where we are today. Some historical, legal, and political points need to be shared to help readers fully appreciate the issues indigenous peoples continue to face today. These will not be found in any mainstream newspaper or among the required readings in educational institutions.

The Quinnipiac Indian reservation is the oldest reservation in North American, established by a treaty made with English Colonists in 1638. Originally, in these treaties, the term "reservation" implied that the Native people reserved tracts of lands for their exclusive use. Treaties are agreements made between sovereign states. However, many of the treaties made with the United States were conducted in less than an honest manner, often under duress. The duplicity in the language of the treaties left the Native people at a disadvantage. Promises that they would be left in peace "as long as the grass grows and water flows," along with an obligation to provide for their health, education, and welfare in exchange for huge parcels of their lands were found to be hollow, in both quantity and quality.

In a series of United States Supreme Court opinions undermining the sovereignty of the indigenous peoples, known as the "Marshall Trilogy," Chief Justice John Marshall ruled the Doctrine of Discovery gave those who "discovered" the lands radical title (sovereignty), and the right to extinguish the Right of Occupancy by the indigenous peoples who inhabited the lands (*Johnson v. M'Intosh*, 1823). Later, he set the precedent that they were "domestic dependent nations . . . Their relation to the United States resembles that of a ward to his guardian" (*Cherokee Nation v. Georgia*, 1831) He then established a doctrine that only the federal government, not the states, have authority in Indian affairs (*Worcester v. Georgia*, 1832).

At the time of the decisions, the United States War Department had been responsible for conducting affairs with the Native people since 1789. It went through different agency names under the War Department before it was transferred to the Department of the Interior in 1849; during that time, it was officially named the Bureau of Indian Affairs (BIA).

Article VI, clause 2 of the United States Constitution, known as the Supremacy Clause, states, "treaties shall be the supreme law of the land." However, the continued demand for more land brought about forced removals, a form of ethnic cleansing, where thousands died in a harsh winter with little or no food or shelter after being forced from their homelands. Article IV of the Treaty of Dancing Rabbit Creek of 1830, which brought about the forced removal of the Choctaws, promised:

> That no Territory or state shall ever have a right to pass laws for the government of the Choctaw Nation of Red People and their descendants; and that no part of the land granted them shall ever be embraced in any Territory or State. . ." (Kappler, 1904, p. 311).

Chief George Harkins, Choctaw, whose people were the first to be exiled to Indian Territory in 1831, wrote in a Farewell Letter to the American People: "We as Choctaws rather chose to suffer and be free than live under the degrading influence of laws, which our voice could not be heard in their formation" (Moquin and Van Doren, 1995, p. 151). These removals became known as the "Trail of Tears and Death."

Today reservations or Indian lands make up about 55.7 million acres of land (*National Atlas*, n). The United States claims 2.3 billion acres of land that, in the eyes of the Natives, is all Indian land (Lubowski, et al., 2010). Reservation life was a traumatic existence compared to the days of hunting and ceremonies. Permission had to be obtained to hunt off reservation to supplement the rations provided by the government through the Indian agents, who were often found to be corrupt. Theft of delivered rations was frequent, substitutions were made of inferior beef for those intended for the Indians, and in some cases, they had nothing to eat. Without means for survival and permission to hunt, warriors snuck off the reservation to hunt to provide for the people, in some cases entire bands left the reservation.

General Nelson A. Miles sent this telegraph from Rapid City to General John Schofield in Washington, D.C. on 19 December 1890:

> The difficult Indian problem cannot be solved permanently at this end of the line. It requires the fulfillment of Congress of the treaty obligations that the Indians were entreated and coerced into signing. They signed away a valuable portion of their reservation, and it is now occupied by white people, for which they have received nothing.
> They understood that ample provision would be made for their support; instead, their supplies have been reduced, and much of the time they have been living on half and two-thirds rations. Their crops and the crops of the white people for two years have been almost total failures.
> The dissatisfaction is wide spread, especially among the Sioux, while the Cheyennes have been on the verge of starvation, and were forced to commit depredations to sustain life. These facts are beyond question, and the evidence is positive and sustained by thousands of witnesses. (Johnson, 2011, p. 338)

The necessity for survival demanded that the Indians go off the reservation in search of food. These excursions led to an era of the bloodiest conflicts of the so-called Indian Wars because the United States Calvary was sent to round them up and return them to the reservations. Two of the most iconic episodes were the Battle of the Little Big Horn in 1876, when Col. George Custer, in disobedience of orders, led his regiment to annihilation, and the massacre at Wounded Knee in 1890, where the reconstituted Seventh Calvary slaughtered Big Foot and his band of Miniconjous.

In a tactic to discourage "going off the reservation," the military encouraged wholesale annihilation of buffalos, poisoning of potable water, and the destruction of food sources. A way of life that had sustained the indigenous peoples was coming to an end, and a mentality of dependency was seeded that created generations of despair and poverty.

Americans' appetite for more land was insatiable; it would lead to inevitable conflicts between Indians and settlers. One solution by "Indian reformers" was that the Indians had to learn to live like the white man. The prevailing thought was that the Indians were lazy, and that all they cared about was hunting and fishing while the land "went to waste" because it did not produce a profit.

Americans believed that by forcing Native people to assimilate into their "melting pot," the conflicts would end. One method was directed at Native children who were taken against their will from their homes and sent far away to boarding schools. All the attributes of being confined in a prison were present in the boarding schools, such as, the confiscation of personal identity. Indian names were replaced with Christian names, they were forbidden to speak their native language to one another under threat of punishment. Their braids were cut from their heads and traditional style of dress taken away. Importantly, their spirituality was replaced with Christianity. These methods of behavioral control, instituted through fear and intimidation, instilled both shame and despair. During a commencement at the Carlisle Indian Boarding School, Reverend A. J. Lippincott said, "Let all that is Indian within you die! . . . You cannot become truly American citizens, industrious, intelligent, cultured, civilized until the INDIAN within you is DEAD" (Adams, 1995, p. 274).

While on the reservations, forced dependency upon government rations established a welfare state. The Code of Indian Offenses (1883) outlawed participation in cultural and ceremonial activities with penalties of withholding rations or serving time in an agency prison. This could have been the end of a way of life, but people began holding their traditional ceremonies in secret for several decades.

With many of the First Nations confined to the reservations and resistance subdued through acts of forced assimilation or ethnocide, Congress passed the Indian Appropriations Act of 1871, which stated:

> That hereafter no Indian nation or tribe within the territory of the United States shall be acknowledged or recognized as an independent nation, tribe, or power with whom the United States may contract by treaty. . .

The era of treaty-making was over and Congress would begin enacting laws directing the fate of the original inhabitants of this land. A following congressional enactment was the 1877 Dawes General Allotment Act that broke up communal land holdings. According to Senator Dawes, Native people had a defect in their character. This flaw as reflected in his comment "there is no selfishness, which is at the bottom of civilization."

In furtherance of the assimilation policy, it was believed that if the Indians were forced to work their lands, they would quickly become American citizens. After each head of the household was granted 160 acres, the so-called surplus lands were opened up for settlement. Through this process, they lost about 90 million acres of land and notched another broken promise when Indian Territory became the State of Oklahoma in 1907 (Denzin, et al., 2008, pp. 430–431).

Just a few years prior to Oklahoma statehood, a move was made by the Choctaws, Cherokees, Seminoles, Muscogee (Creeks), and Chickasaws to form a state under Native constitution and laws in the eastern half of Indian Territory. When it was put to a referendum to create the State of Sequoyah, Native people overwhelmingly supported it. Their hopes were crushed when Congress refused to accept their proposal.

On 16 November 1907, Oklahoma became the 46th state. Ironically, "Okla humma is Choctaw for Red People" (Meserve, 1941, p. 318). I still call it Indian Territory. The allotment process didn't go as smoothly as Dawes and others had hoped. It met with resistance by Chitto Harjo (Crazy Snake) Muscogee, who encouraged others to not participate. This resistance was called the "Crazy Snake Rebellion," which at the time was called the last Indian uprising. Another critical decision that undermined the protections that Native people held in the treaties, that were supposed to be the "Supreme law of the land" was when the Supreme Court ruled in *Lone Wolf v. Hitchcock* (1903) that Congress had the plenary authority to change the treaties at will, thereby making these solemn promises worthless.

In 1926, the Interior Secretary ordered a study on the condition of Indian people. After two years, Lewis Meriam, the study director, reported the Dawes Act had been illegally used to deprive Indian people of their lands, including fraud and misappropriation were rampant among government agents. Historian Angie Debo notes:

> Even murder was systematically employed to channel the inheritance of the headrights into the conspirators' hands—twenty-four unsolved cases, including shooting, poisoning, and blowing up a house with nitroglycerin, in three years beginning with 1921—and the Indian lived in terror of the next strike. (1970, p. 333)

In *And Still the Waters Run* (1991, p. 200), Angie Debo writes about the unsolved murders of Choctaws who had made wills to land dealers in return for $10 per month pension for the duration of their life, but who died suspiciously shortly after making the will. In the forty-seven years since the passage of the Dawes Act, it is estimated that about 90,000 Indians became landless (Denzin et al., 2008, pp. 430–431). It is important to note that the 1924 American Indian Citizenship Act was not recognized by several states for another twenty-four years until a judicial decision was rendered (Deloria & Lytle, 1983, p. 222).

Due to the findings in the Meriam Report (1928), the 1934 Indian Reorganization Act was passed that allowed for the existence of tribal council systems as a form of local self-governance. The federal government would no longer recognize the traditional leaders while creating a system where tribal councils subservient to the United States.

The 1950s brought a period of termination of the federal recognition of the tribal councils. The government believed it would be in the Indians' best interest if they just became a part of the larger American society. Over 109 First Nations were terminated, which comprised about 12,000 individuals, and resulted in a loss of 2,500,000 acres of land when the protective status was removed. This was also the period when the 1956 Indian Relocation Act was implemented, which promised to help Indians relocate out of poverty stricken reservations to acquire a better life. However, racist attitudes in urban areas prevented the goals of better housing and jobs.

Disillusionment caused by these events and the intensity of the Civil Rights Movement in the 1960s prompted the founding of organizations such as the National Indian Youth Council and Americans before Columbus. Richard Oakes, Mohawk, organized what became known as the longest occupation of a federal facility, the former maximum security United State Penitentiary, Alcatraz. Although the occupation officially ended in June 1971, it has been credited with forcing the Nixon administration to cease its termination and relocation policies.

Inspired by the occupation of Alcatraz and other actions of protest by Native people, several Native organizations combined to make up the Trail of Broken Treaties Caravan. They arrived in Washington, D.C. on 3 November 1972 with a twenty-point plan that included redress of treaty violations and related issues, rights of the individual, and their sovereignty. Organizers had sent notice to government officials to arrange a meeting to present their twenty points, and that they intended hold ceremonies at Arlington cemetery and the Iwo Jima Memorial in honor of Ira Hayes, Pima, who had participated in the flag raising at Iwo Jima. The officials had promised to arrange meetings and provide accommodations for them. When they arrived in Washington, they were met again with another in a long line of broken promises. The Park Service denied them a permit to gather at the intended sites and the housing proved inadequate for the number of people that arrived, including the Chiefs and Elders. They went to the BIA office to lodge their complaints through a sit-in. No official came to meet with them; instead, security and police in riot gear tried to evict them. But the police were the ones who got evicted by the Indians, who began fortifying their defenses against another assault.

Years of repressive federal laws and policies boiled over at the heart of an agency established by the War Department. Media attention focused for a week on the issues and grievances of Native people, President Richard Nixon's Indian policy, and government paternalism. Some third-hand anecdotal reports recalling that time claim that Nixon, who coincidentally won reelection during the period of the occupation of the BIA, evinced his disdain by exclaiming: "Get those goddamn Indians out of town!"

After a series of negotiations the government promised it would consider their twenty-point plan, grant them immunity from prosecution for the takeover, and give the Caravan members $66,000 to cover travel expenses for them to leave town. When the Indians left Washington, they took with them many documents that they stole from the BIA, which they said exposed mismanagement of their resources and lands, including evidence of forced sterilization of Native women.

This was a new class of warriors that hadn't been seen since the Crazy Snake Rebellion. It was a new day for many Natives who felt they would never have a voice in how they had been treated. Native youth sought out their cultural and spiritual identities and began talking about sovereignty. Not only did this inspire a new sense of pride among Native people, but it also caught the attention of the FBI's Counter-Intelligence Program (COINTELPRO). Of all the organizations involved in the takeover of the BIA, the American Indian Movement received the most attention and was labeled an "extremist and subversive organization" by the FBI. The methods of COINTELPRO were to "expose, disrupt, misdirect, discredit, or otherwise neutralize" those organizations and its leaders. Even false imprisonments (such as Geronimo ji-Jaga Pratt, a a high-ranking member of the Black Panther Party serving twenty-seven years, who was released after it was revealed that the FBI framed him by withholding exonerating evidence) and assassinations (such as Fred Hampton, another high-ranking Black Panther, who was shot in his sleep during an FBI raid) were not that uncommon.

In 1971, activists broke into an FBI field office in Pennsylvania and stole files that exposed COINTELPRO. A month later, FBI Director J. Edgar Hoover announced it had been "officially" terminated. However, federal agents continue to employ the tactics utilized in its onslaught against the American Indian Movement.

A pivotal incident in this history was the Wounded Knee incident, which began 27 February 1973, when about 200 Oglala Lakota and followers of the American Indian Movement (AIM) seized and occupied the town of Wounded Knee, South Dakota, on the Pine Ridge Indian Reservation. This grassroots protest followed their failed effort to impeach the elected tribal president Richard Wilson, whom they accused of corruption and abuse of opponents, and to focus attention on the state of poverty that infected the reservations with despair. They were also protesting the United States government's failure to fulfill treaties. They were demanding that treaty negotiations with Indian peoples be reopened.

Oglala and AIM activists controlled Wounded Knee for seventy-one days while the United States Marshals Service, Federal Bureau of Investigation agents, and other law enforcement agencies cordoned off the area. They were surrounded with helicopters, Armored Personnel Carriers, and automatic weapons. Two warriors were shot and killed inside Wounded Knee, one while sleeping. Also, one United States Marshal was wounded and paralyzed during the stand-off.

From 1972 to 1975, over sixty Indian people who supported AIM or were opposed to Wilson were murdered. Wilson was known to have used tribal funds to employ a vigilante force that some referred to as the "Goon Squad." In a derisive manner, the vigilantes adopted the acronym "Guardians of the Oglala Nation." During this time, the FBI had a higher concentration of federal agents in and around Wounded Knee than any other location in the country. They were often provided with names of witnesses to the incidents or the name of the murderers, but rarely did an arrest take place, let alone a conviction. In Pine Ridge, as in other reservations, the people felt they had no one to whom they could turn for protection. AIM was all they had to call on and one who answered this call was Leonard Peltier.

As a teenager at the Turtle Mountain Reservation, Peltier remembers attending a meeting where Elders were crying over children who had no food and "if there were no more warriors among our men. . . . Why did they not stand up and fight for the starving children?" (quoted in Matthiessen, 1983, p.

47). The realization of their state of poverty hit Peltier hard, and he made a promise to do all he can to help his people for the rest of his life. So, hearing the call, he arrived at the home of traditionalist Harry Jumping Bull along with other AIM members and set up camp.

What happened at the Jumping Bulls on 26 June 1975, has been the subject of several books, films, and debate among world political and spiritual leaders. Peltier was convicted in the deaths of two FBI agents in a shoot-out that also left another member of AIM dead. During his appeal, fabrication and withholding of evidence and witness tampering by the government was revealed. In addition, a later admission by the assistant United States attorney that they no longer could prove who shot the agents led to support from everywhere. Over sixty members of Congress, several celebrities, and millions of people rallied to his cause. Amnesty International recognized him as a political prisoner, and he was nominated six times for the Nobel Peace Prize for his humanitarian efforts while imprisoned.

Peltier has remained a symbol to Native people of what they can expect if they stand in the way of government and corporate interests. In his case, the interests here amounted to billions or trillions of dollars worth of natural resources that lies beneath their lands in the forms of uranium, gold, and natural gas, etc. Yet, the Pine Ridge reservation remains one of the poorest areas in the United States.

The land of Native people is sought after by corporations for its natural resources. These corporations use bought and paid for politicians to pass laws in their favor. Another blatant case is the one of the Navajo-Hopi people. While in the employ of Peabody Coal, Attorney John S. Boyden created a tribal council and lobbied to have bills passed in Congress, was also appointed the legal counsel for the Hopi people by the BIA. In spite of an obvious ethical conflict of interest, he negotiated a lease for the Hopi with Peabody while profiting from this deal. The Hopi people complained about the illegal leases to the federal government, but were ignored. Historically, the Navajo and Hopi people shared an area of land, but they stood in the way of Boyden's plan. He used a public relations firm to create a fictitious range war between the Hopi and Navajo, then had congressional bill passed to relocate the Navajo off their lands by Sen. John McCain. The lands from which they were forced to relocate are the site of the largest uranium spill in United States history in 1974.

Since the beginning of European contact with indigenous peoples in North America, the demand for land has not diminished. Whenever the few remaining lands of Native people have shown to have potential for natural resources, corporate and political attempts have been made to dispossess them of it. Native people and their lands are trapped in a fiduciary relationship, as a result of the Marshall trilogy, as if Native people are incompetent to manage their trust assets.

A class action suit filed in 1996 by Louise Cobell accused the Department of the Interior of illegally mismanaging the Individual Indian Monies

Account, where payments for leases of lands and mineral rights held in trust are deposited. Papers filed estimated that up to 176 billion dollars had been embezzled or mismanaged from these accounts. The Plaintiffs in the case sought a complete accounting. However, a settlement was offered for 3.4 billion dollars and an end to the case. It has been estimated that members of the class will receive up to $1,500.00 each.

While this resolution has been hailed as a victory by some, others have compared it to being stabbed in the back and removing the ten-inch knife only a fraction of an inch. Cobell had rejected an $8 billion settlement offer in 2006 by Sen. John McCain because it had too many strings attached. In June 2011, a Fairness Hearing was held in Washington, D.C., and the court accepted the settlement, but an objection has been filed that has delayed the settlement indefinitely pending appeals.

President Barack Obama signed the Native American Apology Resolution into law on 19 December 2009, which was included as Section 8113 in the 2010 Defense Appropriations Act, H.R. 3326, Public Law No. 111-118. But the Apology Resolution comes with a disclaimer that nothing in the Resolution authorizes or supports any legal claims against the United States and that the Resolution does not settle any claims against the United States. This disclaimer is much the same as in previous resolutions, such as one by former President Bill Clinton apologizing for the illegal overthrow of the lawful Hawaiian kingdom by the United States military and its agents.

When the Declaration on the Rights of Indigenous Peoples was adopted by the United Nations in 2007, it undermined America's illusionary foundations of freedom and democracy. On 16 December 2010, President Obama announced that the United States would acknowledge, but not endorse, the declaration. However, he remained true to form when his statement cautioned that the declaration will be interpreted according to the laws of the United States, a disclaimer to any meaningful changes to centuries of broken treaties, promises, and lives.

So what is it going to take to resolve the long-standing mistrust Native people have with the federal government? The solution is clouded by years of sociopolitical conditioning as a result of federal policies. The façade of freedom in this country demanded that our way of life dissolve into conformity with dominant society. The divisions we face as Native people involves those others who believe we must forget our past and get with the program.

During a 1993 congressional committee hearing on the religious rights of Native prisoners, I testified that assimilation has created a spiritual and cultural void. When Native prisoners experience traditional spiritual practitioners for the first time, it ignites a yearning for them to learn the ways of their people and to develop their own identity. The natural evolution of our people was disrupted by United States colonization. We continue to go back and pick up the shattered pieces of our collective history. Decolonizing our minds is a critical process towards regaining our freedom and independence from the federal government. At an AIM conference at Tayac Territory in

Southern Maryland, in May 1989, Bill Means characterized the state of affairs succinctly: "To free the land, we must first free our mind."

The brief history outlined here highlights the United States government's treachery and deception towards the indigenous inhabitants of this land. It is one where colonialism and imperialism worked hand-in-hand. The belief by immigrants that the Native people were incapable of making productive and efficient use of the land led them to belief that they had the right to take control by force. This conflicted with the natural laws to which we adhered; we were the first environmentalists, living in balance with the land, respecting Mother Earth, never taking more than we needed.

We were never Americans, and this land was never theirs. It is a myth used to confiscate our natural identity and the reality of our circumstances. We have always been sovereign peoples of this land. This concept of sovereignty has been inherent within each of us since birth, as it was with our ancestors when Columbus and the Pilgrims stumbled upon our shores. It isn't something that can be given to us or taken from us. We cannot be what we never were regardless of attempts to indoctrinate us through the public education, military, and correctional systems.

These prisons of conformity have created learned behaviors that keep us divided as human beings of moral conscience. Racism, sexism, tribalism, and nationalism are the shackles of social control that restrain us from moving forward. The key to loosening these restraints is that we must realize how they have been embedded within us. The reality behind these truths is that America cannot hide behind its facade as a country of the greatest freedoms—not when our spirit of resistance serves as a shameful reminder as to the historical foundations of America and its injustice to the original peoples of this land that we still call ours.

Six

THE TENSION BETWEEN ABOLITION AND REFORM

Liat Ben-Moshe

1. Introduction

There are many ways in which one can fight for social justice or social change. This chapter will interrogate the connections between two main sites in which abolition of oppressive institutions is in effect. One is activism around the abolition of the prison-industrial-complex, and the other is the move to close down institutions for people labeled "mentally retarded" or "mentally ill," known as deinstitutionalization. Within disability and prison activism are many who criticize the nursing homes industry and residential psychiatric hospitals. But not all see a need to abolish or close down these carceral spaces. Some seek to reform these settings or make them less repressive (e.g., with programs for prisoner education or sheltered workshops and day programs for institutionalized disabled people). The prison abolition movement in particular alludes to the abolition of slavery. Some activists and theorists of the prison-industrial-complex see it as a (post)modern form of slavery, especially as it relates to the exploitation and incarceration of poor people of color (Davis, 1998, 2000; Gilmore, 2000; Hames-Garcia, 2004; James, 2005; Sudbury, 2005). Deinstitutionalization activists do not necessarily use the phrase "abolition" in their struggle but often refer to forced psychiatric confinement (Szasz, 1977; 2002). However, their main goal was to close down, or abolish, psychiatric hospitals and institutions for the developmentally disabled.

In contrast to the constant expansion of prisons in the United States, the deinstitutionalization of psychiatric hospitals has been a major policy trend in most states since the 1950s. From the 1970s onward, this has been true in relation to institutions for those defined as "mentally retarded," and later the "developmentally and intellectually disabled." I contend that the deinstitutionalization movements in mental health and developmental disabilities could be construed as historical models to guide us through the transition to decarceration and prison abolition. However, massive closures of large state institutions and hospitals do not necessarily signal freedom for those formerly (and still currently) institutionalized and imprisoned. Therefore, what we need to discuss is the difference, tension, and relation between reform and abolition efforts. Closure in and of itself is part of a larger project of creating a more just society. Prison abolitionists view the prison-industrial-complex as a set of institutional and political relationships that extend well beyond the walls of the prison proper. So in essence, prison abolition is a broader critique of society (Davis, 2000). The resistance to incarceration in mental institutions and psychiatric hospitals also arose from a broader social critique, that of medicalization and medical authority (Conrad, 2007; Szasz, 1961, 1977; Zola, 1991). Deinstitutionalization was also informed by a new understanding of human value, especially in regards to people with disabilities (Wolfensberger, 1972, 1974). Conceptualizing abolition within these movements is an act of social-political resistance.

Norwegian sociologist Thomas Mathiesen conceptualizes abolition as an alternative in the making: "The alternative lies in the 'unfinished', in the sketch, in what is not yet fully existing" (Mathiesen, 1974, p. 1). The alternative, according to Mathiesen, needs to both contradict and compete with the old system it is trying to change or replace. The opposition though cannot be totally foreign to the present system, otherwise no one will adhere to the message. On the other hand, the alternative cannot be fully formed as the new world in the making is not yet here. This dialectic connects abolition efforts to other activist strategies such as attempts to reform a system on the way to abolition. Even efforts to close down repressive institutions do not always result in the abolition of the system as a whole. Below I explicate the connections between these three related strategies, abolition, reform, and closure.

2. Does Institutional Closure Equate with Abolition?

Closure of repressive institutions, such as mental hospitals and prisons, can be conceptualized as a necessary but not sufficient action on the road to abolition. The most important element in institutional closure is to ensure that people do not end up re-incarcerated in other formats such as group homes or other institutional placements (Blatt et al., 1977). In this sense the effectiveness of deinstitutionalization as a movement is in ensuring community living, with all needed supports, not merely in the closure of the institution, which is only a first step. This ideological stance may create a dilemma. Should proponents of deinstitutionalization wait until there are sufficient community placements before advocating for institutional closure? Or, should they go ahead regardless, on the principle that no one should live in an institution at any time? This is the very dilemma posed by Mathiesen in regards to abolition in general. Taylor (1995/6) suggests that in such cases one should ask which path would lead to the least harm done to the fewest people. Such questioning, he believes, would lead one to realize that institutional living is unjustifiable under any circumstances, even if community settings are imperfect at the present time.

The mere closure of prisons and large state psychiatric institutions does not necessarily entail a radical change in policy, attitudes, or the lived experiences of those incarcerated. Penal abolitionist Ruth Morris reflects on her experiences within the prison abolition movement in Canada and the United States:

> My objection to prisons is to something much more oppressive than closed buildings, or even locks and keys. It's important to think this out, because otherwise we delude ourselves about building alternatives when actually we are creating their very spirit in the community, destroying people just as effectively as any building with locks can possibly do. (1989, p. 141)

In this light, closure in itself is still embedded within the same circuits of power that created such institutions, unless there is an epistemic shift in the way community, punishment, dis/ability and segregation are conceptualized. Therefore, closure of prisons and institutions is only one step on the way to achieve a shift in perspective. Closure of large institutions has not led to freedom for all disabled people, nor has it resulted in the radical acceptance of the fact of difference amongst us.

Institutional life, whether in a prison, hospital, mental institution, nursing home, group home, or segregated "school," has been the norm, not the exception, for disabled people throughout North American history. Harriet McBryde Johnson ("The Disability Gulag," *New York Times,* 23 November 2003) describes her experiences and fear of the "disability gulag"—the warehouse for disabled people that is often called "the institution." As she describes in her narrative, many people with significant disabilities fear that one day they will be sent there and lose their independence, if they are already institutionalized. Prison abolitionists also emphasize that activism entails much more then closing prisons. It is about creating a society free of systems of inequity that produce hatred, violence, desperation and suffering. In such a society the idea of caging people for wrong doings will be seen as absurd (Lee, 2008).

When a system is abolished there is a danger that other systems with the same goals would arise to fill the void left by the abolished system. Famed sociologist W.E.B. Du Bois, in his book *Black Reconstruction* (1999 [1935]), discusses abolition not as a mere negative process, one of tearing down. It is ultimately about creating new institutions. Du Bois was very insistent that in order to abolish slavery in modern times, new democratic institutions have to be established and maintained. Because that did not occur, slavery found a new home in Jim Crow, convict lease systems, second class education and mass incarceration. Thus, the abolition of slavery was only successful on the negative aspect, but no new institutions were created to successfully incorporate black people into the existing social order. Prisons today have thrived precisely because of the lack of such resources that Du Bois was arguing for. Prisons today can't be abolished until such equality-ensuring mechanisms are in place (Davis, 2005). Being free of chains is only the beginning.

Dismantling the walls of the prison, therefore, is not a goal that will eliminate the use of coercion and punishment as mechanism of state control, according to some abolitionists (Davis, 2000; Sudbury, 2004). Hence we notice a shift of many prison abolitionist activists and writers, beginning in the

1990s, from promoting prison abolition to conceptualizing *penal* abolition more broadly (Morris, 1995).

Penal abolition is viewed as a more comprehensive practice and discourse than that of *prison* abolition, attempting to revolutionize the way we perceive crime and punishment (Magnani and Wray, 2006). Penal abolitionism, according to critical criminologist Willem De Haan (1990), provides a radical critique of the criminal (in)justice system, while providing other ways, either concrete or envisioned, of dealing with crime and harm. Penal abolitionists believe that social life should not be regulated by penal law, and that other ways of dealing with problematic behaviors and situations should be practiced. However, when discussing penal abolition, some activists maintain that there could be instances where confinement should be used for a select number of cases, at least as a short-term strategy (Sauve, 1988). For the purposes of this chapter then, I mostly refer to the term prison abolition (and not penal abolition) as my focus here is on strategies that envision a world without carceral spaces and institutional mindsets, whether they are affiliated with the larger framework of penal abolition or not. This tension between abolition, closure and reform is discussed further below.

3. The Relation Between Abolition and Reform

In *Instead of Prisons* (1976), an early published attempt to conceptualize prison abolition in the United States, Fay Honey Knopp posed the connection between abolition and reform. Some of the questions this classic primer tries to answer are whether it is possible to work for prison reform without being co-opted, and whether working toward abolition means that prisoners will be left in intolerable conditions in the meantime. This tension is a key characteristic of the penal/prison abolitionist stance and there is no agreement as to how to resolve it. The movement is diverse and ranges from calls for focusing on the present circumstances of prisoners and advocating for gradual decarceration (as described by the attrition model below), to those who contend that any type of reform would lead to the growth of the prison-industrial-complex and should be avoided by activists.

This seeming chasm between pragmatism and vision for the future of a non-carceral society are not necessarily binary opposites. Fay Honey Knopp suggests conceptualizing the long-term goal of prison abolition as a chain for shorter campaigns around specific issues—like jail diversion, restitution programs, or the move of those released to community placements (1976). Such strategic use of abolition and reform can also be applied to the context of abolishing psychiatric confinement and forced medical treatments, as suggested by anti-psychiatry activist Bonnie Burstow in her keynote speech in the 2009 PsychOut conference. She contends that the short term goals of anti-psychiatry activists, such as reform efforts, should be kept as such, as concrete and direct partial abolitions (or reforms) on the road to long term change.

This conceptualization of placing reform and abolition on a continuum can also be traced to the pioneering work *Politics of Abolition*, in which Mathiesen (1974) follows Andre Gorz's distinction between reformist and "non-reformist" reforms. Reformist reforms are situated in the discursive formation of the system as is, so that any changes are made within or against this existing framework. Non-reformist reforms imagine a different horizon that should be realizable for the improvement of humanity, and are not limited by a discussion of what is possible at present. Mathiesen expands this notion to state that non-reformist reforms that are effective need to be of the abolishing kind. He also creates a typology that distinguishes between positive and negative reforms. Positive reforms are changes that improve the system so it will act more effectively, so that the system gains strength and abolition becomes more difficult. Examples of positive reforms in the current penal system include probation and technological monitoring systems (such as ankle bracelets) which, although ensure that those convicted could live outside of the prisons, further the reach of the penal regime to populations and actions that it had not dealt with before. On the other hand, negative reforms are changes that abolish or remove parts of the system on which it is dependent (Mathiesen, 1974). An example of negative reforms could be to demand better health care for prisoners in current prisons and jails, to a point where the prison system will not be able to afford these conditions and will have to start decarcerating inmates who require medical attention. This strategy was also used in deinstitutionalization lawsuits to decarcerate inmates from institutions for the developmentally disabled in the 1970s. Even if it makes the system look more responsive, from a public relations standpoint, such reforms do not contribute to the growth of the system as a whole.

This relationship between abolition and reform is not only a scholarly debate, but also one with pragmatic implications. For instance, Angela Y. Davis (2002), a committed abolitionist, does not believe there is a strict line between reform and abolition. The question is what kinds of reforms are sought, and whether they will strengthen the system in the long run. For instance, fighting for health care for prisoners is something activists should support, as integral to abolitionist and decarcerating strategies. However, some health care initiatives are opposed by abolitionists such as attempts to open new prison hospitals or separate clinical wards, as these would only expand the scope of incarceration in the long run. Many prison abolition and anti-psychiatry activists are insistent that the trend to develop mental health services within the prison only serves to criminalize (mostly) women with psychiatric and cognitive disabilities. Quality health services of this nature are sparse outside the walls of the prison. Why should funds go to operate these services within an already oppressive system?

Some factors leading to the growth of the prison industry were the direct result of attempts to reform the system. Public awareness and advocacy efforts to change the conditions inherent in prisons (overcrowding, need to build specific enclosures for specific populations) had eventually led to prison expansion, according to Rick Sauve (1988), who is a prisoner himself. Senger (1988), a fellow prisoner, also critiques prison activists who, although good-intentioned, had brought on reforms that ultimately reinforced the prison and its power. By insisting on reforms in the prison, these activists reinforce the system as a whole, so that positive change in the daily lives of prisoners actually perpetuates the power structure that keeps prisons as a viable solution to criminality.

As a prime example, Marie Gottschalk (2006) demonstrates how various seemingly progressive social movements in the penal arena inadvertently brought forth changes that concluded in more draconian punishments and increased incarceration. For example, opposition to the death penalty brought forth life sentences without parole, and helped strengthen the deterrence argument in crime control discourse. Similarly, LGBT activists fighting against homophobic and transphobic violence helped in creating hate crime legislation that incarcerated people for longer timeframes; and Moms against Gun Violence ushered in gun control measures that also increased the net effect of the penal system, including surveillance measures on communities of color, who sought the legislation originally. An implied facet of Gottschalk's examples is that being too radical and specialized in demands leads to erasure or cooptation of such arguments by the state, leading to punitiveness. An alternative explanation does not lie in blaming the activists for the unintentional consequence of mass incarceration but in the ideology and overarching goals of public policy. If reform efforts led to the mass expansion of punitive measures, then perhaps the problem is not one of "being too radical" or overarching, but of not reaching far enough, not engaging enough in coalitional and revolutionary politics that will address the root causes of harm. Reformist politics are the main strategy used by the left and liberal politics and are in the greatest risk of being co-opted by the state and its apparatuses (Appel, 2002). Furthermore, in many cases the state's mechanisms are not even necessary because activists embody the state in their actions and interactions. According to some liberal discourses that call for social change, change entails incorporating excluded groups into current structures—the government, corporations and politics. These calls are also prevalent amongst disability activists who advocate for more hiring of people with disabilities in all sectors of the market economy, and activists calling for the election of a black or a woman president. But these calls only change the hierarchy of the structures in which marginalized populations are placed and not the structures themselves.

4. Decarceration, Closure, and Abolition by Attrition

Steven J. Taylor (1995/6), reflecting on the process of deinstitutionalization in the field of developmental disabilities in the 1970s onward, suggests a few successful strategies used in closing institutions in the past and present. The first is to announce the closure far in advance while making sure the move has support from the local community and professionals (this strategy was used in Vermont for example, which closed all of its institutions for those with labels of intellectual/developmental disabilities). A riskier strategy, but one with many benefits, is a swift and massive system change from within. Jerry Miller, director of the Department of Youth Services in Massachusetts in the early 1970s, emptied all but one juvenile detention facility in the state in three years. Miller's method was to create swift changes, so as to not give time to professionals and those in positions of power to revolt against his closure efforts. Miller (1991) stresses that a lengthy phase-down only invited opposition, not only from the staff and parents but also from judges who would send more adolescents into the juvenile facilities about to close, in order to prevent it from happening.

Another successful strategy that was used for deinstitutionalization is more implicit and required the gradual depopulation of an institution to the point where it was no longer cost effective to keep it open (Taylor, 1995/6). This strategy could be characterized as "abolition by attrition," as described by Knopp et al. (1976) in regards to prisons. One component of abolition by attrition is to decarcerate (i.e., release from current carceral spaces and mechanisms) as many prisoners as possible by such strategies as abolishing parole; releasing prisoners perceived as requiring supervision into community peer groups; substituting prison time with restitution to victims; pushing for release of prisoners convicted for victimless crimes.

The second component is to excarcerate (i.e. avoid incarceration to begin with) and examine all alternatives to incarceration by such steps as abolishing jail for those who cannot make bail and preventive detention, creating community conflict resolution centers, establishing community probation programs, and decriminalizing whole categories such as prostitution, sex related crimes, marijuana, public intoxication and other crimes without victims (Knopp et al., 1976).

The attrition model of decarceration has its critics too. Morris (1995) criticizes the attrition model saying that it is indeed an aggressive reform effort, but a reform nonetheless. The point is to decarcerate prison populations one by one—first the young, then the mentally ill and so on. The problem of chipping at the margins of the system is that the center remains intact. Decarceration and excarceration led to deepening a retributive system in programs now billed as alternatives to incarceration, such as boot camps and parole sanctions. This process can also be observed in the co-optation of restorative justice frameworks, which traditionally refer to the process of righting wrongs or healing wounds caused by harm (Leung, 1999). The "justice" system uses the language of healing and restorative justice but without implementing the necessary changes that will alter the system from within. The only change is in the rhetoric used, not in changing the value base of the programs and the system as a whole. For example, restitution and probation are now added on to long sentences, not as real alternatives to incarceration.

In addition, the restorative framework is mainly advocated by white middle class activists, although its roots are mainly within indigenous communities worldwide. As a result, many poor communities and communities of color see this framework as a form of colonialism, as these activists go to indigenous communities and harvest their knowledge to bring it back to their communities. As activists suggest, in order for restorative justice to be meaningful, it should come out of the communities it is trying to restore (Ibid.). In addition, restoring does not deal with the structural inequalities that lead to injustice. It does not question the basic assumptions of the system, such as who gets to be defined as "criminal" (Saleh-Hanna, 2000), and what gets defined as "the community" (Ben-Moshe, 2011a). Due to these problems, Morris (1995) suggested we need to move to thinking of transformative justice more broadly. A deeper stance of prison abolition therefore entails a multiplicity of approaches starting with demilitarization of schools, physical and mental health care for all, a justice system based on reconciliation, not vengeance, decriminalization of drug and sex work, and the defense of immigrant rights (Davis, 2003; Morris, 1995; Saleh-Hanna, 2000).

5. The Most Severe Cases and the "Dangerous Few"

A question raised often in the context of abolition of prisons and institutions is what to do with those deemed as having the most challenging behaviors. In the prison abolition circuits this discussion is known as "what to do with the dangerous few," and in the developmental and psychiatric disabilities realm it is the question of "what to do with the most significantly/profoundly disabled." In both cases the general assumption is that these are the populations that will not be able to "make it on the outside" and therefore will always require some sort of segregation and restraint. There is significant debate though, in both arenas, as to whether this is indeed the case.

Disability and queer studies theorist Robert McRuer suggests that Crip theory, which combines the two, will "draw attention to critically queer, severely disabled possibilities in order to bring to the fore the crip actors who… will exacerbate in more productive ways, the crisis of authority that currently besets heterosexual/ able-bodied norms" (2006, p. 31). By "severely disabled" McRuer is not merely referring to the level of impairment a person is presumed to have, but as a queer position. By reclaiming severe as "fierce" or defiant, McRuer reverses able bodied standards which view severe disabilities as those who will never be integrated (the adage of "everyone should be included, except for…."). From their marginal state, "severe disabilities" and queer subjects are positioned to reenter the margins and point to the inadequacies of straight and nondisabled assumptions. Translated to praxis, some prison abolitionists and activists in the fields of developmental disabilities and anti-psychiatry begin their critique and suggestions for alternative social arrangements from the positionality of "severe" cases.

In this regard, the developmental and psychiatric disabilities fields may appear as more progressive and radical than the prison abolition sector. In *Instead of Prisons*, Fay Honey Knopp writes:

> There is little disagreement that for those very few people who exhibit continual violent and aggressive behavior in society, temporary restraint is not only indicated but demanded. Review and monitoring procedures can be designed with adequate due process safeguards. (1976, p. 135)

Penal abolitionists seem split on this question; some advocate for transformative justice and healing practices in which no one will be restrained or segregated, while others believe that there will always be a small percentage of those whose behavior is so unacceptable or harmful that they will need to be exiled or restrained, when done humanely and not in a prison-like setting.

In the field of developmental disabilities and anti-psychiatry there is also a similar debate, with its origins in the debate surrounding deinstitutionalization (discussed further in Ben-Moshe, 2011b). Those who are deemed as "radical inclusionists" believe that everyone deserves to belong, to be educated with their peers, and to live in the community. For proponents of this attitude segregation is never a viable response, even for those whose behaviors are challenging and are seen as disturbing to others. The goal is to educate the person to not violate any major social norms but simultaneously challenge social views and attitudes that construct normalcy in particular ways. It also entails changing public policy, the education system as a whole as well as housing infrastructure to make them accessible and inclusive to all. In the field of anti-psychiatry such attitudes would involve opposition to psychiatric hospitalization, even of those labeled as "psychotic," and instead advocate for treatment or support in the community, with one's peers, and without coercion.

It is partially this reason that prompted those advocating for community inclusion to begin with the most severe cases when calling for and implementing the move out of institutions. A lesson learned from successful institution closures was that people who are labeled as those with the most significant needs should move to community placements early on in the process of closure and throughout the process. If left to the end, such people would most likely be placed in segregated settings, because of lack of skills, experience, ability or desire to support them in the community (Taylor, 1995/6). For example, those deemed as the most violent and dangerous youth became Miller's symbol as he decarcerated juvenile facilities in Massachusetts, which were the first to be decarcerated.

In regards to prison abolition, Knopp's work is especially telling. After working to draft the abolitionist manual *Instead of Prisons*, she sought to work with the "toughest" cases and has devoted her life to working with sex offenders and sexual abusers. The thought behind this commitment was that if she can demonstrate the ineffectiveness of prisons for this segment of the imprisoned population, there will be no doubt that prisons should not be a response for lesser criminalizable acts such as theft or drug related offenses. She believed prisons took responsibility away from sex offenders by removing them from society and shutting them away without treatment, and when released without treatment, they would offend again. Therefore, the organization that wrote the original prison abolition manual eventually became The Safer Society Program, which deals with the education and treatment of sex offenders to this day.

6. Conclusion

Abolition can be conceptualized as a strategy beyond mere resistance. It not only acknowledges the structure as is, but envisions and creates and new worldview in which oppressive structures do not exist. It goes beyond protesting against the current circumstances to envisioning a more just and equitable world. Abolition can take the form of tearing down the walls of the prison, psychiatric hospital and institution. It is also about building alternatives to incarceration: supporting community living for all, developing affordable and accessible housing, and countering capitalism, ableism, racism, transphobia, and ageism in order to achieve a world in which carceral spaces are meaningless and unnecessary. Abolition enables us to engage in politics of the future—of what could be, of what was dreamed up by deinstitutionalization and anti-psychiatry activists in the past and what is imagined by prison abolitionists at present. It is not just the conceptualization but also the active pursuit of a non-carceral future.

7. Note on Terminology

Throughout the paper I refer to people with psychiatric and intellectual/developmental disabilities and people with labels of mental retardation and mental illness. I use terminology derived either from the people first movement (as in "people with developmental disabilities") and mad pride movement (as in "people who are psychiatrized"). Or, I use more historically accurate terminology that reflects the way to which people were referred in public policy and discourse until a few years ago (for example, the categories of "mental retardation" and "mental illness"). I also utilize the terms "disabled people" in a broad sense to indicate that people are disabled not only by impairments but by social barriers (Ben-Moshe 2005). I refer to "people labeled as developmentally disabled," to indicate that I perceive these categorizations as situational and varied over time, culture, and power dynamics as to who gets to define and who gets to be defined under these categories.

Seven

CAGING SEX OFFENDERS

Dennis J. Stevens

1. Introduction

Since the Renaissance, lepers were criminalized. Lepers, similar to criminals, were labeled as "mad denizens." They were transported around the globe in overcrowded and poorly constructed ships that crisscrossed the seas with their cargo that have been termed a "comic and pathetic cargo of souls" or "Ship of Fools" (Foucault, 1965). When those ships docked at assorted ports for repairs and supplies, their human cargo remained chained and set out to dry among local ridicule and mockery. Public hysteria and fear among the local inhabitants of those ports and among the sailors aboard those ships, powered by the official label of "mad denizen," justified the abuse, demonization, and torment of those wretched souls regardless of their guilt or innocence.

Seventeenth and eighteenth century Western societies experienced vast social turbulence and economic misery that they resolved by imprisoning indigents, primarily women and children, with criminals, forcing them to work and live together. Conventional wisdom has been that the prison sentence should be structured toward rehabilitation and isolation if a violator is dangerous (von Hirsch, 1976). Foucault's "mad denizens" have been replaced by sex violators in the twenty-first century and little has changed about safety, treatment, and recovery since those "ships of fools" sailed. Inherent to modern methods of social control is the reality that social harm through violence, isolation, and intimidation, including a loss of civil and human rights, is the foundation of the prison culture, and that every sex offender is a predator.

A few predators (a cohort of offenders who developed through lifestyles of moral poverty in homes where unconditional love was absent and who inflict unmerciful violence incessantly upon their parents, siblings, neighbors, and anyone who crosses their path, including their own children and spouses) commit most of the serious sex crimes (such as domestic violence, child molestation, family and stranger rape, and sexual homicide). Few of these predators are ever identified or apprehended (Stevens and Ward, 1997; 2011b). When a predator is convicted of a crime, the criminal conviction is rarely linked to a single or even multiple sexual offenses. Most often, predators are charged with or allowed to plea to less heinous crimes resulting in lenient sanctions.

Statistics abound to support the widely known fact that sexual victimization is conducted largely by individuals who know their victims. However, Draconian criminal sanctions and regulations (which translate as sanctions and regulations only against those few convicted of a sex crime) against all behaviors labeled "sex offenses," including those committed by minors, become targets of slander, public hysteria, and demonization.

With the intelligence and capabilities of twenty-first century advancement, you might think that we have learned a thing or two from our societal experiences since the days when those "*ships of fools*" anchored. If we had, convicted sex offenders would become the refinements of reason, empirical research, individual rights, and justice despite realities that four of ten sex crimes (my estimate is one of ten) are reported to the police and less than six percent of those cases end in a conviction (Bureau of Justice Statistics, 2010a). Yet, sex offender policy and sanctions are passed hastily and rarely centered on scientific evidence. Instead, they are based on emotional reactions to high profile, violent, disturbing cases of chronic child molesters and rapists (Fortney, Levenson, Brannon, and Baker, 2007).

Reason, rights, and justice are virtues that have been tipped upside down providing the undeniable rights of public agencies (and individuals at large) as they interface with sex offenders and the communities linked to offenders. Through the slings and arrows of justice, official labels and public panic continue to justify cruel and unusual punishment toward sex offenders and the communities where those offenders reside, both during and after incarceration. Individuals who have been convicted (including those wrongfully convicted) are caged like animals, suffer the pains of deprivation, and once released, are stigmatized through a demonization process as the "worst of the worst." For them, it is almost impossible to find descent living quarters, suitable employment, meaningful relationships, and reasonable privacy because their photograph and personal information are easily available to the public. For their communities, cruel and unusual punishment exacerbates community poverty, community solidarity or cohesion, and community safety. The social well-being of their communities looks worse than bleak.

Prison sentences and police arrests that begin the criminal justice process are not the best answers to reduce sexual offenses because prison employs caged-centered punitive (punishment) orientations that validate violence. The American justice system is not really equipped or expected to go to the root of a violation and "cure" the social problem. One working definition of punishment can mean the infliction by the state of consequences normally considered unpleasant, on a person in response to his or her having been convicted of a crime (von Hirsch, 1976). Punishment of criminals is meant to result in less crime and fewer victims. But punitive sanctions do not deter first-time or chronic violators because punishment or methods of social control have been present among every society since the beginning of time (cf. Durkheim,1895). One implication of this thought is consistent with the idea that punishment has more to do with a social activity based on hysteria and fear and represents "an integral part of all healthy societies" (Ibid., p. 67). Also, because the crime rate is down some say it is linked to a rise of imprisonment. Yet what is real is that reported crime is down which mean that victims have less confidence in the justice system (Stevens, 2011b). Another detail worth mentioning is that the fear of crime—the fear of being victimized is pervasive in American society (Christakis and Fowler, 2009).

2. Fundamental Inquiry

My fundamental inquiry has been intuitively consistent with the issue that the practice of caged custody fosters a present and an imminent danger among individuals and the communities where they reside (Stevens, 1998; 1995). Who is caged and who is not caged has less to do with criminal violations and more to do with other agendas. It stands to reason that a caged existence enhances the frequency and intensity of violence among violators regardless of the nature of the conviction. The act of caging heightens prerogatives among enforcement and correctional personnel, prosecutors, and the general public toward the use of lethal and excessive force against sex violators (Stevens, 2011b). There is little doubt that any criminal offense is determined by a just society, but justice accountability (prosecution and incarceration) is rarely dependent upon whether an individual committed a criminal offense or not, but how the popular media portrays the individual in relationship to the crime (Stevens, 2008; 2011b).

We should be attentive to the idea that violence includes Max Weber's definition of government in terms of its monopoly upon *legitimate violence.* This monopoly justifies its daily routine through a fear of crime glorified and reinforced by the popular media's fictitious accounts of sex crimes and how to control violators. Subsequently, a push-and-pull relationship exists between the popular media and the official rhetoric that continues to define and redefine the limits of cruel and unusual punishment. *Legitimate violence* is provided in legal doses to every prisoner within reach of its supervision especially sex offenders (De Crespigny and Minogue, 1976; Bottoms, Hay, and Sparks, 1990). Since the foundation of the American prison culture is violent, violence especially legitimate violence begets more violence (Stevens and Ward, 1997; Stevens, 2011b). Group membership such as caged-sanctions can and will significantly impact the immediate and future treatment and behavior of an individual through an assimilation process to prison culture regardless of his or her innocence. Getting back to our mad denizen cargo, it can be assumed that many of those wretched souls eventually committed the crimes they were accused of—a self fulfilling prophecy.

3. My Experiences

While teaching at different universities, I spent several years among male and female imprisoned sex violators in some of the most researched penitentiaries in America. At the core of my prison research are the essays and journals of prisoners whom I encountered in prison university classrooms, group sessions such as substance abuse programs and aggression replacement training programs, and advocate meetings. An issue that arose through those years relates to the authority and the integrity of the American justice system to prevent all manner of social harm and to administer justice to its constituents.

What I learned is that prisoners assimilate into a normative prison culture comprised of violence, which produces anticipation of future crime (Stevens and Ward, 1997; Stevens, 1995; 1997a). Donald Clemmer's (1940, 1958) earlier work provided the framework for my research when he coined the term "prisonization." Also, Gresham Sykes' (1966) pains of imprisonment or deprivation model helps better understand that each prison has a unique culture and moves convicts through a prisonization and labeling (demonization) process that heightens barriers of isolation while removing quality supervision. Subsequently, the personal boundaries and rights of sex violators become invisible while in custody (prison) or during local supervision (probation, parole, and sex registers).

4. Social Label of a Sex Offender

Once a prisoner receives (through arrest or prosecution, regardless of guilt or innocence) the official label of "sex offender," prisoners and correctional personnel alike can physically attack and emotionally exploit them with immunity. In part, a sex offender label dehumanizes the individual. The label paints a picture of evil-doer as the result of what can be called the demonization effect. Consequently, an evil-doer label is a conduit to warranted or unwarranted attacks and mistreatment by anybody. Prison personnel can deny convicted sex offenders amenities such as health care, equal protection, restrictive visitation, and refuse work furlough, occupational training opportunities, and work through correctional industries that aid some prisoners in job placement after prison. The sex offender label provides the justification to lock-down or place convicted sex offenders into disciplinarian or segregation units without cause that is not a typical consequence among other prisoners. To clarify a social label, when a violator is tagged or labeled a "sex offender" in part through the judicial process, the labeling phenomenon suggests that the manner in which others interact with the labeled person can encourage and justify actions, lethal or otherwise. Also, the social label can enhance the potential of a self-fulfilling prophecy whereby the actors reject their typical pattern of behavior and conform to the behavior linked to the label (Becker, 1963). The labeled person acts-out or behaves within the expected constructs of the label, regardless of his or her previous behavior.

5. Prisoners and Their Anticipation of Future Options of Crime

With graduate assistants, many of whom had several years' experience as enforcement and correctional personnel, I gathered data for several empirically based studies, the subject pool for which included hundreds of convicted sexual offenders among other convicted felons. Our data showed that male and female non-violent offenders in high custody facilities anticipated criminally violent behavior as future options, once released (Stevens and Ward, 1997; Stevens, 1995; 1997a). These findings can further the myth that "nothing works especially among sex violators" (Katsavdakis, Weissman, and Rosenthal, 2010). Yet, recidivism rates of sex offenses after prison release reveal that an estimated five percent of sex offenders are rearrested for any type of sex crime within three years after release from prison (Langan, Schmitt, and Durose, 2003). Sex violator recidivism rates are consistent with or lower than those of other criminally violent ex-prisoners. Yet the debate rages and is fuelled by the idea that sex violators get "educated" about their apprehension because of their treatment by prison personnel and others. What about sex offenders who were wrongfully convicted or mistreated in the name of justice?

6. Fictionalized Accounts of Sex Offenders

One issue impacting how sex offenders are treated in correctional systems (and on the streets) is that there is a great deal of confusion manufactured by the popular media (newspapers, television, and movies) about the nature of sex crimes and offenders themselves setting the framework for demonization. For instance, *Dateline NBC's* reporter Chris Hansen proclaimed on *To Catch a Predator* that web predators are "a national epidemic." Popular television dramas such *Law and Order: Special Victim Unit*, *Criminal Minds,* and *CSI: Miami* offer sensationalized stereotypes of sex crimes and sex offenders patterned after the heinous attacks of a handful of predators such as Ted Bundy, John Wayne Gacy, and the Boston Strangler (Stevens, 2011b). The *Dr. Phil Show* provides less an understanding of reality and more a concern for Neilsen ratings as hysteria in the sense of a potential of victimization by a sex violator. In one episode, Dr. Phil noted, "You could be sitting next to one in church or standing next to one at the grocery store. Who is trying to prey on your children?" Dr. Phil visited a "maximum security prison and (went) 'inside' the mind of a child predator" to explain how sex offender operate and how to identify them. One truth is that most sexual predators are rarely apprehended let alone identified (Samenow, 2007; Leberg, 1997; Stevens, 2000; 2010). Another truth is that most caged individuals become chronic liars because of their experiences inside prison. Nonetheless, demonization and the wickedness of alleged sex violators can summed in the following Dr. Phil's commentary from a show aired in 2010:

> When Kevin was 10 years-old, he met David Hernandez, who was working as a camp counselor. Because he had grown up without his father in his life, Kevin appreciated the male attention. But when that attention turned into molestation, Kevin began to feel terrible. When David was arrested for child molestation, Kevin testified against him. He says, "I find it hard to believe that David Hernandez isn't in prison for life. I think it's possible he could get out and do it again."

Another episode of Dr. Phil presented the "desperate parents" of a nineteen-year-old son who participated in a three-hour polygraph test to determine whether he was a sexual predator. Because polygraph tests remain highly controversial and unreliable, it is reasonable to ask Dr. Phil in what way he would aid in the reliability of the polygraph. What about the desperate concerns of the boy's parents and the community where the boy lived? Despite the popularity and charisma of Dr. Phil, he is neither a representative of the justice community nor does he hold a psychologist's certificate to practice. Yet as Oprah Winfrey said during an Emmy Awards presentation, "Nothing connects us quite like television" (Scott Collins, "These Emmy Awards are Not a Popularity Contest," *Los Angeles Times*, 22 September 2008).

Conceptually, one way the popular media's obsession is enhanced can be seen through its *war on sex offenders* (Stevens, 2011b). Hysteria about sex violators and their demonization is fueled by hungry tabloids and the popular media through a promotion of aggressive justice policies that include prison policies. The popular media also enhances vigilantism among both justice practitioners and over-zealous constituents who seek their moment of frame (Stevens, 2008; 2011b). The media's version of apprehending sex offenders whereby a suspect falls victim to some ingenious plot centered in an illegal use of force by a Dirty Harry type detective who can justify corrupt behavior resulting in an official denial of due process guarantees. Yet the excessive and illegal use of force after a caged experience and after time-served (if the defendant has not been executed or died in prison), can continue with sanctioned confinement or civil containment after a sex offender has served his or her prison sentence. In other cases, when a sex offender is released, correctional supervision follows through intense probation, parole, and sex registry listings. Presently, sex registry is both a local and a national requirement. In addition to the pains, scares, and slander, caged depravation leads to inhumane treatment of sex offenders including the social label of sex offender ending any promise of apartment leases, jobs, and new relationships.

7. Inhumane Treatment of Sex Offenders

The treatment of sex offenders in prison mirrors the absurd stereotypes of sex offenders promoted by the popular media. This is to say that justification of the inhumane treatment by correctional personnel and prisoners are supported by both the *legitimate* monopoly of violence including official sanctions such as sentencing and the popular media's portrayal of sex offenders. The literature can aid in a better understanding of the effects of prison regime or management linked to prisoner behavior (Stevens, 1997b). For instance, a study consisting of 172 prisoners in one prison versus 229 prisoners in a similar custody level prison were surveyed. Data rejected the hypothesis that a restrictive regime with formal prisoner-custodian relations has greater control over prisoner behavior than a less restrictive regime with informal prisoner-custodian relations. Authoritative supervision produces more interdisciplinary actions than a less-supervised close prisoner-custodian environment. This idea includes the thought the sex violators are at the brunt of those disciplinary actions and victimized by both other prisoners and correctional personnel. An obvious latent outcome would apply to violence. The more legalized violence exercised by the correctional staff in their quest to control prisoners especially sex violators, it is likely that the prison population would mirror that violence and in many ways justifying brutality (Stevens and Ward, 1997; Stevens, 1997a). For instance, when an execution (legal or otherwise) takes place in prison, violence-prone individuals (prisoners and personnel) tend to identify with the executioner as opposed to the prisoner and strike out at the most visible target—sex violators. This clearly pertains to the brutalization effect (Stevens, 2005; 1992). It is a short stone's throw to suggest that the more policy allows correctional personnel to intrude in the privacy and to violate basic human rights as limited as they are among sex offenders, the more prison populations and individuals in a free society replicate those practices.

Government statistics are consistent with the idea that most individuals convicted of sex crimes are young, nonviolent males, usually caught up in a series of bad choices or expectations beyond their gasp at the time of the altercation (Bureau of Justice Statistics, 2010a). I do not intend to minimize the heinousness of any sexual violation, but I contend that most offenders are reachable before being caged or labeled. After incarceration, it doesn't matter because the pains of prison depravation weigh heavily on the life chances of every convicted sex offender. Those pains include the intentional dangers whereby the welfare of the persons sequestered are not the immediate issue, and sex offenders, partly due to the stereotypes through the war on sex offenders, are viewed as the worst of the worst. Consequently in prison as on the streets, to beat-down sex offenders is fashionable, "honorable, and fits the legal standard. It's the right thing to do," opines a prison custody officer who ignores the level (see below for details) of sex offenders similar to most individuals who view all sex offenders as vermin. Prisons are as tough as the streets. For instance, Anthony Mullen found his victims on Washington's online sex-offender list, posed as an FBI agent, and killed 68 year-old Victor Vazquez and 49 year-old Hank Eisses (John Ellement and Suzanne Smalley, "Sex Crime Disclosure Questioned: Maine Killings Refuel Debate Over Registries," *Boston Globe*, 18 April 2006). Mullen was sentenced to life in prison for the murders. During trial, Mullen reported that he left a third sex offender unharmed because he showed remorse. Mullen was comforted by several hundred emails sent to him, the prosecutor, and the judge, which all said in essence that Mullen should receive a medal of honor rather than a trial.

Finally regarding treatment for sex offenders, it has been shown that the family, friends, and the neighborhoods of prisoners also assimilate to the norms and values of a prison violent culture through a resocialization process (Comfort, 2007).

8. Levels of Sex Offenders

Reality about sex offenders can be explained through the *Legal Levels*. Each state and often each jurisdiction categorize sex offenders into three levels based on future risk assessment; i.e., the risk that an offender will repeat a crime associated with sexual assault. For instance, of the 26,841 convicted sex offenders in the New York State registry as of 17 May 2008 (New York State Division of Criminal Justice Services Website), 9,790 were listed as level 1, or low risk of a repeat offense, 9,781 were categorized as level 2, or moderate risk, 6,687 were judged to present high risk, and 583 were included on the registry but with risk level not determined.

In addition to the risk level, the court also determines whether a sex offender should be designated a sexual predator, a sexually violent offender, or a predicate sex offender. This designation, along with the risk level, governs the duration of the registration. Level 1 sex offenders must register for twenty years unless they have been given one of the above designations. Level 2 and Level 3 sex offenders are required to be registered for life. If any have been designated a sexual predator, a sexually violent offender, or a predicate sex offender, he or she must register for life regardless of their risk level. Despite the sophistication of the New York model, along with its Sex Offense Statute 130 and the Sexual Assault Reform Act (SARA), there continues to be disparity in the New York judicial process similar to every jurisdiction across the country. That is, prosecutors are immune from civil liabilities and hold enormous discretion in indicting or charging suspects held by the police with whatever crime is winnable regardless of the guilt or innocence of the suspect (Stevens, 2011b; 2008).

9. Sentencing

Sexual assault accounted for sixteen percent of all violent defendants in 2006 (Bureau of Justice Statistics, 2010). All state prison sentences averaged four years and eleven months in 2006, and 81 percent of those convicted of sexual assault (including rape) were incarcerated compared to 95 percent of the defendants convicted of murder. Rapists received prison sentences that averaged 138 months incarceration compared to 244 months for people convicted of the crime of murder and an average of 71 months of all defendants convicted of a crime of violence. On an average, when sentenced to prison, sex offenders (a state term) serve three years and six months of an eight-year sentence before a conditional release (Bureau of Justice Statistics, 2002).

Sexual offenders are fined more often than are those convicted of murder (37 percent versus 28 percent), ordered to pay restitution to their victims more often (18 percent versus 13 percent), and ordered to do community service more often than murders (19 percent versus 7 percent). Sexual assault defendants are convicted at a six percent higher rate than murderers. Then, too, 39 percent black defendants compared to 30 percent white defendants and 30 percent Hispanics are typically convicted of the crime of rape (Bureau of Justice Statistics, 2010b).

Convictions begin with an arrest. The above statistics imply that blacks as a group are easier to detain, arrest, and prosecute than other races, but then all races show a high unemployment rate suggesting that rape convictions are powered primarily by social class standings of the defendant more than the behavior of the defendant. Status impacts arrest decisions and convictions rather than behavior. One implication of this thought is congruent with the idea that in a "capitalist society prisons function as the reservoir" for the underemployed, unemployed, or those in illicit trades or what has been referred to as the lumpenproletariat (Nagel, 2007).

People convicted of a sex crime generally receive harsher prison sentences than other offenders. For instance, those convicted of drug offenses tend to receive a prison sentence of 34 months compared to a 94 month prison sentence for violent offenders. Under Arizona law, mere possession of pornography involving minors younger than fifteen is punishable by a ten-year mandatory minimum sentence (Sentencing and Policy, 2007). Each individual photograph is a separate offense, and sentences are served consecutively. Morton Berger, a former high school teacher, received a 200-year sentence without parole: ten years for each of twenty images on his computer. There were no reports that Berger victimized anyone.

10. Prison Lifestyle of Sex Violators

Individuals convicted of a sex crime share a different lifestyle once incarcerated than other prisoners. They are perceived by correctional staff and residents as *receptacles* of their violence, frustration, and anger. Upon entering the prison system, the *label* of sex offender (sex offender) impacts the prison classification process and most sex offenders are assigned to a high-risk security penitentiary where supervision is uncompromising even when the crime the defendant had been convicted of is a Level One act. Yet, despite limited constitutional prerogatives, advanced technology, and professional strategies observed by well trained staff, sex offenders are more likely to be prison-raped than other prisoners revealing that correctional personnel often acknowledge the accepted stereotype and ignore careless offenders who quickly learn helplessness and despair. For instance, one source reports that

150,000 prison rapes occur each year on an average and that a high percent of those victims are first-time sex offenders (Fleisher and Krienert, 2009; Melby, 2006). One way to interpret these statistics is to say that it is easier to rape an individual who is considered the worst of the worst and lacks correctional protection than to rape an individual who is not considered to be an outcast (Eigenberg, 2000). Thus, sex offenders are raped in prison without consequence.

Subsequently, sex offenders are beaten, robbed, and raped by the general prison population yet mandated into specific prison programs that blaze a *sex offender label* on their backs. That sex offender label leads to fewer opportunities toward normality including a lack of prison services such as health care and occupational training. Sex offenders are shoveled into a chaotic and fearful world beyond their control and the out-of-the-control of the institution.

Many offenders convicted of sexual offences in the correctional system similar to the above prisoner are denied opportunities to learn a trade while incarcerated. For instance, New York State Department of Correctional Services (NYSDOC) has available the following trade programs: air conditioning and heating repair, building maintenance, cabinetmaking, carpentry, electrical trades, masonry, plumbing, and welding among thirty other programs. Also in the correctional system in New York similar to other correctional systems, there are correctional industries that produce products or provide services such as the cast aluminum foundry. At the foundry, trained prisoners mix dry sand to proper compacting standards, make molds using patterns manufactured to customer specifications, pour aluminum at the proper temperature, and grind and finish the casting. To understand the importance of this training and working opportunity, current wages (2010) for prisoners who leave prisons can expect $19.50 an hour in the trades in the state of New York. NYSDOCS prides itself on helping foundry prisoners obtain jobs. There are fourteen industries within NYSDOC. The goals in each of the industries shops are basically the same. Prisoners are provided an opportunity to acquire 1) job skills and 2) acceptable work habits by working in a production oriented environment, operating equipment and meeting production schedules and quality standards. The point is that sex offender prisoners in aggression replace training and 12 step substance abuse programs are rarely assigned vocational training in correctional systems across the country. Other prisoners in those same programs are assigned to training and prison industries. It appears that a lack of assignment of sex offender to training and work details within prison systems is a standard operating procedure. When I asked one NYSDOC's superintendent why sex offenders were not provided training or jobs, he said:

> Can't mix sex offenders with general pop[ulation] prisoners. Not sure who would survive the battle but there will be battles, and I think sex offender would get their asses kicked in more ways than one (Stevens, 2005).

11. Prison Treatment Programs

One prison treatment for sexual offenders is linked to cognitive-behavioral therapy (Inside Prison.Com, 2010). Sessions are approximately 10–15 hours per week and consist of group participation, homework, and require maintenance therapy after treatment concludes. Treatment relates to faulty cognitions, irrational assumptions and rationalizations about sex crimes, problems with self-regulation and lifestyle management, deviant sexual arousal and deviant fantasization, emotions management, and victim empathy (Inside Prison.Com, 2010). Some of these issues represent triggers to reoffending. These programs follow a relapse prevention framework in that it attempts to prevent offenders from relapsing by making them identify those high-risk situations that potentially cause dysfunctional behaviors to be re-invoked.

However, regardless how elegant a program or how experienced the program-providers, most professional supervisors have learned that *no single strategy* or plan prevents sexual assault alone or works best toward recovery because each participant is different and forcing participation in a rigid environment is contradictory moving a person toward a positive decision. What holds greater promise is the application of multidisciplinary models of sexual offender management but outside prison walls (American Psychiatric Association, 1999). Why? Because another thought held by prison providers is that sex offenders fail to realize the severity of their crimes, and an antagonistic prison environment can exacerbate feelings of being wrongly accused and hamper treatment (LaFond, 2004). Sex offenders are mandated into specific programs that research has yet to have been validated but attending those programs alerts everyone in the prison facility that the individual is indeed a sex offender. Most therapeutic treatments are mandatory and conducted in an unyielding style generally with custody officers listening that tends to result in a stifled participant. For instance, NYSDOCS mandates attendance of aggression replace training for every prisoner convicted of a sex crime despite the sex level of conviction. One twenty year-old first-time prisoner convicted of a sex crime wrote the following in his prison journal:

> I can't believe I'm one of them (sexual predators). They look at me like I'm a piece of pie. What could I say if they jack me up— the COs (correctional officers) treat us all alike. After growing up, I learned things happened that were in my control. Yes, but the way I dealt with my life issues before this place were incorrect. My life became a circus, but now.... At least I learned that three do's to stop abusive behavior: admit the possibility exists; plan to stop it at the earliest signs; replace the time no longer used abusively with healthy activities. Like what— defend my ass from those maniacs (Stevens, 2011b).

In my experience, the spontaneous give-and-take of a group session is redundant in a sequestered environment reducing any opportunity of recovery among willing participants especially sexual offenders. Even one-on-one, prison environments dictate the terms of therapeutic outcomes because the one component lacking toward recovery is freedom of choice.

12. Once Released

Judicial sanctions against sex offender are hardened by stereotypes resulting in longer prison sanctions than sanctioned during the conviction process (because correctional personnel harass sex offenders and write them up more than other prisoners), civil containment (held under prison supervision, see below for details) once prison sentences have been served, and a lifetime of registering and suffering through the abuses of the media, criminal justice community, and the public. Although sex violators once released reoffend at lower rates than most other violent released prisoners, it is a wonder they survive after prison because of the abuse and label depicting them as dangerous perverts who deserve continual punishment and exploitation. But neither suffering nor punishment necessarily enhance reformation or ease a victim's pain.

The popular stereotype of a sex offender influences law enforcement's identification, apprehension, indictment, and conviction of an individual. Rounding up all the usual suspects starts with individuals on the sex registry and those who look like they're on the sex registry. The truth of the matter is that most sex offenders might understand the error of their ways if appropriately treated in an alternative to a punitive environment. Prison is not the best answer for violators especially sex offenders nor does prison serve the greater good because it does not, as a public institution, go to the root of the problem nor does prison deter violent crime. Nonetheless, things that most of us take granted are rarely available to released sex offender such as safe living quarters, employment, and meaningful relationships. Once released into society, the lifestyle of the typical sex offender amounts to a social prison because of the isolation, abuse, and dictates of regulation and policy resulting in a loss of due process rights and a loss of quality lifestyle opportunities (Ravlich, 2008).

13. Civil Commitment

Prisons perpetuate and reinforce violence amongst personnel and prisoners toward sex violators. Prisons compromise the very core of a democratic society and as such the prison system provides both a stepping-stone and the justification of illegal and immoral activities to storm down on a targeted population—the sexual violator. This abuse of power parallels the contradictions of a corrupt political system making it possible to cage a sex violator but once he or she serves the prison sentence, the sex offender is further denied their freedom predicated on some god-like notion that they are a danger to society. Apparently, their prison term had not been a cure from their alleged "madness."

One group of researchers describes several models for the civil commitment after a sex offender serves or maxes out his or her prison sentence (Kendall and Cheung, 2004). In *Kansas v Hendricks* (521 U.S., 326, 331) rather than releasing a sex offender, the Court deemed that continued detainment (after time served) of a sex offender as associated with an (alleged) mental disorder (such as sexual violence) is not a constitutional violation or a due process issue. Somehow, because a sex offender represents a (an alleged) threat to the public safety and can benefit from the treatment (American Psychology-Law Society, 2001), he or she unlike other prisoners are denied their constitutional guarantees of due process and freedom.

Civil commitment follows a psychopathology or mental health civil commitment model. The sex offender is believed to be amenable to treatment and characterizes behavior consistent with dangerous compulsive behavior, consequently he or she represents a continuing danger to the public. The chances of reoffending are supposedly greater among these individuals. One researcher articulates that contemporary cases asked the question of whether a violent incarcerated sex offender could be civilly committed to a mental health facility after this prisoner had served his or her entire prison sentence and was about to be released (Alexander, 2004). For both questions, in 1997 the Supreme Court answered in the affirmative through *Kansas v Hendricks*. The Court's rulings that incarcerated sex offenders nearing release may be civilly committed to a mental health facility have potentially ominous implications for both mental health and criminal justice policy.

One report shows that in 2007 an estimated 2,700 individuals convicted of various sex crimes were held indefinitely, largely in special treatment centers, under civil commitment programs in 19 states. On an average, these programs cost taxpayers four times more than keeping the offenders in prison (Monica Davey and Abby Goodnough, "Double Rise as States Hold Sex Offenders after Prison," *New York Times*, 4 March 2007). Recent legislation in several states providing correctional supervision including rehabilitative treatment or civil containment has stirred legal, clinical, ethical, and public policy controversies (Grossman, Martis, and Fichtner, 1999). While politicians debate, sex offenders continue to be caged after serving prison sentences.

There is little question that high-profile media coverage of crimes against children have heightened public awareness of child safety. That might be a good thing. Yet it also results in blurred realities between heinous sexual predators and young boys and girls who made a single thoughtless decision that has changed their lives, the lives of their family members, and the lives of their victims, forever (Boudreaux and Lord, 2005). At a time in American history when (reported) sex offenses have declined similar to all crimes, prison populations continue to rise including the wrongful convictions of individuals linked to sex crimes.

14. Wrongful Conviction of Sex Offenders

Alana Salzberg (2010) at the Innocence Project in New York reported that there have been 192 post-conviction exonerations (across all offense categories) in the United States since 2000. The primary reasons for wrongful convictions are eyewitness misidentification testimony, invalidated or improper forensic science, and false confessions. Three-quarters of those cases involved sex crimes. For instance, Omar Saunders, Larry and Calvin Ollins, and Marcellius Bradford were convicted of the October 1986, kidnapping, rape, and murder of twenty-three year-old medical student Lori Roscetti in Chicago (Stevens, 2008). The four young men allegedly abducted Lori Roscetti, took her to a secluded location and raped, robbed, and murdered her. In 1988, Omar Saunders and his three cousins were each convicted of the crime and sentenced to life without the possibility of parole. Saunders signed a confession to the brutal sexual homicide of Lori Roscetti. Had any of the young men of been older, the state would have pursued the death penalty.

When seventeen year-old Omar Saunders arrived at Stateville Prison near Chicago, he was assigned to an in-group session I supervised. It was evident to me that Saunders did not possess either the tenacity or the skill to commit a violent act. Fifteen years later, it came to light that Pamela Fish, a forensic crime lab supervisor who had testified that semen found on the victim's (Roscetti) body belonged to Saunders, had lied about her findings.

A subsequent forensic analysis determined that none of the convicted prisoners' blood types matched the crime scene samples. In December 2001, the convictions against all four men were vacated. The governor, so outraged by this case and the hundreds of other cases handled by Fish and the Chicago police, was compelled to vacate capital punishment sanctions of almost 200 prisoners on death row (Warden, 2005).

The Illinois General Assembly proclaimed that an "historic reform of death penalty procedures in a state embarrassed by its penchant for choosing the wrong people to die" fueled the governor's decision. Of interest, three-quarters of those condemned to die had been convicted of sex crimes among other crimes. One source in the prosecutor's office revealed that any alleged sex violation committed by a "worthy" violator powered the prosecutor's pursuit of capital punishment "because it was well established that it was a winnable case and it also meant we got great publicity" (Prosecutor, 2003).

For a prosecutor, great publicity translates into greater resources and votes (Stevens, 2011b; 2010). When prosecutors make errors in judgment and the wrong person is condemned to a cage, what are the consequences? For the prosecutor, there are none, no repercussions—no consequences. For you and me, let's say by circumstance you happen to be in the wrong place at the wrong time with the wrong story where police engage you through an aggressive "zero tolerance" road block or a search of your bags, or targeted you during a "sweep" after a sporting event. This is indeed what happened to a public school teacher. She had been wrongfully convicted of a sex crime. Here's Emma's [although that's not her real name] story:

> The mere innuendo by police or a prosecutor that you are, indeed, a sex offender translates to unemployment, poverty, public ridicule, and shame beyond your wildest thoughts. If you fit the profile of a sex offender for whatever reason like I was a high school teacher and adored my students, it's good-bye freedom, thin crust pizzas, and boring vacations with extended family members. Fair trials are out and godless cesspools of punishment which include rotting teeth, bleeding rectums, warts on both feet, all the while wondering about AIDS and all the other diseases floating below your feet and above your head. You'll want sanity back. This amazing madness plays less significance on your mind than the disrespect your family members bestow upon you. You swallow some deep breaths of incredibly rank air that validates your own worthlessness and helplessness. You struggle not to breathe, not to comply, not to respond as a woman who gave birth to three children and professionally rose in my profession and despite my innocence—every convict is innocent—but eventually you succumb to the madness that promotes survival because you've learned the most ancient of laws—survival of the fittest. (Stevens, 2011b)

A brief analysis of this quote is consistent with the notion that convicted sex offenders including those wrongfully convicted suffer a worst fate than the *mad denizens* aboard those *ships of fools*. Then too, having a wrongful conviction does not make one immune to assault in prison. Additionally, I have discovered that female sex offenders suffer similar fates as their male counterparts. For example, I'll call her Mickey Stone, a young pretty woman who had been a local police officer and mother of four who is currently a sex offender prisoner, advises that "If you're not a whore and a junkie when you come into MCI Framingham [women's prison in Massachusetts, see Stevens (2012) for details] you will be after you leave." In particular, females in the prison system—with a sex offender conviction—changes immediately how the prisoner is treated by personnel and other prisoners (Rathbone, 2006; Talvi, 2007). For instance, Talvi (2007) implies that guards in women prisons sexually abuse sex offenders more than other prisoners. If a raped prisoner reports the crime, the guards retaliate with fierce attacks and allow other prisoners to rape and abuse the sex offender. Should the system believe the allegation that the prisoner had been raped, she is placed in solitary confinement during the investigation and raped yet again and again (Stevens, 2012). Other times, female sex offenders are denied visitation rights of their children especially if she does not submit to the abuse and intimidation of the guards (Rathbone, 2006). If the sex offender is pregnant or disabled in some way upon arrival to a prison system, the punishment she endures is beyond what I can describe. However, why would alleged victims or their parents in the case of a minor, have an incentive to help a prosecutor win a case even if it's a wrongful or suspect conviction? It's called victim compensation.

15. Victim Compensation

California's Victim Compensation Program (VCP) was created in 1965 to lessen the financial impact of crime on qualifying victims. This program has paid nearly $1.8 billion to victims since its inception. In 2008, victims received more than $81 million. By law, VCP is the payer of last resort for eligible out-of-pocket losses resulting from crimes. New York accepted almost 14,000 claims for victim compensation in 2008 and paid out $28M, of which $18M went to victims of personal injury as a result of a criminal action. Michigan reports three victim service programs providing over $20 million in services for over 250,000 citizens each year. And some states, such as Illinois, report that a victim of domestic violence or sexual assault is eligible to receive compensation of up to $27,000. Official statistics about how much has been paid out and to whom (other than a child) are not available. In the case of Gerald Amirault, his mother, and his sister who operated a Massachusetts day care were charged and convicted with nine counts of sexual abuse. Fells Acres Day Care had a $500,000 per-year-per child insurance policy, which covered molested children. In the Amirault case, insurance proceeds and funds from victim services provided, by one account, ten families with an estimated $16 million over their lifetimes. This could produce the best of two worlds: persons indicted of sexual assault accept a guilty plea that produces a lesser charge, and accusers walk away rich.

16. What to Do with Prisons?

One goal of this article is to shrink prisons into non-existence. The idea is that the *prison industrial complex* should be abolished. Rose Braz says, "[t]he use of prisons, policing and the larger system of the prison industrial complex as an 'answer' to what are social, political and economic problems, not just prisons" (Rose Braz, cited in Bennett, 2008). Continuing along this line of reasoning, American society does not require punitive models of social control because few judicial efforts from the justice community (police, courts, and corrections) have stopped crime including sex crimes. Abolitionists of slavery believed that slavery could not be fixed or reformed, and therefore it should be abolished. Similarly, the *prison industrial complex* cannot be fixed or reformed to meet the needs of a healthy democratic society let alone reduce sexual attacks. This thought should not be interpreted to mean that all prisoners should be released from custody. A new vision should take precedence when amending prison sanctions on a case-by-case basis. This thought is consistent with a *Critical Resistance's* vision that calls upon the creation of genuinely safe, healthy communities that respond to harm without relying on prisons and punishment.

17. Final Thoughts

The evidence in this article is consistent with view that the *prison industrial complex* exasperates criminally violent behavior, gives rise to unhealthy communities, and weakens the democratic process through a system of oppression by denying inalienable rights of a targeted group of individuals. Punitive methods of control do not serve the greater good nor do they foster healthy communities or individual recovery. Nonetheless, there's always more to the story as Peter Berger (1963) clarifies with his thought that "nothing is as it seems." Peeling away the social layers of reality can aid in a better understanding of reality. For instance, there are over 200,000 (convicted) sex violators residing in American communities who are on parole or probation, and each year approximately 600,000 ex-prisoners return to their communities. "Unfortunate collateral consequences" arise in those communities such as child abuse, family violence, the spread of infectious diseases, homelessness, and community disorganization (Petersilia, 2000). Consequently, community cohesion is unstable, employment prospects and economic well being are rare, there are no opportunities to join in the democratic process, family stability and childhood development are stifled, and mental and physical health care are inadequate.

Convicted sex offenders on probation, parole, and on sex registrars along with the thousands of returning ex-prisoners, their families, and their victims impact the health of their communities. Christakis and Fowler (2009) argue that there are "tipping points" beyond which communities can no longer favorably influence righteous community member behavior. Attitudes, behavior, and violent lessons learned in prison and violent lessons learned by victims are transmitted to a free society. Previously accepted social values and norms change, disorder and incivility increase, outmigration follows, and crime and violence increase. Moral authority becomes vested in "street smart" young men for whom drugs and crime are a way of life (Petersilia, 2000). This phenomenon can impact the socialization and safety of young people, the power of prison sentences to deter, and the future trajectory of crime rates and crime victimization but most of all, the health of the community is at-risk, advises Hairston (2001). To better understand this perspective, the Bureau of Justice Statistics (2008) estimates that 45 percent of male and 62 percent of female prisoners convicted of sexual assault had minor children prior to their incarceration and that almost 1.7 million minor children have a mother or father in prison for various crimes. That is, real-life social community networks can shape every aspect of each community member's routine: how they feel, whom they marry, whether they fall ill, how much money they make, and whether they vote. Behavioral outcomes and attitudes of each community member are often shaped by their neighbors and often, their neighbors are simply anonymous community members residing and working in the neighborhood. Sociologists conceptualize the collective civic value of social networks that includes the influence, social resources, and social solidarity (social cohesion or glue) within a community as *social capital*. Those networks include the social bonding of similar community members and the bridging between diverse community members. Bonding and bridging are linked to socially accepted values and norms or social reciprocity (Claridge, 2004). A compelling argument is that communities are governed by what Christakis and Fowler call the *Three Degrees Rule*. Each community member influences and in turn is influenced by other community members up to three degrees removed from each of them, many of whom are unknown individuals.

When government perceives a community as marginal in terms of social capital, community members and their community at-large are subjected to political disenfranchise, fewer municipal amenities, more street pot holes, an abundance of slum building owners, and boarded up buildings that house thugs. Marginal community members also experience greater intrusion by the police in their private lives because those members both individually and collectively posses few social networks which include political clout or protection. Although the following example deals with drug searches in a marginal community, imagine how police-stops or *sweeps* of alleged sexual violators would be conducted? The results of one study "paints a disquieting picture, with nearly one-third of (marginal community members) searches (115) performed unconstitutionally and almost none visible to the courts" (Gould and Mastrofski, 2004). The researchers offer the following description of an unconstitutional "egregious" search:

> A black male in his late twenties while riding a bike was told to pull over by two officers from their patrol cruiser. The biker refused. The officers called for backup. When another police vehicle appeared, the biker stopped. One officer told the biker that the police dispatcher had received a report that a biker was selling drugs. The biker denied that he had any drugs. Nonetheless, one officer searched the rider's knapsack while another officer padded the biker's pockets. Nothing. "I bet you are hiding them under your balls. If you have drugs under your balls, I am going to f___ your balls up," the officer told the biker and added, "You sure are nervous. I wonder why you are so nervous." The officer ordered the biker to stand behind the police car door, and to pull his pants down to his ankles. The officer put on rubber gloves, and searched the biker's private parts. Finding nothing, the officer said, "I bet you are holding them in the crack of your ass. You better not have them up your ass." And with that the biker turned, bent over, and spread his cheeks. The officer put his hands in the biker's rectum, but found no drugs. As the officers returned to their vehicles, one commented, "I know he had some drugs."

It should be noted that the illegal searches discovered by Gould and Mastrofski were highly concentrated in a few officers. An implication linked to sex offenders suggests that law enforcement tends to target subjects whom they can intimidate without fear of public outcry and in most cases that means marginal community members. To some marginal community members, the police represent an occupational army violating due process rights (Hunter, 1994).

In conclusion, traditional models of social control grounded in punitive violent orientations exacerbate the use of violence, isolation, and intimidation among prisoners and communities. It appears that only the eradication of the prison systems and control over the police would provide humanity with an opportunity to better control crime, reduce recidivism, and provide benefits toward recovery and quality lifestyles. An emphasis should be placed on working to build healthy and autonomous communities, where the basics are provided, such as food, shelter, self-determination, and a wider spectrum for economic and political participation that will aid in lasting community safety. Fundamentally, this thought gives rise to a *renaissance of community* whereby the legitimate authority of violence through punitive responses is abolished from the hard hand of government, and justice is shared by the people, for the people.

Eight

QUEER (IN)EQUALITIES: IMPRISONING LGBTQ PEOPLE

Amit Taneja

1. Introduction

Lesbian, Gay, Bisexual, Transgender and Queer/Questioning (LGBTQ) people face violence and discrimination on a continual basis. Not only interpersonal in nature, but these problems also take the form of state sanctioned forms of violence that construct them as deviant or threatening, which increases public perception that they deserve such physical, emotional, spiritual, financial and other forms of violence and constraint. This chapter explores how LGBTQ people—their lives, dreams, and aspirations—are "imprisoned" by a web of interconnected restraints consisting of both written and unwritten laws and social norms. I will demonstrate how queer imprisonment is an extension of the racist, sexist, ableist, patriarchal, classist, imperialist, and colonizing agendas of the nation-state.

Both the mainstream and gay media have done an excellent job of representing LGBTQ people as part of one uniform community with a unified "gay agenda." This is far from the truth. LGBTQ people represent a wide array of racial, gender, class, ability, religious, political, and national affiliations, among many other differences. Many different sub-communities fall under this conceptual umbrella. For example, LGBTQ people of color and LGBTQ people with disabilities resist and distance themselves from the mainstream white, able-bodied, male-centric, educated, and upper class representations of the "gay" community. They choose other labels to self identify themselves, including "same gender loving" and "queer crips." Rooted in these acts of resistance to "homo-normativity," the idea that all LGBTQ people must conform to a narrow definition of what being "gay" means or looks like, I purposely choose to write with the term "queer" people in this chapter as a broader and inclusive term.

A quick scan of recent national media headlines speaks to the prominence of queer issues as core to the cultural and social struggles embedded in the fabric of our society. Issues ranging from ordination of LGBTQ clergy members, civil unions, Don't Ask Don't Tell, and domestic partnership benefits have one thread in common—regulating the humanity of queer people. These laws not only permit the subjugation and imprisonment of queer people, but even when they are supposedly gay friendly laws, they often narrowly define the acceptable limits of what "good queers" look and act like (as in the case of same-sex marriage). Often complex LGBTQ issues are reduced to single identity politics that lack deep analysis and reflection, and small queer victories often come with a hidden price-tag (for example, the revocation of Don't Ask, Don't Tell may allow queer people to serve openly in the military, but it also allows the US government to continue to build its military industrial complex that serves its imperialist agendas).

We must consider not only what queer issues and struggles look like, but also ask *why* they are vital to the nation's current struggles. Queer issues are central to the rhetoric of defining and regulating acceptable citizenship and morality with the United States context. They have consistently been used by political candidates as a moral yardstick to benefit their political agendas. Claims to family values, tradition, and yearning for a return to the American dream (aka, the white, Christian, heterosexual, middle class, white picket fence, 2.3 children fantasy) are essentially a call to arms for politically conservative candidates and their supporters in waging their wars on the morally and spiritually corrupt, including queers. Claims that conflate "queer" with abnormal, deviant, promiscuous, and diseased are just some of the ways in which society is able to create the boundaries between "good (heterosexual) citizens" and those who threaten the American dream. Thus, queer imprisonment has become a topic of grave national security, as is often substantiated by claims that acceptance of queer people and the "gay lifestyle" will lead to the destruction of the moral fabric that makes America great. Such claims strongly position queer imprisonment as in the state's interest. It also calls upon ordinary citizens to enact violence upon queer people and communities as a way to protect national and personal interests. To be queer friendly is often construed as being un-American.

The political left is neither disconnected, nor any less guilty in the subjugation of queer people, bodies, and communities. Good minded leftist politicians pander to the gay voting block by making lengthy campaign promises that rarely come to fruition. Much like their conservative counterparts, leftist politicians use queer issues as a political game play to showcase their so-called progressive politics as on a candidate's agenda; but we see no follow-through after they are in office. Many LGBTQ measures are lost in the political battlegrounds of law making procedures while queer people wait and hope for transformative policy and leadership. Small advances in public policy are often touted as evidence of growth, but do little to create a transformative political agenda.

2. Creating the Prison: One Bar at a Time

Many issues beyond same-sex marriage impact queer people and communities. Marilyn Frye (1983) proposed an excellent "birdcage" metaphor that helps us understand the imprisonment metaphor that I apply to LGBTQ people. She explains that a bird is not held captive because of one individual wire, but because a series of wires come together to create a cage. The same is true for queer people.

Homophobic laws at the federal and state level impact heavily queer people. It is also crucial to note that laws created to undermine the humanity of queer people often intersect with other racist, sexist, xenophobic, and ableist structures to create literal and metaphorical "super prisons." An intersectional analysis beyond single identity politics is therefore not only preferred but is essential in understanding queer lives holistically.

While an exhaustive review of the legal status and societal constraints that impact queer people would be beyond the scope of this chapter, I will present a summary overview that will help us to understand some of the bars that help create "queer prisons." The following sections outline how laws, homophobia, nationalism, the war on terror, and queer on queer violence all act in concert to create the prison and to operate it on a day-to-day basis.

3. Queers as "Diseased": The Medical Prison

The early medical and psychological models labeled "homosexuality" as a mental disorder that was both dangerous and in need of medical intervention. Freud's theories of maladjustment perpetuated the thinking that all people were born heterosexual, and therefore deficits in upbringing and "normal" human development lead to the mental disorder of "homosexuality." The simple step of labeling queerness as a disease also meant that it took on other properties of diseases: threat of contagion and need for treatment. Under the guise of helping, many LGBTQ people were subjected to an array of treatments including induced vomiting, electro-shock, reconditioning, and other techniques generally clumped under the term of "reparative therapy."

These treatments have now been removed from the approved list of interventions available for the mental health profession because of their damaging impact on queer people (Ford, 2002). However, they continue to be advertised and practiced by pseudo clinical professionals as a large financial industry that is often supported by the organized religion industrial complex. In particular, organizations such as the National Association for the Research and Therapy of Homosexuals (NARTH) continue to promulgate ideas that scientific and medically valid interventions exist to cure gender nonconformity and same-sex attractions, while organizations such as Parents and Friends of Ex-Gays (PFOX), provide similar relief from homosexuality from the spiritual realm. Organizations such as PFOX and NARTH operate under the guise of wanting to help queer people get rid of their disease but in reality are extremely damaging to their mental, spiritual, and emotional well being.

The American Psychiatric Association considered homosexuality to be a mental disorder until 1973. Furthermore, transgender and gender variant people continue to be labeled as mentally ill through diagnostic labels including

Gender Identity Disorder, Transvestic Fetishism, etc. The organized medical industry requires transgendered people to have an identified psychological diagnosis that allows them access to medical interventions such as therapy, hormones, and Gender Confirmation Surgery (also sometimes known as Sex Reassignment Surgery). Trans and gender variant people therefore continue to be subjected to demonization by the medical industrial complex (Lev, 2004) and these organizations continue to alienate trans people from access to basic medical care, while operating a large subset industry often glamorized as the "sex change" complex. Trans and inter-sexed bodies thus serve both the capitalist and moralist agendas of the medical industrial complex.

The medical complex therefore plays a huge role in not only informing public opinion and social norms about queers and queer bodies, it also impacts legal structures that govern those bodies. For example, Yoshino (2006) argues that the 1978 decision by Justice William Rehnquist to grant credibility to a public university's assertion that it did not need to recognize its gay group because of fears that the group would spread homosexuality is tantamount to equating queerness with disease. Rehnquist wrote in the University's favor, noting that the issue was "akin to whether those suffering from measles have a constitutional right, in violation of quarantine regulations, to associate together and with others who do not presently have measles . . ." (p. 37). Rehnquist's argument is consistent with the disease model. In essence, it reduces the citizenhood of queers as less than desirable human beings.

HIV/AIDS has heavily shaped queer history in both the United States and international context. Hundreds of thousands of gay men in particular died because of this devastating disease. While HIV/AIDS is a medical issue, it is also an equally relevant political and policy concern. The reason for the significant delay in response to the epidemic and lack of attention to HIV/AIDS interventions was that it largely impacted queer men (Krieger, 1988). HIV/AIDS continues to disproportionately impact queer men, and especially queer men of color. Cuts in funding for AIDS research and service continue to create added pressures for those infected and affected by HIV/AIDS (Turkewitz, 2011).

4. Heteronormativity: The Social Prison

Heteronormativity is the belief and practice that heterosexuality, gender conformity, and traditional family structures are the only correct way of existing in our society (Oswald, Blume and Marks, 2005). This belief demonizes queer people and privileges heterosexuals through laws, conventions, and everyday practice. Heteronormativity thus supports and perpetuates homophobia and transphobia, respectively defined as the irrational fear and hatred of homosexuals and transgender people. Heteronormativity and homophobia/transphobia are two sides of the same coin.

Homophobia and transphobia manifest themselves in many different forms ranging from individual acts of violence against queer people to institutionally sanctioned forms of violence, such as employment discrimination. In particular, jokes around same-sex attractions and gender non-conformity run a central theme in several sitcoms, movies, and other forms of mass communication. For example, the recent emergence of the phrase "no homo" in hip-hop music speaks to the ways in which heteronormativity and homophobia are both produced and reproduced as social constructs. While many hip-hop artists claim that their use of "no homo" is not meant to be homophobic, it is a stark reminder that men/masculinity are closely monitored for conformance to strict raced, classed and gendered expectations.

Additionally, the erasure or suppression of same-sex relationships from the public realm is another way to control and regulate queer bodies and visibility. For example, Facebook only recently added the option of "domestic partnership" and "civil union" in their options of relationship status for individual's online profiles and still continue to only provide the male-female gender binary options for self-identification. In essence, transgender and gender non-confirming people are forced into boxes that do not apply for them.

A common fallacy is that homophobia and transphobia occur only at the individual level, but it is the larger social environments and underlying imperialist and colonizing agendas that create conditions for these acts to occur. For illustrative purposes, let's consider the prisoner abuse at Abu Ghraib prison in Iraq. While many government officials characterized the acts of abuse as out-of-the-ordinary acts performed by low level soldiers, it is anything but isolated forms of violence (Puar, 2005; Richter-Montpetit, 2007). The use of chains, nudity, forced sexual contact, hoods/masks, restraints and tortures are explicit forms of raced and gendered heterosexist violence (Puar, 2005). Given the strong links between the military industrial complex and the prison complex, these forms of violence and subjugation are deeply rooted in homophobia that is practiced domestically and internationally. Acts such as the hooding of faces and forcing brown naked bodies upon one another are designed to reduce the humanity of the prisoners by demonizing them as the homosexual "other." The literal and metaphorical overlaying of "queer" and "terrorist" therefore are used as a means to conflate the two identities that threaten the United States' imperialist agenda (Puar and Rai, 2002). The emergence of Abu Ghraib comedy skits and prisoner Halloween costumes for kids and adults speak to both the acceptance and celebration of a culture of violence against brown bodies, queer bodies, and brown queer bodies.

5. Queer Youth

Queer youth in particular are subjected to extreme and persistent forms of interpersonal and structural violence on a daily basis. A recent report by the

Gay, Lesbian and Straight Education Network on the national school climate for queer youth outlines some of the major challenges experienced by queer youth: Eighty-nine percent heard negative remarks and use of the word "gay" in a negative context on a frequent basis (GLSEN, 2010). Roughly two-thirds experienced negative remarks about their gender expression. One in five youth experienced physical violence because of their sexual orientation and thirteen percent have experienced the same for their gender expression. Eighty-five percent experienced verbal harassment. LGBTQ students were four times more likely as their heterosexual counterparts to miss an entire day of school in the past month because of the harassment that they experienced. Sixty-two percent of the students did not report incidents of harassment or violence because they believed that the administration would do little to nothing, or that the situation would get worse. Of those who reported incidents, one-third reported nothing was done (GLSEN, 2010).

These data outline the significant daily struggles that some queer youth have to experience within the educational environment. Additionally, the data suggest that complicity of the educational industrial complex in condoning violence on queer bodies. Most schools are not required by federal or state laws to address these issues, nor are the teachers or administration provided the tools to create safe environments. Organizations such as the Gay Lesbian and Straight Education Network (GLSEN) provide some limited support to high school Gay-Straight Alliances (also known as GSAs), and these forms of support have come with legal and political challenges (Grattan, 1998). For example, in 1996, after a prolonged court battle that affirmed the rights of LGBTQ students to be able to form GSAs as student clubs, the Salt Lake City school board voted to ban all extra-curricular activities from their schools in order to prevent the GSA from being formed. Such actions deploy strategies of silencing, isolation and demonization to deny LGBTQ students access to the public square and rights as full citizens (Burrington, 1998).

Importantly, merely establishing a GSA does not necessarily create a welcome or inclusive political or social climate for queer youth. Lance T. McCready (2003) argues that often GSAs are created on Eurocentric and homo-normative values and principles, and continue to alienate and marginalize queer youth of color, and especially gender non-conforming queer youth of color. Laura Gipson (2002) has argued that low income, queer youth of color in particular are at risk, as they are over-represented in the child welfare and juvenile justice systems. Transgender and gender non-conforming youth also face significantly more barriers than their lesbian, gay and bisexual counterparts. Roughly half of all transgender youth who were bullied or harassed in school reported attempting suicide (Grant, Mottet and Tannis, 2011). The failure of the schooling industrial complex in addressing transgender inclusive policies and practices results in the unchecked harassment, significantly lower GPAs, missed schools days, disproportionate dropout rates, and much lower enrollment in post-secondary education (Greytak, Koswic and Diaz, 2009). In essence, the intersections of race, class, ability, and gender co-exist with queer identities to create the metaphorical and literal "super-prisons" for the multiply marginalized youth and adults.

Given the persistent harassment and lack of support from adults for some queer youth, it is no surprise that queer youth are at higher risk for both attempted and completed suicide. The recent media attention on a series of highly publicized queer youth suicides advertised the phenomenon as a new epidemic; however this is neither new, nor shocking news, for those who work with queer youth (Morrison and L'Heureux, 2001). As support for queer youth in schools and higher education increases, so does the push back from those who seek to contain queer bodies and visibility. A recent example includes Texas House Bill HB1 that mandates all public colleges and universities that have Gender and Sexuality Centers to provide an equal funding for "family and traditional values" centers on those campuses (Ura, 2011). The positioning of LGBTQ centers as antithetical to traditional and family values is not only of rhetorical significance in creating a polar divide between "good heterosexual citizen" and "bad queers," it is also a political strategy to effectively defund these centers given the large budget cuts to higher education.

6. Queer Elders and Aging Issues

Many queer seniors grew up in a society that viewed them as mentally ill and morally deficient. Law enforcement agencies have a history of disenfranchising and oppressing queer people, including the gay witch hunts in the 1950s led by a closeted gay man and head of the FBI, J. Edgar Hoover. Police officers were known to raid queer gathering spots and bars where they would arrest any gender non-conforming individuals and then publish their names in the newspapers. Such actions would often mean that these individuals would lose their jobs, get disowned by their families, and many committed suicide as a result of the demonization and isolation that they experienced. These forms of oppressive behaviors lead to the Stonewall riots in 1969, and created one of the first waves of mass queer political organizing. In addition to the law enforcement, queer baby boomers were also subjected to demonization by the medical/psychological professionals who labeled them as mentally ill. It is therefore understandable that the same queers who are seniors today are quite skeptical of legal and medical authorities, and often resist social services available to seniors because of a well founded fear of these same institutions that marginalized them in the past (Grant, 2010).

Many individuals in the aging queer community came out at a time when it was not acceptable to be LGBTQ and were often disenfranchised from their families of origin. This vastly reduces their financial and emotional support networks; many queer seniors struggle in silence. As well, the lack of same-sex marriage recognition means that queer couples, especially queer seniors, are unable to collect partner benefits including health insurance and social security benefits in the event of the death of one of the partners. Collectively, queer seniors are marginalized and at risk because of the oppressive past and current socio-political constraints that they have to negotiate.

7. Same-Sex Marriage: Building Better Prisons?

Same-sex marriage and relationship recognition is a complicated issue. On one end of the spectrum, advocates for same-sex marriage list the myriad of ways that same-sex couples are disenfranchised from society through denial of rights including tax benefits, ability to make medical decisions for one another, property and spousal death benefits, immigration rights, adoption and family recognition, health insurance benefits, divorce and alimony, etc. The list is extensive and demonstrates state sanctioned violence and discrimination against queer couples. On the other side, many others have argued that marriage itself is a historically flawed system, and that it becomes even more problematic when governments are able to dictate not only what legitimate relationships look like but how those relationships should function and be rewarded (Ettelbrick, 1989).

Public discourse over same-sex marriage is readily accessible from the political, religious, and legal stand points. Instead of reiterating those debates, it might be more revealing to consider how either denial or access to marriage can operate as forms of oppression. For illustrative purposes, let us consider New York's current stance on same-sex partner recognition. Until 2011, same-sex marriages were not legal in New York. However, same-sex unions from other jurisdictions were recognized by the state. Prior to the recent establishment of same-sex marriage laws in New York, the only partner recognition written in to New York state law was the public health law No. 4201, also known as the "Disposition of Remains Act" which gives same-sex partners the right to designate each other as the legal authority over each other's dead bodies. It is especially ironic to consider that New York state laws barely recognized any rights for same-sex couples over one another while still alive, but only affirmed such relationships in death. It is exactly this kind of tension that illustrates the problems with designating the government as an arbitrator of what a legally sanctioned relationship looks like.

Marriage as a societal institution is deeply rooted in hetero-patriarchy where women were traded as property and objects (Hamilton, 1999). Paula L. Ettelblick (1989) argues that the basic struggle over marriage is that it creates a divide between the "haves" and the "have-nots." For example, marriage allows one partner to have access to health care benefits from the spouse's health care plan, but it does not allow for or recognize other familial relationships that might be significant to that individual such as people caring for sick or retired parents. Centering of a spousal relationship over other familial relationships is a deeply Eurocentric construct that ignores or devalues other multi-generation family structures prevalent in other cultures. Same-sex marriage therefore opens the doors for recreating and reinforcing a two-tier system that allows the state to regulate and define legitimate relationships. Within this model, "good" queers take on heteronormative models by mimicking straight relationships, while other queers and straight couples who are unmarried continued to be demonized (Etterblick, 1989). Same-sex marriage also opens up the possibility of demonizing any same-sex sexual contact that happens outside of the context of marriage, thereby regulating the autonomy of individual sexual expression. Same-sex marriage is a way for the state and the corporate industrial complex to regulate benefits and spending while distributing the meager funding made available to working class citizens. If marriage is itself a flawed concept, does same-sex marriage ask the question: are we just working to build better prisons, instead of working toward abolishing them?

Reward and punishment are essential components of the same-sex marriage debate. Heterosexual citizens are rewarded when they meet the narrowly defined structures of marriage through childcare tax benefits, joint tax filings, access to health care, partner survivor benefits, etc. Additionally, the state increasingly functions as a way to control and punish those who seek to conceive of marriage in alternate forms, including same-sex partner recognition. For example, the Defense of Marriage Act (DOMA), the very name of which evokes feelings of fear from a queer attack on the institution of marriage, is a way for the nation state to protect itself from having to legally recognize any relationships outside of the hetero-patriarchal male-female configuration. Additionally, many states have passed "super-DOMAs" that not only define marriage as between a man and a woman, but also seek to impose penalties on local governments or public institutions that allow for any other form of same-sex partner recognition. A recent example of this includes the Michigan state senate that passed a bill penalizing state colleges and universities five percent of their budget if they continue to offer same-sex partner health benefits to their employees (Haywood, 2011). Measures such as these demonstrate the ways in which the state exercises control over queer bodies by punishing those who treat queers as human beings/citizens.

8. Queer on Queer Violence: Doing the Master's Bidding

> *Jails and prisons are designed to break human beings, to convert the population into specimens in a zoo—obedient to our keepers, but dangerous to each other.* - Angela Davis

Queer people face state sanctioned violence and discrimination on an ongoing basis, but this oppression not only happens from outside of the community but within queer communities as well. There has been a particular lack of attention paid to the ways in which the "gay rights movement" has played a large part in doing the master's bidding by being agents of oppression for other queers. The gay rights movement has largely been funded and supported by educated, white, middle to upper class, able-bodied, gay men. The gay rights movement has largely been a single-issue movement for the large part.

Kenyon Farrow argues that the marriage recognition benefits only a small percentage of white, middle class queers because the denial of marriage rights is really the only barrier stopping white male queers from being full citizens. By prioritizing marriage as the central and often the only issue addressed by "the movement," many other issues of concern to queer people are sidelined. Mimicking heterosexual arrangements of relationships by claiming "we are not so different that you" reinforces the superiority of hetero-patriarchy and continues to harm queers who have larger or other struggles in their lives:

> Even if same-sex marriage becomes legal, white people will access that privilege far more than Black people. This is especially the case with poor Black people, who regardless of sexual preference or gender, are struggling with the most critical of needs (housing, food, gainful employment), which are not at all met by same-sex marriage. Some Black people (men in particular) might not try to access same-sex marriage because they do not even identify as "gay" partly because of homophobia in the Black community, but also because of the fact that racist white queer people continue to dominate the public discourse of what "gay" is, which does not include Black people of the hip-hop generation by and large. (Farrow, 2005)

The mainstream Gay Rights Movement therefore can sometimes function as an agent of the state by creating the dichotomy between "good" queers (those who live in traditional two partner households, often with kids) and the "bad" queers (gender non-conforming, poly-amorous, non-monogamous, or other family structure oriented queers). Strategies on the part of gay rights advocates, and even heterosexual allies, have often centered on noting the similarities between same-sex relationships and heterosexual relationships (Kudrek, 2004). This well meaning strategy is one of the ways that queer on queer violence manifests itself with queer communities as it marginalizes and demonizes queers whose family structures or gender/sexual expression differs from hetero-patriarchal norms.

In addition to marginalizing queers on the periphery of the queer community, centering marriage as the key and only issue sidelines other concerns vital to diverse queer communities. The fights for gender justice, economic justice, safety, transgender rights, and employment protections become less relevant in both public discourse and policy. For example, while many queer youth find love and acceptance within their homes and communities, many do not. There is an epidemic of homeless queer youth, especially low income queer youth of color, that has largely been ignored by social service agencies and the LGBTQ rights movement (Ray, 2006). The priorities of the gay rights movement and heterosexual allies becomes evident when roughly $43M alone were spent on the California Proposition 8 battle in 2008 to keep same-sex unions legal in the state of California, while tens of thousands of homeless queer youth struggle for basic survival needs. Prioritizing the needs of white, middle class queers over poor queer youth of color is further evidence of queer on queer violence.

Transgender communities in particular have been subject to ongoing forms of queer on queer violence in the form of silencing or sidelining trans issues. Transgender individuals have experienced persistent transphobia within queer communities and organizing. A recent example is especially poignant because it exemplifies the ways in which queer on queer violence operates and is rewarded by the state. In 2007, the United States Congress was considering the "Employment Non-Discrimination Act" (ENDA), which would have barred employment discrimination on the basis of sexual orientation and gender identity/expression, in addition to other already protected classes such as race and gender. Some legislators expressed concerns that they were supportive of such protections for lesbian, gay, and bisexual individuals but not for transgender individuals. At this moment of fissure, the Human Rights Campaign, the most well funded gay rights organization decided to lend its support to ENDA without protections for transgender individuals, thereby prioritizing the rights of LGB individuals over transgender people. This case of queer on queer violence is especially telling from a strategy point of view because the state was willing to reward such violence by creating fissures within the queer community. In essence this strategy illustrates the ways in which the state seeks to divide and conquer marginalized communities.

9. Conclusion

The preceding discussion illustrates the ways in which queer people are imprisoned in many ways to create a birdcage effect through multi-layered and pervasive oppressive strategies. The anti-queer agenda is deeply rooted in heterosexist, Eurocentric, ableist, patriarchal, and capitalist agendas of the nation state. Similar to the prison industrial complex, the anti-queer industry relies on concepts of rewards, punishments, boundaries, and borders to control and oppress queer bodies and queer lives. These forms of oppression are not only exercised directly by the state or individual actors, but are also sustained by queer on queer violence. It is therefore crucial for us to consider alternatives for queer organizing that will lead to radical and transformational changes within our society. One such alternative would be the creation of multi issue grassroots organizing that forges alliances within and between social justice movements. The quest for queer liberation is intricately linked to other movements that are also impacted by the imperialist and capitalist projects of the state and the global corporate industrial complex. The metaphorical queer prison is just one cell block within a larger system of prisons, and it is therefore essential that a Queer Liberation Movement be intricately tied to racial justice, economic justice, gender justice, (dis)ability justice, anti-war, and other (in)justice movements.

Nine

IMPRISONING NATURE

Amy J. Fitzgerald

1. Introduction

This chapter critically examines the imprisonment of "nature," broadly conceived. At first, conceptualizing nature as being imprisoned may seem strange because it has been dominated and subjugated so thoroughly that we generally fail to critically examine its positioning in the world. The term "prison" also evokes visions of austere brick buildings and barbed wire—not what we think of when we hear the word nature. Additionally, when the words imprisonment and nature are joined, images of the environment inside prisons might be conjured up. Imprisonment, however, extends beyond those walls. Michel Foucault, for instance, demonstrated that disciplinary power extends beyond prisons and produces "a docile body that may be subjected, used, transformed, and improved" (1977, p. 136). To say that we have subjected, used, transformed, and allegedly improved nature is a gross understatement.

I discuss two processes of the imprisonment of nature: enclosure and designating Protected Areas, using these examples to develop an argument to explain why the imprisonment of nature is important to consider intellectually and address in an applied manner. I begin by discussing the theoretical grounding for examining nature as imprisoned, first by addressing why the imprisonment of nature is relevant to criminology, which has concerned itself with the imprisonment of people for quite some time, and next by integrating ecofeminist theorizing.

2. Criminology and Nature

As a product of Western culture, criminology was built upon a presumed impenetrable barrier between nature and culture. The social sciences more generally developed in opposition to biological and social Darwinist theories, and social scientists consequently sought to distinguish their work and their disciplines from the realm of biology and nature. As a result, perhaps unwittingly, they participated in constructing a rigid culture/nature dichotomy and concerned themselves strictly with culture. The result of the reification of this dichotomy is the prevalence of anthropocentrism (privileging human beings) and speciesism (prejudice or discrimination based on species) within the social sciences. Anthropocentrism and speciesism are still apparent in criminology today. However, recently a shift has occurred within criminology, under the banner of green criminology, that challenges the anthropocentric and speciesist undercurrents.

The term "green criminology" (Lynch, 1990) has been defined as "the study of those harms against humanity, against the environment (including space) and against non-human animals committed by both powerful institutions (e.g. governments, transnational corporations, military apparatuses) and also by ordinary people" (Beirne and South, 2007, p. xiii). A central premise of green criminology is that the purview of criminology should not be determined by rather arbitrary legalistic boundaries. It is therefore framed around a social harm approach and expands traditional disciplinary boundaries beyond that which is officially defined as criminal. Four main types of harms that could be addressed through a social harm approach include the following: those resulting from the dynamics of the market, from the inequalities fostered by the market, those produced during the production and distribution of goods and services, and those that result from the consumption of said goods and services (Tombs and Hillyard, 2004). The degradation of nature is but one illustration of these harms, and it has resulted in harm not only to the natural environment but also to human beings and other species.

Scholarly interest in green criminology has grown in recent years (Chunn, and Menzies, 2002; South and Beirne 2006; Beirne and South, 2007; White 2007; Boyd, Fitzgerald and Baralt, 2010; Fitzgerald, 2010), and it has been argued that the relevance of criminology depends upon its inclusion of harms against the environment and non-human animals: "A criminology relevant to the [twenty-first century] should have the intellectual breadth and constitutional space to be able to embrace environmental, human and animal rights issues as related projects" (South, 1998, p. 225). Criminology will be assisted in this task by engaging with the rich literature developed by ecofeminists (see Lane, 1998), who have laid the groundwork for understanding how the subjugation of nature, non-human animals, and marginalized groups of people are interrelated.

3. Theorizing the Imprisonment of Nature

Ecofeminists argue that sexism and the exploitation of nature are related, as evinced in language and several oppressive dualisms pervasive in patriarchal culture, including the distinctions between culture and nature, public and private, and mind and body. Robert J. H. King concisely summarizes this perspective as follows:

> Ecofeminists argue that there is a connection between the patriarchal oppression of women and the economic and social habits and beliefs which underlie the exploitation of nature. Conceptually, the basis for the drive to dominate nature derives from the "normative dualisms" which lie at the heart of a patriarchal culture and provide the conceptual framework for a logic of domination (1991, p. 79).

I will focus my attention here on the culture/nature dualism, while recognizing that it is interconnected with other oppressive dualisms.

Barbara Noske (1989) explores the culture/nature dualism in detail and she explains that as a result of this dualism human beings consider themselves unique and vastly different from non-human animals and nature. Human beings are believed to belong to an entirely different order, the realm of culture, whereas other beings are regarded simply as nature. However, membership in the realm of the cultural has not been equally afforded to all human beings: hegemonic conceptions of masculinity (see Connell and Messerschmidt, 2005; Messerschmidt, 2004) have been associated with culture, whereas women and subordinated masculinities have been largely identified with nature. Subordinated racial and ethnic groups have also been associated with nature (see Griffen, 1997; Spiegel, 1996). As a result, nature, along with those who are associated with it, has been constructed as the Other and lesser.

The two frequently delineated types of ecofeminism—cultural and social ecofeminism—interpret the relationship between women and nature somewhat differently. In brief, cultural ecofeminists consider the relationship between women and nature a natural and biologically-based one that should be celebrated. By contrast, social ecofeminists consider the relationship between women and nature to be the result of their similar social construction and their shared experiences of oppression. From this perspective, Carol Adams opines, "I value nurturing and caring because it is good, not because it constitutes women's 'difference.' Similarly, I do not value animals because women are somehow closer to them, but because we experience interdependent oppressions" (1996, p. 175).

While the foregoing may sound extremely abstract, there are real, lived consequences of the othering and subjugation of nature. For instance, like nature, women have been treated like natural resources. The productive and reproductive capacities of women and nature are expropriated, and their contributions are simultaneously undervalued (Salleh, 1995).

Due to the interconnectedness of these experiences, attending to all forms oppressions is the best way to undermine them; a point Lynda Birke succinctly states as follows: "my belief [is] that politics that ignore other oppressions cannot be liberatory politics for anyone" (2002, p. 429). Ariel Salleh (1995) states more specifically that change will only come when the commodification of nature and perception of nature as being external to human beings are overcome. Thus, according to ecofeminists, both of the cultural and social variety, liberatory politics for human beings will require that we grapple with our treatment of nature. Our current treatment of nature might best be described as imprisonment propelled by an unfolding process of hyper-commodification.

Nature is being increasingly degraded as a result of this imprisonment and commodification. Environmental degradation and resource overuse have come to be referred to as "management" problems, which is illustrative of the anthropocentric assumption that it is the role of human beings to manage non-human nature. The term "nature" is even becoming extinct in a way: nature is being replaced with the term "environment." Natural resources that are useful to capital fall under the category of environment, while everything else goes overlooked (Escobar, cited in Goldman and Shurman, 2000, p. 577). When "environmental problems" result from the commodification of nature, the commodification itself is not questioned, instead capital seeks to overcome these problems by extending its reach (Goldman and Schurman 2000). Capital seeks to remake nature in its own image (O'Connor, 1994; Schnaiberg, 1980), and in the process it is changing the way we think about nature (or fail to do so). Some examples will assist in understanding this process.

4. The Enclosure of Nature

"Enclosure" has been defined as "the capture of common resources and exclusion of the communities to which they are linked" (Heynen and Robbins, 2005, p. 6). The term refers not only to physical enclosure but also to the placement of land under the ownership of one person or group of people. The term generally evokes thoughts of the quintessential historic example of the Enclosure Movement in England in the seventeenth and eighteenth centuries. It is estimated that during that movement, the British parliament enclosed 6,794,429 acres (Wordie, 1983), resulting in the rural poor losing their grazing land and being pushed into the factories to work. There is also a history of enclosure in North America, where the land was stolen from indigenous peoples and given to speculators. "Private rights" to land and minerals were subsequently developed, which was a sweeping process of commodification and imprisonment of peoples and land (Robbins and Luginbuhl, 2005, p. 46).

Termed "accumulation by dispossession," enclosure has continued through late capitalism, taking inventive forms, augmenting the separation between the natural and the social, and simultaneously threatening both. Capital has increasingly had to accumulate by reaching outside itself into previously untapped areas. Some recent examples include attempts to commodify and restrict rights to water, plants, and even the genetic composition of organisms (Shiva, 1997). This process has found a friend in neoliberal logic, which unfolds as follows: the only way to protect nature (read natural resources) is to privatize aspects of it and then trade rights to these items within the free market. The market would assign high prices to scarce resources, thus affording them protection (Himley, 2008, p. 422).

Wildlife provides a particularly good example of this process of enclosure. The transformation of wildlife into a commodity was among the earliest acts of the enclosure of public property (Robbins and Luginbuhl, 2005). Of course, the enclosure of wildlife is different from the enclosure of land; it is more complicated because the materials being enclosed are mobile beings. Technically, wildlife belongs to the state in which they reside, although some species are given special protections (e.g., through the Endangered Species

Act). State agencies, variously given titles like Department of Natural Resources and Department of Fisheries and Wildlife, have authority over wild non-human animals, and with that the ability to determine access to the non-human animals and even set a value for it.

The commodification of wild non-human animals and their imprisonment within rather arbitrary legal definitions and boundaries has tangible consequences. As sport hunting (as opposed to subsistence hunting) developed and became increasingly profitable, access to wildlife was restricted for profit. As a result, collective interests in wildlife were overridden by individual, profit-based interests. Hunting licenses are sold by states to individuals who can kill (an extreme end result of imprisonment) non-human animals who are deemed to be "wildlife."

In some states, the state-acting-as-middleman is cut out and hunting rights are given to landowners and commercial guides who then sell the permits for profit. Proponents of this type of arrangement argue that it is an effective way to manage and protect wildlife because individuals who stand to benefit economically from their maintained existence (so that they can then be killed) have a stake in the health of the population (Robbins and Luginbuhl, 2005). In other words, it is viewed as a way to avoid the "tragedy of the commons" (Hardin, 1968), a situation where shared resources are at risk because individuals will seek to maximize their own benefit at the cost of the greater good (the commons). However, the profit-based model of managing wildlife is not entirely rational: the killing of large trophy animals results in an unbalanced ecosystem, as does artificially increasing the population of species prized for hunting and killing off predator species (Fitzgerald, 2005; Robbins and Luginbuhl, 2005).

The enclosure process even blurs the line between wildlife and domestic non-human animals. An extreme, but unfortunately not uncommon, manifestation of this is the "canned hunt," where "farmers" breed "game" animals in literally enclosed, fenced-in areas, which hunters are given access to for a price. Some operators even guarantee the kill of large trophy animals. These developments have lead Paul Robbins and April Luginbuhl to conclude that wildlife is "a final frontier for rapacious privatization" (2005, p. 61).

Enclosure is, therefore, not just an historic movement of imprisoning nature and dispossessing human beings. It continues today, as some people are allowed to benefit economically from what used to be protected communally. The seizure of nature for profit ought to concern all of us because we ultimately depend upon nature for survival. Greta Gaard (1997) further points out that the so-called wilderness (nature presumably untouched by culture) should concern ecofeminists in particular because wilderness has been othered and exploited as women have been. What is perhaps most ironic is that even the alleged protection of nature can reinforce the problematic culture/nature dichotomy, a dilemma we examine next.

5. "Protected" Nature

Designating certain parts of nature as Protected Areas has been a central element in conservation strategies. As early as the nineteenth century, public parks were being established in the United States. Since that time, the number of protected areas has grown dramatically, especially since World War II (Adams and Hutton, 2007). Currently, over 105,000 protected areas exist globally (West, Igoe, and Brockington, 2006). Yellowstone and subsequent national parks in the United States became the model for national parks globally (Adams and Hutton, 2007). This model is one that protects "wilderness" nature from human "culture." The motivation for the creation of these Protected Areas is the belief that to protect nature for the greater good, the government ought to step in and protect specific areas of land. For instance, it is suggested that the creation of Protected Areas could reduce deforestation in developing countries (Coad, Campbell, Miles, and Humphries, 2008).

However laudable the goals might be, the process of designating Protected Areas is political. In some cases, the ramifications are quite problematic:

> The relationship between people and nature, particularly in the context of PAs [Protected Areas], is highly political, embracing issues of rights and access to land and resources, the role of the state (and increasingly non-state actors in NGOs and the private sector), and the power of scientific and other understandings of nature. (Adams and Hutton, 2007)

Notably, the designation of Protected Areas may actually further support the culture/nature dichotomy and the process may even export the culture/nature dichotomy to areas unfamiliar with it:

> Protected areas have increasingly become the means by which many people see, understand, experience, and use the parts of the world that are often called nature and the environment. This virtualizing vision, although rarely uncontested, has imposed the European nature/culture dichotomy on places and people where the distinction between nature and culture did not previously exist. (West, Igoe, and Brockington, 2006, p. 255)

The reification and exportation of the culture/nature dichotomy in this way is problematic for two central reasons. The first issue that arises is that relatively small areas of nature (that perceived as wilderness, untouched by culture) would qualify as being worthy of conservation under the standards of Protected Areas because culture has thoroughly infiltrated so much of nature. William M. Adams and Jon Hutton (2007) articulate this point when they refer to national parks as being "founded on a conception of nature as something pristine that could be distinguished and physically separated from human-transformed lands." The divide between culture and nature is difficult to sustain in practice, and it is challenging to make the case for protecting nature that does not meet the "pristine" or "pure" nature threshold.

The second problem inherent in reifying and exporting the culture/nature dichotomy is that envisioning and supporting such a division assumes that human beings should be physically excluded from Protected Areas. In some cases, indigenous human inhabitants have been forcibly removed from lands on which they resided. Interestingly, however, not all human beings are banished: scientists and tourists are frequently permitted in Protected Areas. There are consequently situations where people who pay are granted access, whereas people who used to live there are excluded.

The development of Ecotourism is further illustration of the commodification and imprisonment of nature, which is then marketed as spectacle. Here conservation meets capitalism. Ecotourism can change the way the native population engages with and views nature; it effectively transforms nature from becoming a form of sustenance to be respected to a commodity to be exploited (King and Stewart, 1996). Not surprisingly, there have been cases where indigenous peoples conceptualized their lives as being inextricably linked with the natural environment prior to the creation of a Protected Area, but afterwards they began to view nature and culture as quite separate domains (West, Igoe, and Brockington, 2006). This places nature at risk of exploitation. Therefore, to effectively protect nature it should not be cordoned off from culture, conceptually or literally. So what should be done?

6. Protecting Nature while Challenging the Culture/Nature Dichotomy

The foregoing should not be taken to suggest that programs designed to protect nature should be abandoned. Instead, it suggests that we need to do so in ways that challenge rather than prop up the culture/nature dichotomy. Challenging this dichotomy may be done in Protected Area programs by modifying their governance structure. The management of many protected areas has followed a "'fortress conservation' model, i.e., a top-down protectionist, quasi-colonial approach to National Park management" (Timko and Satterfield, 2008, p. 239). Some research indicates that top-down approaches to governance are problematic and can result in economic and social costs for the local people and conflicts between the locals and the managers (Coad et al., 2008). Instead, community-based management is recommended as an alternative (see Adams and Hutton, 2007; Coad et al., 2008). Involving the local population in planning and implementation would foster a feeling of investment in the program and would make it more likely that the benefits from the program would be shared. Similarly, some have argued that indigenous peoples should be involved in the governance of the ecotourism industry (King and Stewart, 1996). Importantly, involving indigenous peoples in designing these programs would be more likely to preserve the connections between people and nature, instead of imprisoning nature behind fences and creating antagonism between nature and culture.

More generally, treating nature as a commons instead of as property to be accumulated through enclosure can provide a way forward in protecting instead of imprisoning nature. The commons discourse has emerged as a counter to the discourse of sustainability, which has been co-opted by capital to ensure its own survival (i.e., protecting the natural resources it depends upon). Instead commons "are cooperatively organized to maximize access of all commoners to the means of life" (Johnston, 2006, p. 50) and "commons discourse represents a direction for human/nature interactions that is more egalitarian, democratic, and oriented toward ecological survival across generations" (p. 41). The goal of the commons, "to maximize access to life goods" (p. 51), stands in stark contrast to the goal of capital (i.e., profit). There have, of course, been concerns raised about the sustainability of the commons. For instance, as discussed earlier, Garrett Hardin (1968) articulated the potential "tragedy of the commons," where users could seek to maximize their own gain and therefore degrade the commons. However, Hardin's hypothesis overlooks the potential of users to reach agreements to benefit the greater good (for specific suggestions, see Dietz, Ostrom, and Stern, 2003; Ostrom, Schroeder, and Wynne, 1993).

Still, protecting nature as commons does not entirely solve the problem. Nature should not be viewed as something that ought to be protected because it has value to us as "users," but because it importantly has value outside our personal interests. We need to recognize the overlap between culture and nature without presuming that the interests of the latter should be subjugated to the former. Ecofeminists such as Lori Gruen (1997) suggest that we can make our way forward by including nature in our conceptualizations of community and developing community-based ethics that would take nature into consideration. Doing so would begin to bridge the perceived divide between culture and nature.

7. Conclusion

Protecting nature will require that we actively deconstruct and challenge the culture/nature dichotomy. Ecofeminists have pointed out that this dichotomy not only puts non-human nature at risk of devaluation and subjugation, it also undergirds the oppression of human groups who continue to be associated with the realm of nature instead of culture.

Imprisoning nature, whether motivated by enclosure and commodification or under the banner of protection, reifies the culture/nature dichotomy. Enclosure, which can be conceptualized as the imprisonment of nature through privatization and commodification, has not protected nature. Privatizing and commodifying nature widens instead of bridges the presumed divide between culture and nature, and as such, places nature at greater risk.

At the other end of the spectrum, designating areas of nature assessed as being unmarred by culture as Protected Areas leaves a great deal of nature vulnerable and risks institutionalizing adversarial relationships between culture and nature, which ultimately undermines the protection of nature. In sum, imprisoning nature to protect it from culture risks further harming nature and all humanity by extension.

Instead of reaffirming the culture/nature dichotomy through the drive to imprison nature, we need to deconstruct and challenge this process. The way forward, as thoughtfully laid out by ecofeminists, is to include nature in our notions of community. Additionally, the human members of these communities must share in the responsibility of decision making about protecting nature. This type of decision making process can simultaneously protect nature and culture from top-down governance regimes – which have demonstrably exacerbated tensions between nature and culture – and from capital's desire to enclose and privatize nature, which threatens both nature and culture.

Ten

CONTROL AND INCARCERATION OF HUMAN AND NON-HUMAN BEINGS

Jenna McDavid

1. Introduction

The human world exists today in a virtually never-ending series of hierarchies and power structures that serve to keep some populations imprisoned physically and socially. Race, class, gender identity and expression, sexual orientation, ability, and myriad other characteristics have been used to lump people into categories, often arbitrarily bestowing privilege upon one while the other languishes in submission. Sadly, parallels to that dynamic can be found in human beings' treatment of the non-human animals with whom we share the planet. Billions of non-human animals currently live in systems designed to exploit them for human use, a number so large as to be nearly incomprehensible. From food production farms and factories to zoos and circuses ostensibly used for human education and entertainment, non-human animals—by virtue of their being non-human—are imprisoned, exploited, and killed. We as human beings have established barriers between us and the animals, a belief of "misothery" that, like misogyny and the submission of women to men, is deeply entrenched in our culture and serves to keep animals in their "places" as means to an end (Mason 2000). As abolitionists, our circle of compassion must extend to these prisoners as well, for as long as one system of dominance is allowed to flourish, others will never be far behind.

2. Animals Exploited for Their Flesh

Of the billions of non-human animals currently living and dying in the various prisons established for them around the world, the greatest percentage is comprised by those whose bodies are used for food. In the United States, over nine billion animals are killed every year in the meat and dairy industries—a number that exceeds the human population of the planet (Mohr 2010). Far from the idyllic green pastures of Old MacDonald's farm, the United States agribusiness industry operates primarily through the euphemistically-named "Concentrated Animal Feeding Operations," or factory farms, that push the bodies of non-human animals through the system as quickly as possible with no regard for what activists recognize as non-human animal autonomy or for the inability of non-human animals to give informed consent. These operations treat non-human animals not as individuals with an interest in living but as a renewable resources whose bodies—or the byproducts of those bodies—exist solely for human consumption. In *Discipline and Punish*, Michel Foucault provides a vivid account of the execution of a prisoner:

> Then the executioner, his sleeves rolled up, took the steel pincers, which had been especially made for the occasion, and which were about a foot and a half long, and pulled first at the calf of the right leg, then at the thigh, and from there at the two fleshy parts of the right arm; then at the breasts. Though a strong, sturdy fellow, this executioner found it so difficult to tear away the pieces of flesh that he set about the same spot two or three times, twisting the pincers as he did so.... The executioner Samson and he who had used the pincers each drew out a knife from his pocket and cut the body at the thighs instead of severing the legs at the joints; the four horses gave a tug and carried off the two thighs after them, namely, that of the right side first, the other following; then the same was done to the arms, the shoulders, the arm-pits and the four limbs; the flesh had to be cut almost to the bone, the horses pulling hard carried off the right arm first and the other afterwards. (1995, pp. 1–3)

While the book goes on to suggest that the rise of social and criminal prisons has emerged as an alternative to those public displays of punishment, torture, and execution that once reigned supreme, in the case of non-human animals, prisoners are still drawn and quartered by the billions in slaughterhouses, and yet their only "crime" is being of the non-dominant species.

Non-human animals' bodies are displayed—on our plates—as a constant reminder of their status as "other" in our society. Those valued for their flesh—chickens, turkeys, fish, cows, pigs, goats, and others—are the most recognized victims of this imprisonment, often crammed into as little space as possible, fed a diet of antibiotic-laced grain or seed that they would never choose for themselves in free-living situations, denied many of the behaviors intrinsic to their species, abused, neglected, and ultimately murdered (Mason 1980). The bare minimum of care is given to farmed animals because profit, not their happiness is the goal; the health of an individual animal is rarely of concern to the farmer or corporation. One factory farm for chickens had just one veterinarian on staff for over 700,000 birds. At that rate, it would take the veterinarian approximately twenty-eight years to conduct a five-minute examination on each bird (Durand 2004). Animals raised as food are often driven to insanity from the boredom, the captivity, and the cries of their fellow prisoners on the farm. Just as human prisons tend to negatively impact the communities in which they are built, feedlots for cows, sheds for chickens, and hatcheries for fish are all overwhelmed by the waste products of the animals crammed into their boundaries, often destroying the natural environments surrounding the facilities. When profits are held in the highest esteem, as we see so often in the capitalist system, everyone suffers.

Another casualty of the human desire for animal-based foods are non-human animals exploited for the production of dairy products. Milk-producing mammals and egg-laying birds are treated to much of the same confinement and mistreatment as their flesh-production counterparts, except that these animals are often in impossibly-worse health, since their only the milk or eggs and not their bodies are of value to the corporation. Processes such as forced molting, perpetual pregnancy, and debeaking maximize productivity at minimum cost, but to the detriment of the non-human animals' physical, mental, and emotional health (Mason 1980).

The lives and lived experiences of these animals—and, by extension, females of every species—are so devalued that industry goes so far as to call the mechanism on which cows and pigs are inseminated a "rape rack," a term coined by animal experimenter Harry Harlow and later adopted by agribusiness (Runkle 2005). Despite the obvious exploitation involved in the production of these foods, dairy animals are often overlooked by human beings practicing a vegetarian diet because they wrongfully assume that dairy production does not result in the animal's death. Sadly, this is not true: male chicks born in the dairy industry are killed immediately because they produce no eggs; calves born to pregnant cows are sold for slaughter so that their mothers' milk can instead be sold to human beings. Once the dairy-producing animals become too old or too sick to be profitable, they, too, are sold to slaughter. Dairy production is hardly the harmless industry that the corporatocracy would have us believe.

At the end of these non-human animals' short lives in either the meat-production or dairy-production system, they are often transported to slaughter en masse in large, drafty, dirty trucks. Left without food or water for the transport process—if they are just going to die, why feed them?—the slaughter-bound animals are often stressed, scared, starving, and sick. To move them onto and off of the slaughter trucks, they are beaten with sticks and canes, shocked with electric prods, and sometimes physically lifted with farm machinery in the case of those too weak or ill to stand (Cuolo 2000). Few regulations exist for this part of the process, and those that are written into law are incredibly difficult for the limited government staff to enforce. As a result, animals are often left conscious while their throats are being sliced, or while they are being dunked in vats of scalding water, or while their stomachs are being sliced open and their skins removed. This sounds like a nightmare, but for upwards of fifty billion animals each year, this is their reality.

3. Animals Exploited for Their Hides

Far from being a simple by-product of the flesh industries, fur, leather, and other animal-based textiles are obtained through the exploitation of a set of non-human animals completely separate from those whose bodies we consume as food. Hundreds of thousands of rabbits, mink, foxes, dogs, cats, chinchillas, and other fur-bearing mammals are imprisoned in intolerably-small cages and kept alive just long enough for them to grow a pelt that can be removed and turned into hats, gloves, or trim (Morrison, 2009). Driven mad by stress and boredom, fed an unnatural diet, and denied contact with other human or non-human beings, these fur-bearing animals live short, miserable lives, at the end of which they are often drowned, gassed, or electrocuted—to preclude blood from slaughter ruining their coats.

Still thousands of other non-human animals in the wild are snared by leg-hold traps—steel mechanisms that catch animals by the paw or leg and crush them with up to ninety pounds of pressure. Some consider these traps to be so inhumane that several states in the United States have banned their use, although this has done little to curb the practice of trapping—or the use of fur in fashion (Hyslop, 2011).

Cows used in leather production, especially those in India, are subject to brutal living conditions on farms and in transit to the slaughterhouse. The slaughter of cows has been banned in all Indian states and territories except for West Bengal and Kerala, so trafficking of cattle is necessary to get them to slaughter. These journeys can span hundreds of miles, during which the cows are transported by trucks or tied together and transported on foot. They are beaten, their tails are broken, or chili peppers are rubbed into their eyes to keep them awake and moving; they are not allowed rest, food, or water. One activist writes of this trafficking:

> It's a hideous journey. To keep them moving, drivers beat the animal across their hip bones, where there is no fat to cushion the blows. The cows are not allowed to rest or drink. Many cows sink to their knees. Drivers beat them and twist their battered tails to force them to rise. If that doesn't work they torment the cows into moving by rubbing hot chili peppers and tobacco into their eyes. (Popham, 2000)

Sheep raised for wool undergo similar mistreatment during massive shipment to other states and countries for slaughter. They are also subject to genetic manipulation to make them produce more wool than would naturally occur, resulting in overheating and insect infestation in the folds of their skin (Hartman, 2010).

When non-human animals are valued only for the products of their bodies, well-being will be disregarded in favor privileged groups obtaining as many products at the least cost as possible. Parallels to this structure can be seen in the way privileged groups of human beings benefit from the labor and bodies of groups considered to be less privileged because of their race, class, gender, or citizenship status. For example, immigrants are often valued for their willingness to work at undesirable jobs for low wages and no benefits—and literally sacrificing their bodies—cleaning toilets and picking fruit, for example, so that privileged groups can benefit from their labor. These workers are likely to have difficulty obtaining health care, education, protection from abuse, or citizenship. Workers' rights—and the abolition of the social constructs that keep workers imprisoned in low-paying jobs—go hand-in-hand with animal rights, just as do civil rights, women's rights, and other movements to end oppression.

4. Animals Imprisoned in Laboratories

The bodies of non-human animals are also exploited by experimenters in laboratories around the world. Vivisection is defined as the practice of subjecting live animals to cutting operations, especially to advance physiological and pathological knowledge. Hundreds of thousands of animals are currently languishing in laboratories where their brains and bodies are manipulated under the auspices of science, a practice supported by René Descartes' assertion that "animals are without feeling or awareness of any kind" (Kemp Smith, 1952, pp. 136, 140) in the 1600s and flagging little since.

Despite the emergence in recent years of many alternatives to non-human animal testing and the extensive knowledge already gained from hundreds of years such testing, experimentation on non-human animals continues apace. Many scientific experiments conducted today merely validate what we have already discovered before, such as the continued testing done on tobacco and nicotine. Still others seek answers, such as the ways in which a particular disease can be alleviated or cured, but those results may not be applicable to human beings. In an interview with Dominick Miserandino (2008) Ray Greek, co-author of the book *Sacred Cows and Golden Geese* (2000), said that animal testing does not actually provide us with information relevant to human health:

> Animals, like people, can be infected with viruses and bacteria. So, yes, one could argue that by so doing, nineteenth century researchers proved the germ theory of disease. But just because a concept works in an animal does not mean that it will in a human. Rabies produces many of the same symptoms in human beings and animals, but a vaccine that works in animals may kill a human. Polio can be produced in monkeys, but since the disease is subtly different, experimental results cannot be extrapolated to human beings. Herpes B, rabies, and many other diseases exist in animals and can be transmitted from an animal to a human. But Herpes B is asymptomatic in monkeys and kills human beings. Animal

> experiments did help convince skeptics that infectious diseases were real phenomena, but the reasonable scientist was already convinced based on human data. Animal experiments did help convince researchers of certain scientific principles in the ninetheenth century but in the final analysis, even being generous, I am unable to see any present-day benefits to animal experimentation. As a paradigm, it fails miserably. It steals money from legitimate research modalities and results in harm to people.

Aside from the possible irrelevance of the results of testing on non-human animals, the conditions in which laboratory animals are kept are often unspeakable. The 15,000 monkeys currently imprisoned in laboratories in the United States find themselves in stacked cages with barely enough room to turn around, much less climb, swing, or jump as monkeys in free-living situations would do. Caged monkeys are often so stressed by their living conditions that they mutilate themselves: pulling their ears, biting their bodies, pulling out their hair. When they are removed from their cages, it is often to undergo painful medical procedures such as having limbs broken in crash simulations, having toxins injected into their veins, or being subjected to electric shocks (Reinhardt, 2009).

Still other animals are used in traumatic, painful psychological testing such as the infamous Harlow experiments conducted between 1951 and 1963 to study maternal care and need for comfort, in which baby monkeys were removed from their mothers and given nourishment from either wire mesh constructions or soft terry cloth dolls. Surprise: Harlow discovered that the babies will still try to hug their mothers, despite the injuries, and that sentient beings can die from loneliness (Harlow, 1958).

Still other animals are used in the testing of household chemicals or perfumes. Rabbits' eyes are doused with cosmetics to find out at what concentration mascara can safely be applied to a human eye. Dogs and pigs are routinely used in military weapons testing.

In the 1930s Alabama, doctors and public officials watched 400 black men die of syphilis during the Tuskegee Syphilis Study. This experiment, which was initiated by the United States Public Health Service, ran from 1932 until 1972, sought participants from a primarily black, low-income community and infected them—without their knowledge or consent—with syphilis. Treatment was deliberately withheld and, in some cases, prevented. Ultimately, the experiment provided no new information about syphilis but left scores of men dead, blind, or insane (Brandt, 1978). These experiments were, rightfully, decried as racist, unnecessary, and unethical—no longer considered okay to perform on human beings without informed consent.

Still, millions of non-human animals currently languish in laboratories, subjected to similar experiments—and few are coming to their defense. What gives human beings the right to perform these tests, for their benefits, on non-human beings?

5. Non-Human Animals Exploited for Entertainment

A fair number of non-human animals are also imprisoned for the purposes of human entertainment. In the case of circus animals and carriage horses, some are forced to work long hours without any ability to give consent, often pushing their bodies and brains beyond the limit. Zoos and aquariums take animals from free-living situations and force them to live in enclosures that rarely emulate the natural space or climate from which they were kidnapped. Even the "best" facilities in the United States cannot compare to hundreds of miles of traversable Savannah desert or the depth and diversity of the Pacific Ocean. The average enclosure size for mammals in zoos in the United Kingdom is one hundred times smaller than their minimum home range in a free-living situation, often resulting in repeated, meaningless gestures such as pacing or twitching, and other unnatural anxiety-driven behaviors (Whiting, 2009). They have been observed to pace in circles for hours on end, pull out their hair, chew on the bars of their enclosures, spontaneously terminate pregnancies, or fall ill and often die from the stress of being caged.

Consider that in 1906, Ota Benga, a twenty-two-year-old male human being from the Botwa people was put on display at the Bronx Zoo in New York (Richman, 2006). Plucked from his home in what was then the Belgian Congo, he and other Botwan people were brought to the United States to be displayed at the St. Louis Worlds' Fair of 1904. After that, because his tribe had been annihilated and his integration into American society was virtually impossible, he was put on display at the zoo for 40,000 daily visitors to ogle. Though a protest eventually closed Benga's exhibit and allowed him to live freely, he ultimately killed himself. It is a dangerous and tenuous situation to cage sentient beings for the viewing pleasure of other sentient beings.

Because animals are not given a choice in the matter, how are we to know if they are happy, healthy, or content? How are we to know that we are doing right by them, and what's more, is that for us to decide?

Some systems of captivity force non-human animals to work without their consent, often under conditions that are stressful, dangerous, and unnatural. Carriage horses, especially those in New York City, where the economy relies on tourists demanding a ride around Central Park in a horse-drawn carriage, are trotted through busy Manhattan streets, alongside dangerous traffic and mobs of pedestrians, and are forced to pull heavy carriages through inclement weather, injuries, and dehydration. Circus animals live in cramped, dirty boxcars—often for days at a time while a circus travels from one town to another—and are beaten with whips, hooks, and electric prods to get them to perform tricks in front of bright lights and screaming crowds. When you consider that animals as large and undomesticated as lions, elephants, and tigers are being held in these inhospitable conditions, it is a minor miracle that more people have not been killed by circus animals resisting their oppressors; since

1990, eighteen people have been killed and another eighty-six injured by rampaging circus elephants (Robinson, n.d.). One orca whale kept in captivity at a marine mammal park was responsible for the death of three human trainers; these whales do not attack human beings in the wild (Haq, 2010). These animals are resisting—just as human prisoners riot against their abusive guards, just as political dissenters riot in the streets—which is a powerful indication of their unwillingness to remain imprisoned. As abolitionists, we should support their resistance and do everything within our power to eliminate their very real prisons.

6. Animals Exploited for Companionship

A more contentious issue, even among those who fight to end the oppression of non-human animals, is the legitimacy of keeping pets and domesticated animals. Dogs, cats, rodents, birds, and fish are popular animals for human beings to have in their homes as companions. While the breeding of animals for sale as pets is an obvious problem—breeding animals are enslaved for the use of their reproductive organs, a troublesome relationship as illustrated above by the animals exploited for dairy products—even with animals rescued from a shelter, a power dynamic exists in the relationship between human beings and their non-human companions that gives some animal advocates pause.

I believe that keeping non-human animals as pets constitutes a form of exploitation, albeit one marked by affection. The animals in our care, while given names and taken for walks and lavished with sweaters and toys, still rely upon us for their very existence; because their genes have literally been modified to fit into our homes and our society (NOVA, 2004), it is unclear whether the domesticated animal population would be able to survive outside of the current arrangement.

Author Ida Hamme eloquently compares the enslavement of non-human animals to the enslavement of other underprivileged groups by espousing:

> it is not just non-human animals who are treated as pets. Children, women, and workers, to name a few, are also often treated as pets. Adults, men, and bosses as agents of exploitation may treat each respective target of exploitation with affection, but that doesn't mean the relationship is not oppressive. (2008)

Because the overall goal should be the elimination of these structures that perpetuate inequality and allow for people or animals to be treated as pets, we have to recognize that even the forms of exploitation that are marked by affection must be eradicated. Just as the feminist movement is undermined by "nice" men (who use and abuse women) and as the workers' rights movement is undermined by paternalistic corporations that provide wages and benefits but prevent unions from forming, the movement for animal liberation is undermined by making allowances for human beings to keep pets.

Even animal sanctuaries, which are often billed as the panacea to animal prisons, may infringe upon an animal's right to live a natural, healthy, happy life of her choosing. Many small and underfunded sanctuaries rely upon visitors and donors to keep the sanctuary functioning, and thus the animals there must constantly be available for viewing. While the animals living at a sanctuary are obviously spared a life of exploitation for their body parts, they may still be asked to spend time with human beings, pose for photographs, and generally live in conditions that are far less than perfect. This situation feels more like a reformation than an abolition of the conditions that we oppose.

To truly achieve abolition, a larger structure would need to be in place to answer the question, "What happens when the slaughterhouses, farms, and laboratories close?" The rescue and rehabilitation of these traumatized animals cannot be left to private donations and funding. Animals who can be allowed to return to free-living situations should experience just that; others, such as chimpanzees raised in human households as unwitting participants in language experiments (Fouts, 1997) or cows whose udders grow so large so as to produce enough milk to satisfy demand drag on the ground and develop infections (Robinson, 2011) should be given a place to live not dependent upon financial contributions made by people who find them "cute" or "useful." Otherwise, we are just replicating those systems of oppression: we may no longer be turning animals into supper, but we are still forcing them to sing for it.

These atrocities—the exploitative and violent system that has created farms and factory farms, laboratories, zoos, and circuses, the one we must work to topple them all if animals are to be freed from their prisons and human beings from ours—do not exist in a vacuum; they are a symptom of our larger willingness to treat living beings as commodities or as a means to our ends. Much of this attitude can be traced to capitalism and its mantra of profits, profits, profits.

When large corporations are allowed to dictate the rules of the game—by owning all of the resources, for example, or filling the pockets of the elected officials—the reality is that the human beings and non-human beings not in power will be the ones to suffer. The "invisible hand" of the marketplace has allowed wealthy businessmen (who are, largely, men: Forbes noted that in 2010, of the ten richest CEOs in the world, none are women) to pay people less than a living wage, to destroy the natural environment, to tear apart families, to crush dissent, and, as illustrated above, to treat leaving, breathing, sentient animals as nothing but renewable resources to experiment on or to eat. Blogger Melissa McEwan (2011) opines that businesses have also created a hostile climate for workers to unionize; after a poll of the American public revealed that 53 percent view labor unions as negative:

> This hostility toward collective bargaining is a significant part of the reason we're living in a … corporatocracy, where people are overworked and underpaid, wages are stagnant, benefits are waning, unemployment is at 10 percent, and workers toil in unsafe or exploitative conditions, afraid to report workplace violations, while corporations rake in profits hand over fist.

As long as there are profits are to be made by the capitalist system, human and non-human beings alike will be viewed as a means to producing those profits, to the detriment of health, happiness, consent, and freedom. Schools will continue to churn out mindless worker bees; people will toil at thankless, dangerous jobs and still not be able to feed their families. Non-human animals will languish on farms, in laboratories, and in circuses. The hierarchies of speciesism, racism, classism, sexism, heterosexism, and ableism will see to it that the current structures are maintained and the underprivileged bodies exploited.

So why should any of this matter to prison abolitionists? Power structures and hierarchies feed off each other; as long as one system of oppression exists, it is possible for any system of oppression to exist. As long as female-bodied animals are being exploited and imprisoned for the milk and eggs that come from their reproductive systems, there exists a rape culture that keeps human females incarcerated by perpetual fear of exploitation—raped, trafficked, ogled on the street, assaulted, degraded—because they have a female body. For as long as some non-human animals are forced to work without consent pulling carriages or entertaining circus-goers or testing household chemicals on their skin, it will be possible for some groups of human beings to be viewed as "less-than" and forced into similar slavery, as existed outright on the plantations of the United States of the eighteenth and nineteenth centuries and as exists in less-noticeable forms in the United States and elsewhere today. As long as we are able to separate animals into this category of "other," potential exists for separating people into categories of "other" and treating them accordingly. A popular quote reads, "No one is free while others are oppressed," and those of us working toward the abolition of prisons both physical and social would do well to remember the billions of non-human beings who find themselves enslaved and imprisoned for our appetites for flesh, fur, and entertainment.

If it feels like a stretch to imagine that human beings will ever be treated as heartlessly as non-human animals are being treated, consider the plight of prisoners around the world and ask again if we don't already lock human beings in cages, take away their rights, mistreat them, and kill them. In the United States, 2.4 million people are currently incarcerated (Solinger, 2010). Prisons are violent institutions that perpetuate violence, not resolve it, and they do nothing to address the cultural conditions that lead to so-called criminal behavior (CR10 Publications Collective, 2008).

Instead, the prison-industrial complex is a political tool designed to keep poor people, people of color, and gender non-conforming people under control. It systematically denies people wealth, education, and freedom. Sexual assault and murder run rampant through prisons and jails. Prisoners are denied adequate health care, opportunities to make contact with their friends and families, education, or income. Women are physically shackled to tables and beds during childbirth. Immigrants are deported to countries in which they may know no one after serving their jail sentences here. It's a system that completely devalues the lives and bodies of the people struggling within its walls. And just as species is the deciding factor for who will end up on a factory farm or in a slaughterhouse, class, race, and gender weigh heavily on our chances of ending up in prison. More than 60 percent of the people in prison are people of color. One in eight black men in their twenties is behind bars on any given day. Three-fourths of people in jail for drug offenses are people of color, though white-identified Americans buy and use drugs at the same rates (Butler, 2009). Ostensibly put in place to address violence in our communities, the prison-industrial complex rarely actually addresses this violence, and when it does, it does not address it equally. Toppling these cage walls is as crucial as emptying the cages of the animal-industrial complex.

While some instances of animals resisting their oppressors has been recorded, on the whole they are outgunned in their fight for liberation. Human beings have tools and technology at their disposal that enable them to remain the dominant species; while their voices are far from silent, they certainly need human allies to help bring about the end to their oppression. Thousands of human activists have raised their voices to bring attention to the plight of animals trapped within these oppressive power structures, to varied effect. A tangible split in the non-human animal activist communities in the United States and abroad has created two separate camps: those who are pushing for complete abolition of the systems that imprison animals, and those who seek reform of those systems to make them "more humane." These efforts have given rise to myriad small, local, organic farms producing animal products that can be labeled as "humane:" meaning, perhaps, that the animals were not raised in factory farms, or that they were not fed grain laced with antibiotics. These efforts—much like efforts of reform movements throughout history—have ultimately failed to eliminate the structures of power and privilege that enabled the disparity between human and non-human animals to occur in the first place.

A more "humane" imprisonment for non-human animals does nothing to alleviate their imprisonment; they are still considered "less-than" human, or "other," and are still subject to our whims, desires, and (lack of) mercies. Keeping animals in bigger cages does not, ultimately, remove them from those cages and actually may assuage some of the discomfort human beings may feel about the "fundamental wrong" of viewing them as nothing but resources for our exploitation. As author and philosopher Tom Regan stated

(1989), "giving farm animals more space, more natural environments, more companions does not right the fundamental wrong, any more than giving lab animals more anesthesia or bigger, cleaner cages would right the fundamental wrong in their case" (pp.113-114).

Agitating instead for the abolition of non-human animal exploitation and the complete dissolution of animal agriculture will not only free those animals from their current confines as resources and bring about an end to the barriers we have established between "us" and "them," but it will also pave the way for the barriers between other "us" and "them" systems of the world to also come tumbling down.

Eleven

PATRIARCHAL IDEOLOGIES AND WOMEN'S DOMESTICATION

Mechthild Nagel

Didja ever notice
how Justice is a woman?
Not a man
Not a malecopsmalejudgesmalelawyers
Justice is a *woman* — Cathy Marston, 2012

1. Introduction

North American courtrooms depict Lady Justice (a cross between the Greek goddess Themis and the Roman goddess Justitia) wearing a blindfold and carrying a sword and scales. Given imprisoned intellectual Cathy Marston's verdict, it would appear to me that Lady Justice stands for women as prisoners of a massive male error—the male, white, capitalist dominated injustice system that perpetrates crimes againstthose who fall outside normed categories: the poor, the queer, the disabled, the racialized Other, and the elderly.

This chapter focuses on the domestication and institutionalization of women by the interlocking systems of capitalism, patriarchy, and other systems of domination. These systems reinforce each other, so resistance often seems futile—in particular, because as a group, women, and all those others who are on the bottom of the "great chain of Being" are particularly ill equipped to support each other.

Independently minded elite, working class, anarchist, and intersexed women from Hypatia and Hildegard von Bingen, to Mary Wollstonecraft, Sojourner Truth, Herculine Barbin, Emma Goldman, Aung San Suu Kyi, and Wangari Maathai have criticized, resisted, or rejected social control emanating from patriarchal regimes the world over. Feminist agitators have created language and practices to advocate for the "rights of woman" or to resist "the rule of the fathers." They note that "the personal is political," and criticize interlocking systems of oppression (i.e., the ways in which race, class, religion, ethnicity, national origin, or disability intersect with gender). They look at sexual or gender harassment, date rape, marital rape, misogyny, femicide, "the second shift" of housework, gendered division of labor, feminization of poverty, the "glass ceiling," the gender gap, as well as "pink color" (female) versus white and "blue color" (male) job classifications.

Some of the areas of patriarchal social control faced by women discussed in this paper crisscross the public and private spheres: (1) the "domestic;" (2) the workplace; (3) the criminal justice complex; and (4) (residential) schools as other historical-social forms of oppression, which intersect with racism and colonialism. I focus mainly on the endurance of sexist ideologies and give empirical examples from the United States and Canada, but there are cross-cultural implications of this analysis. For instance, one recent anthology investigates the cross-border political economy, the effects of globalization, the killings of over 500 women and girls in Ciudad Juárez, and notes how grassroots organizations and mothers of the disappeared raise trouble to this femicide, when the state failed to respond to these crimes (Gaspar de Alba and Guzmán, 2010).

What ideological presuppositions make such failure possible, and what constitutes an effective response to the patriarchal status quo? Resistance to oppressive conditions tends to be individualized by popular discourses, whether it is through Hollywood, corporate media, popular authors such as Nicholas D. Kristof and Sheryl WuDunn (2009) or by United States Supreme Court decisions. Arguably, women's agency seen solely through the individualized lens is disempowering and will not lead to transformative justice.

After decades of calling "the personal political" much of contemporary feminist theory and practice still revolves around the strategic opposites of "sexual difference" and "equality." It has its roots in the cooptation of the "separate spheres" ideology (male breadwinner, female housewife), which led to zealous support of temperance championing Victorian sensibilities of propriety and social reformers' support of protective legislation. This hampered working class women's participation in the labor force and secured the male-led labor union's demand for the husband's "family wage."

Another debate that has dominated feminist philosophy has centered on the question of essentialism: what is the meaning of "woman," if any, and who might have license to speak on behalf of women? Iris Marion Young (1994) has argued in favor of the Sartrean term of "seriality" to suggest that "women" find ourselves thrown into a series (e.g., structurally through the sexual division of labor) and a coherent identity is only formed when we band together as women for a common goal or objective. I take my cue from Linda Martín Alcoff whose advocacy for a "positionality approach" provides language for a nuanced approach that avoids sweeping generalizations, white solipsism, and a bucolic retreat into reactionary individualism:

> Being a "woman" is to take up a position within a moving historical context and to be able to choose what we make of this position and how we alter this context. From the perspective of that fairly determinate though fluid and mutable position, women can themselves articulate a set of interests and ground a feminist politics" (1997, p. 150).

Alcoff thus argues for a politics of identity, where identities serve as a point of departure but never become reified or static. There are, of course, many examples from women's organizing for change that have not heeded her cautionary advice. Much activism has been guided by a fearful politics of entrenchment that serve the political interest of the few.

The fissures within Women's Rights Movements (such as the first organized one at Seneca Falls in upstate New York in 1848) often overshadowed the momentum gained by gathering hundreds if not thousands, as witnessed at the Fourth World Conference on Women, Beijing in 1995. Whether it concerns woman's suffrage (the key controversy of the nineteenth century) or lesbians' and sex workers' rights (the latter constitutes a twentieth-century provocation), which at times brings the Holy See and radical feminists to the same side of the table, many strategic sessions have catered to fear, racist and religious fervor, and co-opted the progressive socio-political agenda that could have had a far reaching impact on the majority of women.

Again, as with the earlier campaigns against vice and dangerous occupations for women of childbearing age, the competing theories undergirding the principles of "ethic of care" (cultural feminism) and "equality for all" (liberal feminism) continue to dominate the political discussions and perhaps impede feminist agitation for change. What will the twenty-first century bring in terms of feminist or solidarity organizing? To understand the challenges of resisting social control, a review of dominant ideologies such as the unities doctrine, the separate spheres doctrine that engendered the Cult of True Womanhood, and the racist theory of the pathology of the black family is necessary. How have women adapted and responded to these ideologies of social control?

2. Imprisoning Ideologies

A. The Unities Doctrine

> *Woman has ovaries, a uterus; these peculiarities imprison her in her subjectivity ... It is often said that she thinks with her glands. . . . Humanity is male and man defines woman not in herself but as relative to him; she is not regarded as an autonomous being ... He is the Subject, he is the Absolute—she is the Other.* - Simone de Beauvoir, 1972

A key underlying ideology that concerns us here is that of patriarchy, the domination of men over women based on the presumption that men have the right to dominate women because they feel superior to them: "he is the subject, she is the Other" (de Beauvoir, Ibid.; cf. also Sheffield, 1995). Enduring worldviews, even those that obviously oppress people, fauna, and flora, seem everlasting precisely because they seem natural, obvious, and commonsensical—it would be comical to think otherwise.

Thus, John Adams chides his uppity wife Abigail, who implores him to "remember the ladies," with the following high-toned rhetoric: "I cannot but laugh. . . . We know better than to repeal our Masculine systems . . . [and] completely subject Us to the Despotism of the Petticoat" (cited in Mandel, 1995, p. 405).

Judge William Blackstone's legal invention of the "unities doctrine" in family law is such an example (Williams, 1997). It seemed part of the divine and natural order to give the head of family (*pater familias*) a special status: "husband and wife are one and the one is the husband," as this fiction has famously been summarized by Justice Black (cited in Freeman, 1995, p. 466). Marriage contract obliges the wife to be "covered" by the husband, submit to him at will, assume his family name, surrender her own name and belongings. In turn, the husband is legally responsible for his kin. She cannot vote, get loans or her own bank account, testify in court, face incrimination, nor pursue advanced schooling or professional work outside the home. In other words, the wife is reduced to the status of a minor. Upon the husband's death, male kin will receive all assets so that the wife may be reduced to a pauper depending on kindness of kin and strangers. Thus, the unities doctrine also guarantees that she is deemed "civilly dead" (Williams, 1991).

Western condemnation of misogynist interpretations of Shar'ia law or of Muslim women's practice of "veiling" seem hypocritical given the casual neglect of human rights afforded to European and colonized women especially since the advent of Christianity as the state religion, as for instance documented throughout the history of persecutions of hundreds of thousands of women, often of those who were unattached to a man and the pernicious history of "coverture"—the symbolic, legal veiling of Christian and other non-Muslim women. Whether it was the implementation of religious manuals such as the *Witches' Hammer* (Kramer and Sprenger,1486), which intensified the modern era witch craze, the Blackstone legal codes, or the 1804 Napoleonic Code, which relegated the legal status of women to that of "children, felons, and the insane," misogynist fervor is part and parcel of the Western, Christian-based, patriarchal tradition (cf. LeGates, 1995, p. 496).

The unities doctrine seems to be outmoded and of little concern to modern day feminists. Yet, coverture continues in the marriage-industrial complex. Wedding vows often speak of submission and devotion and naming ceremonies erase the family name. A vast majority of women, at least those who are not from Latino countries, abandon the father's name in favor of the husband indicating the adherence to patriarchal social order (of control and obedience). Political women such as Hillary Rodham are pressured to adopt their spouse's last name and thus eschew their independence and to avoid being scandalized as so many of their political foremothers have been, who refused to be bound to coverture—even when it was the law.

By contrast, Paula Gunn Allen (1984) reports that in matrilineal nations of the Iroquois Confederacy, women who took the spouse's name after marriage were forbidden from pursuing political positions in the nation such as the position of the Matron.

B. The Separate Spheres Doctrine

There can be no doubt that our Nation has had a long and unfortunate history of sex discrimination. Traditionally, such discrimination was rationalized by an attitude of "romantic paternalism" which, in practical effect, put women not on a pedestal, but in a cage. - Frontiero v. Richardson, 1973

Early nineteenth-century industrialization and Western expanse, trespassing indigenous lands, arguably changed the public discourse and ideological fervor regarding EuroAmerican gender relations. While immigrant unmarried girls increasingly pursued factory work (not unpaid domestic work), hegemonic anxious discourses shored up support for a slightly more progressive version of social control ideology than the unities doctrine (Freeman, 1995). The separate spheres doctrine recognizes women as "alive" (not civilly dead) in the safe purview of the home. The upper-class white "lady" is put on a pedestal and enjoys decision making in the tranquility of the home, away from the loud, immoral demands of the public world, where the husband is busy being at war with his (male) workers and averting labor discontent. She has a civilizing, ennobling and religious duty on her husband and is in charge of moral education of the young, including the sons.

This doctrine enshrines a "cult of domesticity" at a time when the radical abolition movement against slavery got off the ground to be followed by the suffrage movements after 1868. It also served a purpose for working class men who did not wish for female competition. "Protective Legislation" at the end of the nineteenth century should be considered a natural and euphemistic outgrowth of this separate spheres doctrine of a now public patriarchal state, because women were forbidden to work long hours, overnight, were not allowed to lift heavy weights and could not pursue certain professions at all (Freeman, 1995).

Women social reformers and anti-suffrage women activists also participated in the defense of this restrictive labor law at the same time that they began the first organized effort of daycare for working-class working women's children (Freeman, 1995; Marshall, 1995). It took another 100 years for enlightened Supreme Court judges (Frontiero, for the majority opinion) to acknowledge that much of this legal dance affected women's capacity and movement in public, whether at the workplace, the bank, or the jury pool, and served strictly to cage women and make them separate and unequal. One curious effect of this transatlantic domestic(ating) ideal of the passionless proper lady is that Queen Victoria refused to sign a bill meant to criminalize lesbianism in 1885, because she didn't believe such behavior existed (Weitz, 1995, p. 449).

The cult of domesticity, also known as "Cult of True Womanhood," seems bound to stay. It has a complex feminist lineage of support from the monarchist Olympe de Gouges to conservative anti-feminist Phyllis Schlafly and self-proclaimed feminist Sarah Palin on the one hand, and, ironically, to suffragist Elizabeth Cady Stanton and modern day cultural feminists such as

Carol Gilligan on the other. By making this sweeping and controversial claim, I simply wish to probe and revision the feminist "sexual difference versus equality" debate. At stake is whether the defense of psycho-social and biological difference overrides a single-minded liberal concern for eradicating socially existing forms of gender discrimination.

Cultural feminists charge that girls and boys do behave differently from birth on, independent of social pressures. Carol Gilligan (1982) developed her famous ethic of care approach based on observations she made of girls' moral deliberations, which she thought to be remarkably absent in boys' decision-making skills. However, she also advocated that a best possible ethics would involve both the justice paradigm followed by boys and the care paradigm followed by girls. Here we detect a functionalist, biological determinist argument that plays into separate spheres ideology (cf. Scott, 1996, p. 1057). Clearly, Aristotle's differentiation of the sexes with his defense of the natural complement theory provides an ideological foundation for the rational, autonomous man versus emotional, relational woman framework that is part and parcel of the cult of domesticity—and, I would add, equally of modern day celebratory expressions of feminist psychology.

Elizabeth Cady Stanton, best known for authoring the Declaration of Sentiments and Resolutions (Stanton, 2007), thus initiating a protracted struggle for the women's vote, also relied on the (racist, sexist) cult of domesticity when it served her. This is already implicit in the 1848 declaration: "He has withheld from her rights which are given to the most ignorant and degraded men—both natives and foreigners." Twenty years later, Stanton engages in an outright racist, elitist, and chauvinist attack on freed black men. She held that they were not entitled to the vote, despite the 15th Amendment, because they were "ignorant sambos"; and in response to the heckling of George Downing, a black supporter of male superiority, she responds:

> When Mr. Downing puts the question to me: are you willing to have the colored man enfranchised before the women, I say no; I would not trust him with my rights; degraded, oppressed himself, he would be more despotic with the governing power than ever our Saxon rulers are. If women are still to be represented by men, then I say let only the highest type of manhood standard at the helm of State. (cited in Davis, 1981, pp. 84–85)

Eclipsing the voting rights of black women, Stanton positions herself as a defender of the purity standards of the white dominant race and as Angela Y. Davis (1981) points out completely disregarding the material conditions of abject poverty, lack of reparations, the formation of the Ku Klux Klan and overall political uncertainties that engulf black people who remain in the former Confederacy.

Does the cult of domesticity constitute progress over the unities doctrine? Looking closer at lived experiences, it seems as if with the emphasis of confining EuroAmerican women to the home and garnering the family wage for EuroAmerican men, women suddenly had less decision making power—this was particularly the case for aristocratic women who could no longer effect change on the estate of the absentee husband and for skilled women, who were no longer encouraged to pursue their trades (Bryson, 1992).

However, the Cult of True Womanhood proved to be elastic enough to accommodate racist oppression and to endure even though economic, social, and political conditions changed for the better for many women through hard fought struggles for unionization and concomitant benefits of family leave, day care centers, and better education so that women have now entered most of the disciplines. But double standards still prevail in the public and private spheres. Mothers especially are still expected to do the bulk of household chores ("the second shift") and are the first to be blamed if their child fails to live up to the moral education mothers "ought" to provide. This is particularly true with respect to racially sexualized expectations of the black family—the controlling images of black womenhood (Collins, 1990).

C. White Supremacist Anxieties about the Black Family

> *Portraying African-American women as stereotypical mammies, matriarchs, welfare recipients, and hot mommas has been essential to the political economy of domination fostering black women's oppression. Challenging these controlling images has long been a core theme in black feminist thought.* -Patricia Hill Collins, 1990

Stanton's racist exclamation about the "ignorant sambo" haunts the feminist imagination about sisterhood even now. Frederick Douglass was asked not to show up on platforms with speakers such as Susan B. Anthony when she toured the South to garner financial support for suffrage among wealthy white male patrons (Davis, 1981). A century later, the known supporter of racial segregation Democratic senator "Judge" Howard W. Smith, made an infamous move to add "sex" to the Civil Rights Act of 1964. The National Woman's Party supported him. However, other feminist and civil rights organizations opposed his move, because they feared that it would detract from addressing racial discrimination (Bryson, 1992).

Angela Y. Davis has argued that much of racialized discourse has focused on pathologizing the black family. New York's liberal Senator Patrick Moynihan's report provides inflammatory analysis by suggesting that the black family faces high divorce rates precisely due to the weak status of the male and an overbearing female, whose matriarchal tendencies are out of step with the rest of society. This constitutes an unabashed defense of white public patriarchy as the cherished norm of society. In the context of a racialized sexuality, black women could never aspire to the white Victorian motherhood cult, and their putative sexual independence as family matriarchs brings up memories of yesteryear's fierce, uncontrollable witch (Collins, 1990; Barstow, 1994).

Contemporary films such as *Precious* (Lee, 2009), which are meant as stinging social criticism, and that attempt to humanize black women, run the risk of reinscribing a known racist, sexist ideology. *Precious* has received mixed reviews, some praising it for its stark realism and unrelenting focus on social problems, others criticizing it as "the most damaging film to the black image since the *Birth of the Nation*" (Armond White, 2009). It portrays a young darker skinned woman (Gabourey Sidibe as Precious) who is raped and impregnated by her mother's boyfriend. Her opening line conveys the pains of internalized racial hatred—she imagines herself as glamour girl alongside a light skinned boyfriend who has nice hair.

Black women in the United States are victimized at the same time that they are blamed for the ill-named "black on black" violence and being mothers qua "welfare queens" of "young superpredators" (Feder, 2007; Nagel, 2011). What does not get named in these media-driven discourses of victim blaming is the government's War on Drugs (begun in 1971), which has ensnared more black men and women than any other group, as well as other policing measures with the result that one in three black men will find himself jailed during his lifetime and black women have faced the fastest increase of imprisonment thanks to the War on Drugs (Davis, 2003).

In the following, while highlighting aspects of the state's biopower, the subjection of women through regulatory techniques, I will focus on the "private" sphere.

3. The Discourse of "Domestic Violence"

In *Discipline and Punish*, Michel Foucault famously writes, "Is it surprising that prisons resemble factories, schools, barracks, hospitals, which all resemble prisons?" (1977, p. 228). He persuasively argues that these are places of social control, where deviancy is constructed and policed to the point that the pupil, prisoner, or the person dubbed mentally ill will all be monitored to the point that they will become "docile bodies."

Such is the implied intent of institutional power and the expression of hegemony. Whether it is successfully executed is another matter, since "where there is power, there is also resistance" (Foucault, 1978, p. 96). However, Foucault, too, has blind spots as he succumbs to the division of "public man, private woman" (Elshtain, 1993), by highlighting (Western) institutions in the public sphere. He is mostly silent on the private realm (except of course, in *History of Sexuality*, when he remarks on the trope of the heterosexual Malthusian couple), and overplays the docile effect of Jeremy Bentham's panopticon—of the all-seeing gaze that disciplines the prisoners in a way that they turn the gaze inward. He leaves out the colonial state's racialized brutalization of prisoners (James, 1996), and is silent on the effects of the modern prison on women (Dodge, 2006). Surprisingly, Foucault also leaves out the asylum (which he also writes about) in the above quote, because arguably, it is the modern asylum, rather than the factory halls, upon which American penitentiaries were modeled (Cohen, 1992, cited in Dodge, pp. 22–23).

Arguably, the asylum has been the depository for European women after the end of the witch persecutions. With the emergence of the enclosures of the common and industrialization, women increasingly became a threat to male breadwinners. Stanton has this radical, hyperbolic, feminist insight to "correct" a Foucauldian view: "Society, as organized today under the man power, is one grand rape of womanhood, on the highways, in our jails, prisons, asylums, in our homes, alike in the world of fashion and of work" (cited in Bryson, 1992, p. 43).

What is the discourse of confinement and violation today? When it comes to the social realities and to identity formations of the girl child and women, it is the home, the "domestic realm," that is a premier site of contestation and violence. California was the first state to enact the Domestic Violence Center Act to provide safe houses for battered women at the local level; it used funds from marriage license fees (Stevenson and Love, 1999). Linking domestic violence to marriage taxation was probably because it used to be narrowly defined as "spousal abuse."

Labeling something as "domestic" has the ring of "harmlessness"—domestic violence, as harm done between friends, acquaintances, or blood-related persons is described. After all, it is not akin to "stranger rape" or random assault on the streets—unless of course, the victim "asked for" the sexual assault in terms of how she dressed, and why was she on the streets (or the bar, as extension of the "street') at 2 a.m. by herself?

Such questions were raised in a court of law regarding the gang rape of a woman in a bar in Bedford, Massachusetts (Butler, 1993). In this notorious court case, the defense implied that the wild woman who is roaming bars is not properly "domesticated." She chose to defy her role foisted upon by heteropatriarchal Eurocentric social norms, and this is where another definition of "domestic" comes to play: this has to do with the Latin roots of "domus" (house) and "dominus" (master of the house and by inference lord over cattle, children, and certainly his wife and any unwed sisters).

Domestic then has a ring of "ownership" and putting it together with "violence" invites confusion; how can somebody be castigated as violent, if he couldn't do what he pleases with his property? Indeed this is the grounds for 2000 years of Euro-American legal wrangling whether to endow the female partner with personhood or continue to consider her chattel who could be chastised with a stick no bigger than the man's thumb—clearly, a compromise solution of the "justice system" that was clearly intent to keep the woman (or girl, traded from the father to the future husband) in a subjugated role. Finally, using terms like "domestic" violence rather than "battering" may just "obscure the relationship between gender and power by failing to define the perpetrators and victims" (Meyers, 1994, cited in Marston, 2011, p. 82).

Radical feminists have pointed out that we live in a rape culture. Catherine MacKinnon famously espouses that rape, "from women's point of view, is not prohibited; it is regulated" (1983, p. 651). That explains the legal reality of the difficulty of obtaining rape convictions against acquaintances, family members or boyfriends.

Still hotly debated on listservs today is whether spousal rape is an oxymoron. Until the late 1970s, rape laws exempted husbands if they violated their own wives, and even today, husbands are exempted from rape prosecutions if they assault their wives while they are asleep, unconscious or mentally disabled, i.e. when the women (or girls) are unable to give consent.

Finally, there remains a patriarchal urge to legislate morality of women who pursue sex work—it is an odd adage that prostitution is the oldest trade, yet radical feminists content that the institution of heterosexual marriage as a form of patriarchally sanctioned prostitution—a father "trading in" his daughter to the best bidder, the future husband. Practices of bride prize (or lobola) and dowry turn brides into chattel, even if justifications are given that these guarantee her subsistence living or insure her husband.

Bridal negotiations may result in grave conflict, or they could be results of restitutions for premarital rape or consensual sex. It's surely a sign of patriarchal codification of such payments that are legally sanctioned and celebrated through the rites manifested in the marriage-industrial complex, even as benign as the fatherly gesture of "giving away the bride" rather than scandalized as women's sex work certainly is (cf. Narayan, 1997; Kempadoo and Doezema, 1996; Dewey, 2010).

One impetus for penning the 1848 Declaration of Sentiments was Stanton's envy of Haudenosaunee women who lived (and continue to live) in egalitarian relationships free from male abuse, rape, or custody battles, leading suffragist Matilde Joslyn Gage to exclaim: "never was justice more perfect, never civilization higher" (Gage, 1893 [1998]; cf. Allen, 1984).

In the 1990s, we have the curious situation of a putative egalitarian enforcement by police officers: when it's not clear to them who started the "trouble" both parties may be arrested; several states have mandatory arrest policies—with the troubling effect that children are not only being traumatized by the parents' fight but also by the state's zealous intervention (Bernstein, 2005).

The watershed case that brought state violence into sharp relief (through "benign neglect" of spousal torture) was that of Tracey Thurman:

> [Thurman] won her suit against a Connecticut police department for negligence and violation of her civil rights in 1985. Her husband receives a fifteen-year sentence for attacking her, stabbing her and repeatedly kicking her in the head during 1983 while police and neighbors were in the vicinity and ignored Tracy's pleas for help. (Stevenson and Love, 1999)

Cathy Marston (2011) decries the blatant disregard for battered women's well-being as chronicled in her own story, eerily reminiscent of Thurman's torturous ordeal. Rather than suffering under "benign neglect" of the police, she finds herself convicted through trumped up charges of burglary, as a "by-product" of the mandatory arrest policies (although her male assailants never got arrested):

> As I was going unconscious and could taste the blood in my mouth . . . smothering me into the concrete, a police officer pulled-up to the curb five feet from my head. The officer laughed with my assailant, just as the . . . arresting officer had done with this batterer and my abusive ex. If the first unlawful arrest had been quickly and properly adjudicated to exonerate me and arrest my batterers, the second attempt on my life would never have occurred. Where would these abusive men get the idea that they could beat and kill a woman, and that these cops would arrest HER? From the larger American context of blaming women for the male violence committed against them and obviously from the Texas justice system. (p. 75)

The Texas Council on Family Violence reports that, sadly, Marston's criminalization as victim is not an aberration but occurs 20 percent of the time when police respond to a "domestic violence" call (Ibid., p. 73). Andrea Smith (2005) paints an equally grim analysis regarding violence against Indian women on reservations, and yet, she is also quick to note that mainstream anti-violence movement's collusion with the state for funding feeds into an expansion of the prison industrial complex that social movement groups such as INCITE! and Critical Resistance have resisted against (cf. pp. 170–171).

4. Death by Culture?

Occasionally, a "death by culture" argument will be employed in the courtroom when the Empire sees it fit in non-Western occupied countries. Narayan (1997) notes this argument when well-meaning British colonialists, peak into localized practices such as decrying *sati* (widow burning) in the nineteenth century and castigated all Indian men as being complicit in such practice; the widows suffered a worse death than that of personal choice to commit suicide: they were marked women by the woes of their culture.

By contrast, Uma Narayan also takes stock of the high numbers of women murder victims in the United States and argues that no "cultural defense" of gun-toting, Christian, heterosexual, patriarchal men is used; instead the murders are constructed in a most personalized, individual ways completely bereft of cultural codification. "Death by culture" argumentation (and take any non-Western, non-Christian rite dubbed as "barbaric") finds a hearing in the contemporary courtroom, which otherwise prides itself in taking seriously personal responsibility:

> Brooklyn Supreme Court justice Edward Pincus sentences Chinese immigrant Dong Lu Chen to 5 years probation for using a claw hammer to smash the skull of his wife. *Pincus concludes, that traditional Chinese values about adultery and loss of manhood drove Chen to kill his wife.* Pincus justifies Chen's probationary sentence by stating that Chen was just as much a victim as his wife due to extenuating circumstances. The Chen decision sent a message to battered immigrant women that they had no recourse against domestic violence. (Stevenson and Love, 1999; emphasis added)

So, Dong Lu Chen's defense, which appeals not only on cultural grounds to Chinese (patriarchal) values but given the culture of the United States courts is informed by patriarchal values. Thus, he is able to "fraternize" with the jury and judge to receive leniency. However, immigrant women who attempt to use cultural values (male breadwinner status, etc.) rarely accomplish the task to persuade the United States courts to listen to their stories and consider mitigating circumstances.

Interestingly, the first time the "battered woman syndrome" was allowed into the courtroom by the presiding judge was in the late 1980s, when the defendant was on trial for killing her lesbian partner. But she was convicted anyway. In that case, the judge allowed the battered woman's syndrome defense changing it to "battered person defense." The defense attributes the guilty verdict to the jury's homophobia (Ibid.). Overall, since the introduction of the "battered woman's" defense, juries have been reluctant to acquit the defendant und unwilling to acknowledge the environmental thesis (of long-term abuse and suffering) and its abolitionist implications (Nagel, 2000).

What do girls and women face upon being committed to jails and prisons? The next section will describe the collateral damages of the carceral regime—in its most isolating and punitive form.

5. Not Part of My Sentence?

In 1999, Amnesty International published a provocative report "Not Part of My Sentence: Violations of the Human Rights of Women in Custody." The report made it clear that women who enter the prison system are not immune to further violence by state actors. Similarly, Human Rights Watch's report "All Too Familiar: Sexual Abuse of Women in United States State Prisons" (1996) details endemic sexual abuse by male prisoners who work in women's prisons and the casual approach of prison authorities to remedy corruption and coercive control. Furthermore, currently, the prison is ill equipped to handle the special needs of female, of transgendered persons, and of those who have mental disabilities.

The vast majority of women prisoners are mothers of small children; some of them are teen mothers; many enter jail and prisons while they are pregnant without any pre- or postnatal care, which can have dire consequences for their health. Miscarriages are disproportionately higher than "in the free world." They may be forced into poorly fitted tight clothing which further harms the mother and fetus or they are subjected to being shackled while giving birth (Amnesty International, 2010).

While abortion on demand in prisons has been curtailed by the Hyde Amendment (1976), some prisoners report being coerced into abortions, especially African American women (Johnson, 2002). This magnifies and eerily echoes the history of reproductive violence and genocide committed against indigenous, black, and brown women since 1492 (cf. Ybanez, 2007).

Ana María García's film, *La Operación* (1982) chronicles the United States population control policy "Operation Bootstrap" of the late 1950s, which succeeded so well that "over one-third of all Puerto Rican women of childbearing age have been sterilized. The procedure is so common that it is simply known as *La Operación*." Conducting coerced sterilizations is a major violation of Article 3 of the Geneva Conventions and constitutes a war crime if done during armed conflict.

However, some women prisoners disagree that they face further violation and oppression in the prisons, as noted in "Criminalizing Women—Past and Present" (Kilty, 2011). It chronicles the lives of aboriginal women in particular who have had to work through decades of substance abuse, of sexual violence by relatives, endemic poverty, neglect, and more. Still they find the prison can be a refuge from the terror, grief, and highs that numb their bodies temporarily.

For Sharon Acoose, who was sexually abused since age three, jail provided a structured, safe place with accommodations so far beyond the street life that she developed bulimia because she didn't want to get fat. Her eating disorder stopped once she left jail and was again living on the streets. Acoose notes with great honesty, "I liked jail because I was tough and jail gave me status, a name so to speak. I was *the* girl. People would move when I walked by" (Kilty, 2011, p. 50). Her greatest joy was to be feared and she felt invincible as the jail's premier bully. Only when she became sober she realized that those desires made her into a "full time looser" and life was passing by (p. 51).

Acoose's life "on the installment plan" (living between the streets and jails for some eighteen years) began once her father moved off the reservation, and it was during the hated times spent in segregation for infractions or self-harm, she pondered the wages of "Indianness": "I didn't want to be an Indian because of the extreme racism my people faced and I knew I couldn't be white, so who could I be? I felt only isolation of the body, mind, soul and spirit" (p. 53). In segregation, she could feel the extent of "spirit murder" that the prison system represents.

The prison system for First Peoples of Canada is an extension, a continuation of the legacy of the repressive residential school system to which Indian children were subjected (both in Canada and the United States), which robbed the youth of their culture, belief system, and language, amounting to cultural genocide. Not surprisingly, facing criminalization of drug addictions, grinding poverty, and stigma-related sex work, they are vastly overrepresented in the Canadian (and United States) prison system (Kilroy and Pate, 2011; Ybanez, 2007) at the same time that Indian women are also "underpoliced" (Kilroy and Pate, 2011) and victimized to the point that Amnesty International calls for an urgent investigation of vast numbers of missing and murdered women.

More than one in three Native women will face rape assault in her lifetime, and rapists most often escape judicial process due to the federal/colonist imposition of a complexity of laws (Amnesty International, 2004). Wholesale criminalization of a people, be it Puerto Ricans, blacks in the United States, indigenous people, or others who are oppressed as a group, shows the interaction of racism, imperialist motivations and buttressed by patriarchal ideology, so that the giddy multitude commits violence against each other but does not band together against "the system of injustice."

The system, on the contrary, creates the illusion of the rights-bearing individual who may seek redress through the courts (Davis, 2003) and may also be punished qua individual for trespassing against the law. Classical liberal ideology disguises the benign social contract, which in fact is a racial/sexual contract by propertied white heterosexual men against those who are Othered (Pateman and Mills, 2007).

6. Rape Laws—Protection or Repression of Women?

Rape of prisoners has been a serious issue that finally was acknowledged in the Prison Rape Elimination Act (PREA) of 2003. However, its focus is on rape in male prisons and is particularly concerned with rape occurring between prisoners. It remains silent on the rampant violations occurring between staff and prisoners in female prisons. The way it has been translated by Texas is that *any* act (even holding hands) is punishable not only as sexual misconduct but as sexual abuse and a lifelong label as sexual offender. When two lovers were written up for misconduct and sent to segregation, one of them fearing the label accused the girlfriend of rape, the accused hung herself. A friend of the woman who committed suicide writes:

> Ever since the feds enacted that "Prison Rape Elimination Act," it has done nothing to help us [women]. Now someone is dead. With her girl crying rape to save herself from being convicted of a sexual abuse charge, it leaves Jamie with a sexual assault charge and having to register as a sex offender when she gets out and it'll be on her record, affecting her parole chances and chances of getting into a halfway house. (Law, 2009, p. 71)

What then can we say in general about legal reforms that might benefit imprisoned women?

7. What Does Gender-Responsive Service Mean to an Abolitionist?

Gender responsive service is a complex and contested issue. It can be a platform for meaningful improvements in women's prison and important services given to transgender prisoners. On the other hand, it can be a way of *increasing* penalties. Whereas a pregnant mother might be released early from prison, a prison with excellent pre- and postnatal arrangements might sway the parole board to retain the prisoner to give birth in prison. Mara L. Dodge (2006) notes that nineteenth-century judges in Illinois were reluctant to send pregnant women to prison, not based on humanitarian concerns, but due to cost-benefit accounting: pregnant women and the subsequent prison care (crèche) of babies would not be cost-effective in a prison environment that was supposed to extract as much menial labor from the convicts as it could (pp. 31–32).

Hardly a bleaker picture on gender disparities can be found than that from a chaplain in 1930: "To be a *male* convict in this prison would be quite tolerable; but to be a *female* convict, for a protracted period, would be worse than death" (cited in Dodge, 2006, p. 14). This sentiment is reiterated in May Barr's harrowing account of surviving New York's prison, Riker's Island—the largest jail in the world, housing over 20,000 remand and convicted women, men, and children (Barr, 2007).

The recurrent theme in all these critiques is that of creating the modern penitentiary along norms that would seem "reasonable" to house large numbers of men. Nineteenth-century women reformers such as Elizabeth Fry, beholden to the Cult of True Womanhood ideal, heaped much blame on the loud, unkempt women prisoners rather than on the material conditions in which they were forced to survive. Even so, Fry would have been aghast at "gender-neutral" accommodations, so that men can work in shower areas in women's prison because of "equal opportunity" provisions for employees.

By the 1970s, gender-specific prisons, inspired by disciplinary regime of reformatories, vanished and "co-educational" prisons appeared (Dodge, p. 21). So, it is ironic that gender-specificity would be demanded again; my worry is that if one operates under a *reform* paradigm, one is always inclined to make excuses for sending women (and men) to prison and for long stretches of time, because it will be a tolerable experience. Julia Sudbury argues that creating gender and trans-sensitive spaces in prisons goes counter the spirit of "maroon abolitionism":

> This interaction between racism and trans-phobia in the prison is the basis for an antiracist, gender-queer, anti-prison agenda promoted by black transgender and gender non-conforming activists. In contrast to calls to develop a "normative transgender prison order,'" or trans-sensitive prisons (Edney, 2004, pp. 336-37), the participants point to the systemic nature of gender violence as part of the structures of imprisonment, and reject the possibility of gender liberation under conditions of captivity. In

> so doing, they seek to transform anti-prison politics by calling for the abolition of gender policing as part of a broader abolitionist agenda. (2010, p. 18)

Clearly, resistance to enforced gender behaviors instead of advocating for trans-sensitive prisons is necessary. Following recommendations by Andrea Smith (2005) and others, gender-responsiveness in the abolitionist context can mean to care for girls in non-punitive open healing sites such as a Healing Lodge for indigenous Americans and First Nations girls, where they can get holistic treatment for trauma, for state-generated violence, etc., and get educational opportunities that are meaningful rather than coercive and test-oriented.

Most Western feminist criminologists calls for expert-driven gender-specific, trauma-informed treatments in prisons and would take into account the girl's personal history of abuse and drug dependency. However, many girls and young women have been intensely studied by (white) expert personnel to very little avail (Koo, 2010).

Working with a community justice paradigm that empowers the "non-experts" such as children as peer trainers guided by an abolitionist framework may have more lasting results to bring about healing; I avoid language of "restorative justice" or "rehabilitation" because those terms suggest that there has been bucolic non-violence in our cities, towns, and rural areas some mythic time ago, when in fact, the United States was founded on slavery and genocidal practices for which it has never been held accountable.

8. Resistance and Survival

From Native America (Neve and Pate, 2005; Amnesty International, 2008) to urban America, the psychic and social costs of brutalizing and institutionalizing children of color are immense. The following excerpt is from Roslyn, participating in a writing group while incarcerated. She faced victimization as a child, fought back, and was criminalized by a vindictive court system, sentenced to fifty years for an offense she committed at seventeen. Roslyn imagines the same judge as her audience, showing him that she has moved beyond victim status:

> Did you see no potential in me? You noted my high IQ, how "articulate" I was, how "mature." I'd run away from home because I refused to let my mother keep hurting me. You put me in a home for bad kids; my roommate wasn't even sane. I left there, too, so you put me in a group home. You call that help? No matter who I tried to tell, no one got it. So then you sentenced me, said no hope for rehabilitation, said I'm as good as dead. Just like my mother: kicks, flights of stairs, words that made me flinch. Well, you were both wrong. I have a life. I have a beautiful daughter, a college education. I teach parenting skills. I make a difference in people's lives. You never gave me a chance, so I made my own.

> My poverty, skin color, background, past—who at age seventeen can't change, won't grow? You robbed me of my youth, of my belief in justice. But from the graveyard, the barbed wire, and the cinderblock, I'm resurrected. I'm worthy. I'm somebody. (cited in Boudin, 2010a, p. 298)

Roslyn is exemplary in refusing to make the prison and prism (of violence, of racism and sexism, of institutionalization, of gate keeping, and revenge) her home and destiny. Instead, she transcends and transforms, turning, in Assata Shakur's words, "walls into bridges" to bring hope to others.

Many prisoners turn to bibliotherapy to escape the noise of the prison environment; these might range from romance novels to urban fiction, self-help books or African American writings from slavery narratives to the contemporary critiques of white supremacist societies (Sweeney, 2010). Here, of course, as with any prison surveillance, censorship of reading material that is considered "insurrectionist" is commonplace.

Rather than insuring the maintenance of docile bodies—just as during ante bellum times on the plantation—imprisoned intellectuals (James, 2003) are thought of as disturbing the peace that the pervasive lull of illiteracy brings to prison administrators the world over. The Roslyn's of the world and their indomitable spirit are utterly threatening to the prison regime—even though ironically, once a majority of women prisoners is involved in college-bound education, they stop fighting with each other, frown on idleness, and develop a real sense of purpose as the prison becomes another institution of higher learning. Kathy Boudin (2010b) reports that as soon as college education disappeared at Bedford Hills prison thanks to the draconian, vindictive laws of the 1990s, violence ensued among the women and a real sense of hopelessness settled in.

How do schools fit into this picture of social control, surveillance and a sense of purposelessness? The next section provides an insight of the carceral regime as a continuum through a girl's coming of age in a punitive, hetero-patriarchal and racist society.

9. The School-to-Prison Pipeline

As many critics of the prison industrial complex have noted (e.g., Davis, 2003; Weissman, 2008), the recruitment for imprisonization cannot start early enough. Urban schools are a quasi-militarized zone with "resource officers"—otherwise known as armed police—stationed at metal detector gates who have increasingly displaced school counselors, so that California now has more of these resource officers than counselors in schools (Schnyder, 2009). Some children are being singled out for special attention. If they display good behavior, military recruiters will invite them to join the army, if they are in defiance, it is the reform schools and detention centers that will await them.

The ideological expectation of girls and women's turpitude give us insight into the history of modern policing and criminalizing women and girls.

Once women's reformatories were firmly established, it so happened that the state zealously expanded the domain of punishable moral offenses during the Progressive Era, and ironically, female reformers happily assisted prosecutors in naming outlaw women who dared to walk the streets, deal in alcohol or showed other signs of waywardness.

Politicians believed that "reformatories" weren't actually prisons and would assist women to fall in line with the expectations of the Cult of True Womanhood. "Women often served longer sentences for misdemeanor crimes than men did for more serious felonies" (Dodge, 2006, p. 20). Mara L. Dodge focuses her study on Illinois, and what is important to point out is that "freed" black women in the South served time in the convict lease system, not being afforded time in the troublesome, but much better conditions of the reformatories reserved for white women, if they were incarcerated at all (Davis, 1998).

What does this brief retrospective mean for contemporary images of "fallen" girls? I would argue that the relational aggression hypothesis fits into the continuation of moral double standards, namely regarding behaviors expected of girls and boys and what happens if either one falls from graces or pedestals. While the "moral fall" is harder for girls of all colors, girls who transgress sexual norms, e.g., showing lesbian tendencies, face harsher policing (Himmelstein and Brückner, 2011).

Homelessness, then, is a particularly acute problem for gay and lesbian youth as well as for transgendered and gender non-conforming persons, because of the homophobic/transphobic hostility faced in the (foster) home and threat of subsequent expulsion from home as well as school grounds (Sudbury, 2010; Baus et al., 2006).

Orlando Patterson (1982) has written persuasively about the psychic effects of United States slavery in terms of natal alienation. We can extend this analysis to United States imprisonment, precisely because of state-sponsored slavery in the Thirteenth Amendment (1865), which set enslaved people free at the same time that it codified slavery in prisons (James, 2005; Nagel, 2008). Just as Sojourner Truth lamented in her speech "Ain't I a Woman?" in 1851, that she lost all of her children to the auction block, today's prisoners risk losing custody of their children because of a federal reform measure: Adoption and Safe Families Act (ASFA). Victoria Law (2009) movingly describes the cruelty of lack of visitation rights with loved ones and hunger strikes engaged to demand placement in a prison closer to home. From a mother's perspective, we can now talk about "pre-natal" alienation (Paley, 2010) given conditions in United States jails and prisons as well as conditions outside the prison that include abject poverty, battering by male partners, preventable communicable diseases, which are all rampant when living in stressful, war-like, crowded quarters whether it is "minimum security" (shelters or barracks) or "maximum security" (prisons or detention centers).

10. Social Movements and Counter Movements

From the discrimination of women that led to imprisonment behind "domestic walls" to persecution for witchcraft and other forms of social exclusion have been propagated by religiously motivated ideologies, political regimes, and economic relations of production favoring men (fathers and sons). Elite white women have not only exploited the "sexual difference" by appealing to "patriotic" or Victorian womanhood—most recently Phyllis Schlafly who helped to derail the Equal Rights Amendment in the 1970s—but have also benefited from supporting eugenics, race, religious, class, and caste based hierarchies and medical practices that are harmful to girls and women.

Much of Schlafly's slick rhetoric is based on Aristotle's natural complement theory of men and women. She claims that women qua "patriotic" homemakers are *equal* to their husbands, and feminists shore up *inequality* by becoming like men, e.g. by supporting the military draft for women—an "unpatriotic" move (cf. Marshall, 1995, p. 552). She rallied her troops against the feminist evils of "comparable worth, subsidized child care, family leave, and abortion" (p. 557). Since the 1990s, she toned down her attack by supporting the "mommy track" and "family friendly workplaces" (Ibid., p. 558).

Much of feminist organizing has also been fraught by internal divisions and racist fears as well as homophobic politics of appeasement. This was true during the seventy-two-year-long struggle for the single issue campaign of women's suffrage, when women's organizations decided to purge lesbians from their rolls because they feared that the "lavender menace" would derail their credibility for other pressing feminist demands such as pay equity and abortion rights; lesbian rights was not a priority (Ransdell, 1995, p. 642).

Thus, given the internal divisions among women and girls, surprisingly, the oppression of over half of humanity has not led to a revolt of the "ladies," which Abigail Adams had threatened to organize for seeing that her husband conspired successfully in excluding the fairer sex from the United States constitution. However, working class or un-casted girls and women having no class or caste privilege to lose have organized trade unions, fostered social unionism and welfare rights organizations, and rallied for laws changing employment conditions rather than focusing single mindedly on the right to vote (since they knew that suffrage within the capitalist system meant little improvement for their own material conditions) (cf. Zinn, 2003; Robowtham, 1973; Hannam, 2007; Davis, 1981). The Lawrence, Massachusetts "Mill girls" were in the forefront of militant labor strikes during the 1840s—an interesting irony given that the 1848 Declaration of Sentiments was silent on working women's grievances and trade unionism in many sectors today tends to be in solid male leadership. To counter this, labor women created the Coalition of Labor Union Women to generate the next generation of female leaders.

11. Conclusion: Resistant Voices to Public Patriarchy

Whether women or girls are behind walls of the injustice system, called the prison-industrial complex or other version of "domestic" walls (Nagel, 2007; Nagel, 2008), they have always resisted their repressive conditions, and now, they do even more so, in a world that is increasingly interconnected. Groups such as INCITE! Women of Color against Violence continue the intersectional work of the 1970s Combahee River Collective with a new focus on the challenges of the prison-industrial complex which has increased ten-fold in the last forty years and the militarization of communities of color. INCITE! also works in coalition with transgender and gender non-conforming persons of color who face the brunt of criminalization at all ages.

I shall close with a caveat: while cell phones have increased cyber-activism from Porto Alegre, Brazil, to Teheran, Iran, the demand for these products has also lead to the increasingly publicized rape committed as an act of war against many Congolese women and girls. What is rarely remarked upon is that one of the contributing causes of rape is an ingredient of cell phones. Coltan is mined in the Eastern region of the Democratic Republic of Congo, where transnational companies supply men with guns to guard their property. Also, various armies (including the United Nations "peace keeping" forces) occupying Eastern Congo do little to stop the flow of raw materials from the Congo. Again, facile "Death by Culture" arguments mute any sustained analysis of the neoliberal context of resource exploitation and its effects on the lives of rural women and girls in Central Africa.

I began this chapter by asking that we remember that the women and girls' murders in Ciudad Juárez have transnational implications. Major culprits are trade agreements that led to the exploitative maquiladora system as well as the United States led War on Drugs, which has actually exploded drug-trafficking in Latin America, especially in Mexico. All those colonial-military-policing forces might not work completely in concert, but they have quite devastating consequences for women.

Kristof and WuDunn's (2009) celebrated book *Half the Sky*—now a veritable movement according to their website—leaves out all these messy networks and institutions and focuses instead on the lone heroic "Third World" woman, who wins an education and starts a business by herself with a few kindly Western strangers lending support. Incidentally, Kristof (2006 and 2009) also supports sweatshops or maquilas because, according to him, they provide much needed work opportunities to women in developing countries.

To conclude, any critique of women's domestication and criminalization in one area of the globe, say the global North, will have to take into consideration the complexity of women's politics of location, not only living and acting in the global North, but the way their way of life impacts life around the globe. My argument has discussed only a limited portion of the rich tapestry of diverse women's and girls' lives and the impact of social policies on their lives and their reaction or resistance to them. Yet, my hope is that we continue to join forces in the worlds' social forums and intentional communities in order to abolish unjust institutions that hinder women and girls' avenues for creative self-expression, self-esteem, and playfulness. That may be a messianic hope, and for now, a footnote to new girls' and women's manifestos yet to be written.

Twelve

THOUGHTS FROM AN ELDER ABOLITIONIST

Tiyo Attallah Salah-El

1. Introduction

This is the first round of what will be a long battle. My goal is to strengthen the Prison Abolitionist Movement by exposing the powerful relationship between capitalism, the criminal justice system, and the development of the prison industrial complex. There has been and continues to be a profound disconnect between the majority of the public toward the modus operandi of capitalism and the prison industrial complex. The time has arrived for all prison abolitionists to ratchet up the level and revolt against the current conditions of ecological degradation, exploitation, racism, sexism, poverty, wars, hunger, the death penalty, the building of more prisons, and violence against women, children, gay men and lesbians, and the corruption of politics through the money of special interests.

First, people need to come to grips with the fact that America is not a democracy. A true democracy is a form of government in which the people have a true voice in the exercise of power, not only through electing representatives (who mostly represent big business) every four years. "We the People" do not have a true voice in the exercise of power in Congress or the economy. When only one percent of our population has ninety-five percent of the wealth, then the one percent are the ones who control the economy and have large and loud voices in Congress. Most modern day politicians who are in Congress have legislated out the rules and regulations that were supposed to keep the huge financial corporations and banks from amassing unparalleled wealth and power, and who now engage in legalized greed.

2. What We Need to Do

We must organize collectively instead of organizing in private or in small groups. We must review and learn from the productive social and political movements of the past (for example, the Civil Rights Movement in the

South). Most evident was that individuals, joining with others, actually were making a difference. The labor movement between the 1930s and the 1960s had improved the lives of millions. The anti-war movement brought down a sitting president, Lyndon B. Johnson, in March 1968, and was actively engaged in stopping the Vietnam War. In the forty years since, the women's movement, gay rights, disability rights, the Black Power Movement, environmental and animal rights movements have all made social and political gains. In the absence of knowledge of how these historical movements were built, young people and some older people assume that these movements arose spontaneously, or perhaps, that charismatic leaders suddenly called them into existence. Racial solidarity is part of the mood and the movement that helped Barack Obama to become President. Let us struggle in new radical and inventive and revolutionary ways to disable the mechanisms that perpetuate our exploitation and divisions. Let us call for a life where our survival does not depend on constant war on the people of the earth and our own youth. We must speak out against the wars in Iraq and Afghanistan and against the repression of the Palestinian people. Let's speak loudly and incessantly against the politics of mass incarceration. Let's speak against the obscenity of pumping money into prisons when it could be productively investment in our communities and youth. Most importantly, we need to redefine crime, exploding the propaganda that crime is characterized as horrendous when a poor person robs a liquor store, but calls the crimes of capitalists that lead to death and destitution of tens of thousands, "accidents," "mistakes," and even "business as usual."

Let us keep in mind that the needs of those on the bottom—the poorest, economically, the least powerful socially and politically—should be first, in an explicit way that builds and sustains unity. We must work toward accelerating the process of building long-term autonomous and decentralized livelihoods based on collective relations of productive exchange and consumption that are forged in meaningful work. We need only ask immigrants and historically oppressed races as to their view of progress. Clearly they would say that there is a long way to go before there is an inclusive justice movement that includes those on the bottom. We must aim to ensure that we all treat one another with dignity, and that those most deeply affected have a real voice in the conversations and decision made in their name.

Abolitionists struggle to achieve real justice. Too often exploiters and oppressors acted with impunity. Thus the real criminals must be brought to justice for reeducation, new understanding, healing and progress to occur. Revolutionary justice is bottom up. We must also be aware that revolutions by their very nature will create unforeseen realities and characteristics. That is why we must protect our struggle from not being turned back against us as too often has happened in the past. We have to learn to become far smarter than before. Not just smart "intelligent," but more perceptive, more conscious.

Struggles inspire and spark other struggles against the systems of oppression. Starting with the people of the First American Nations, we need to liberate the descendants of slaves of black, brown and Asian descent. The days of waiting for their "forty acres and a mule" are gone! We need to regain the sense of wholeness of our lives, the wholeness of what we do, so that we stop living in a state of systematic irresponsibility toward the consequences of our actions which capitalism fosters, for example, denying that our garbage/pollution/toxic waste will end up in some people's food, as smoke in somebody's lungs, or as carbon dioxide in everyone's atmosphere. This is a powerful idea we need to bring to everyone.

3. We Need to Stop Thinking of Struggles as Separate

Where did this system of domination and control, from the police to prisons, come from? How have we gotten to the place of ever-growing prison expansion nationally and internationally? It's easy to blame the Quakers for the first penitentiaries in America, but the oppression by elites out of greed began long before Quakers set sail for the shores of America. Many religious leaders of various sects benefited from and perpetuated the expansion of the penal system since its beginning. For example, in recent years evangelical Christians have supported private prisons, and the chaplains who restrict prisoner access to outside support have gained more and more power often being rewarded by government supported "faith-based" programs.

The movement for the abolition of prisons and the prison industrial complex (PIC) is not simply about tearing down the walls and cages that hold 2.4 million people in the United States. The movement for abolition is about responding pro-actively to the systems of violence that permeates our society. These systems of violence are manifestations of oppression. When people work to secure quality housing, health care, education, water, etc., for all people, they are also working alongside the abolition movement. Campaigns to "ban the box" on job applications about past convictions are part of the abolition movement. Abolition is not about one particular campaign, issue or struggle. The abolition of chattel slavery was not complete with the passage of the Thirteenth Amendment or the end of the Civil War. The movement for abolition today is an extension of the same movement of which Nat Turner, Harriet Tubman and John Brown were leaders. Organizing must go way beyond annual conferences. We are taking on two extremely powerful intertwined institutions of oppression—capitalism and the prison industrial complex. Let us never forget this cold, hard fact.

As we break down the power of state surveillance and policing we must create and put into practice new, innovative and flexible strategies. The communities most impacted by the violence of prisons and prison industrial complex are people of color, especially poor people, prisoners, former prisoners, gender non-conforming people, gays, lesbians and the millions of young and old men, women and children who live on society's margins and who bear the brunt of police scrutiny and government sanctioned coercion. During the past thirty years, a historically unprecedented politically popular, extraordinarily punitive, and hugely racially disparate system has been institutionalized requiring the mobilization of billions of dollars for policing, imprisonment and post-release supervision. The collective and combined systems of capitalism/big business, prisons, and criminal justice *create* the prison industrial complex that has no historical precedent, and so we must *fully* use our intelligence, creativity and persistence in order to dismantle it.

In the United States, the major cause of poor undereducated, frequently employed and troubled, but still human young and old men of color being sent to prison is poverty. They are treated without respect. They have to fight for everything. They are not getting the same chances. They are being left out and told one way or the other, "You don't count." For many it is death. It is the brutal truth of thirty-three million hungry people trapped in poverty in America—a bitterly real place where every forty-three seconds a child is born; but for some children, every fifty-three minutes, another child dies from the impact of poverty. And, for many children, every year spent in school means risk of failure and never graduating. Poverty is America's forgotten state. For many it's a life that moves from poverty to prison.

When President Obama spoke to the N.A.A.C.P. in July 2009, reaffirming the standard racial narrative while lecturing the black community on the need for better values, he barely uttered a word about ways in which public policy, over which he might exert no small influence, has resulted in the hyper-incarceration of poor African American and Latino young and old men, women and eleven to sixteen year-old children.

We must begin to invest much more in educating our fellow troubled brothers and sisters who are caught in the web of poverty and law enforcement. We must change the ways in which the criminal justice system deals with juveniles convicted of offences—sometimes only status offences—so a foolish act in childhood doesn't put them on the road to a lifetime in prisons. Clearly, after almost forty years, we can say that the "war on drugs" is a complete, widely expensive failure. Reforms of various sorts will never succeed. Such programs add to more prisons being built to house more poor people. So called "humane prisons" don't work.

4. Regarding Various Past and Present Reform

During the 1920s and 1930s, black prisoners received the worst jobs and had separate living facilities from white prisoners. In many prisons white prisoners enjoyed wider privileges, relaxed supervision and special amusements. This principle of segregation existed both in the Northern and Southern states. Cruel, state-sanctioned forms of convict leasing continued in the South until the 1940s. Following the Civil War prison farms were built where convicts could labor for state and private profit. As strange as it may seem, in the Jim Crow South, the chain gang had the dubious distinction of being one of the few state-sponsored interracial encounters in the Southern penal system. This system became notorious for the terrible conditions and the horrendous conditions given to prisoner—some of which continue to the present day.

Beginning in the 1970s came small amounts of so-called state and federally sanctioned reforms. Bankrupt counties no longer able to afford chain gangs began sending their prisoners to the state prisons. Crime and punishment were nationalized and politicized early on in American political development. Various kinds of "reforms," for example, the rise of psychological, medical and sociological explanations of criminal behavior pushed hard to have much of the control over the length of prison terms turned over to administrative authorities, usually parole boards. A 1971 report by the American Friends Service Committee, "The Struggle for Justice," charged that the rehabilitation model was "bankrupt "after a "century of persistent failures." The report condemned individualized treatment because it gave the state enormous discretionary power to "control not just the crimes but the way of life" of prisoners. The report charged that the rehabilitative model perpetuated race and class discrimination by giving criminal justice professionals, the majority of whom were white and middle class, enormous power to decide who has and who has not been deserving of early release.

Today, some states are rethinking parole reforms after years of harsh ever-longer sentences and placing greater obstacles prisoners must overcome before being paroled. As of this writing, California may be forced to make changes to its parole system that experts and government officials now say are key to reducing the dangerously and needlessly overcrowded prison population. It appears that in California and other states, correctional authorities are being compelled to realize that more parole is one necessary step in reducing overcrowding. For years, efforts to change the parole system have met with fierce resistance from "tough on crime" legislators, prison guards unions, special interest groups representing private prisons, privatized prison services, and many "victims' rights" groups. But the state now faces a perfect storm of problems surrounding the system of incarceration it has built. It appears that the history of so-called reform focused on improving prisoners and the criminal justice system, has instead created major economic, social, political destruction and unmeasured pain and punishment upon poor people and present day prisoners. Reform is inadequate as an end in itself. The best and only intelligent way is to not to have any prisons.

As abolitionists we must move forward keeping our eye and our work on the ultimate goal: the abolition of prisons. Moving toward this end we must organize to stop people with non-violent convictions from being sent to prisons, create bail reform programs so that jails are not debtors prisons, expand parole, reinstate commutation, end the unnecessary systems designed to send parolees back to prison based on minor violations, decriminalize addiction, decriminalize sex work, end mandatory minimum sentences, shorten the length of sentences, end life without parole, institutionalize compassionate release, end three strikes and habitual offender sentences, create more community-based mental health and addiction treatment centers—all of these things can be accomplished now and are practical first steps on the way to abolition.

5. The Prison Industrial Complex Produces Its Own Customers

The prison industrial complex's role in the so-called "war on crime" in some ways parallels that of the military industrial complex's role during the cold war. Both derived their power from the quiet collusion of the self-interest of corrupt politicians and big business, and both created and exploited fear to enrich themselves at taxpayers' expense while gaining more and more power.

In the post-Cold War Era in many states, prison guards unions were formed and have grown enormously. Most are distinct from the organized labor of earlier periods and during the cold war. In this period of the growth of the Prison Industrial Complex traditional labor has lost power as globalization has caused good paying jobs to move out of the United States in search a workforce desperate to work for pennies. Simultaneously, as traditional labor has decreased, strong, powerful unions of guards have developed. These "unions" work to protect the jobs of guards by contributing millions to pro-prison politicians who vote for longer and harsher sentence, prisons and prison jobs in their towns. They lobby pay packages that in certain states can be as high as $100,000 a year. The greater irony is that some of the very people now incarcerated come from the communities that once had strong trade unions and a powerful industrial base.

Over the years, we see that a bloated correctional system does little to reduce crime. In fact, there are increasing signs that the prison industrial complex may be contributing to crime. People cycling in and out of prisons and jails destabilize families and communities, makes legal regular work almost impossible to get for someone with a criminal record. It pushes people further to the margins and for some communities prison becomes the norm rather than the exception. Every year, America's prisons release approximately 700,000 prisoners who have completed their prison sentences. For example in New York state "24,223 prisoners were released from the Department of Correctional Services (DOCS) in 2005, 2.7 percent were returned to prison for a new felony within one year following release; 7.7 percent were returned within two years; and 10.9 percent were returned within three years. The proportion of prisoners returned for a rule violation is substantially higher. For those released in 2005, 16.4 percent were returned to prison for a rule violation within one year following release; 26.8 percent were returned within two years; 30.3 percent were returned to prison for a rule violation within three years." That is, the majority was returned for parole violations, although clearly some were returned for new crimes (Federal Interagency Reentry

Council, 2011). This is also really true in California "where between 60,000 and 70,000 California parolees return to custody annually for violations (Farrell, 2009). They may have failed a drug test, gone missing, or even committed a new crime for which they were not prosecuted." The issue is that all of these former prisoners—people committing new crimes and people violating parole—all get lumped together as "recidivist" which the media and others who benefit from tough on crime policies use to foster fear of crime and criminals out of control. This in turn works to drive harsher laws and longer sentences. And as luck plus good capital planning would have it, the Prison Industrial Complex stands ready to welcome them all back to the big house. What the correctional system has created is the perfect capitalistic business plan. Prisons are literally producing their own future customers. As long as the public is brainwashed into fearing those branded "criminals," they will continue to be willing to spend $65-75 billion a year or more on this fraud on the American public, and prison populations continue to grow unabated. Crime may not pay, but prisons sure as hell do.

Organizing is a process that is creating long-term campaigns that mobilize a certain constituency to press for specific demands from a particular target, using a strong creative defined strategy and escalating tactics. Let me be very clear. We have to move toward organizing masses of people. We should focus on building relationships with local and inner city people and help them develop into leaders within democratic structures. *We have to make clear that what they do is important.* In order to move forward politically and powerfully people must believe in themselves and the mission. We must involve long-term strategy, patient base-building, personal engagement between people, full democratic participation, education and coalition building. We must create and build a permanent anti-imperialist, anti-capitalist, anti-racist, anti-sexist and anti-homophobic abolitionist movement.

The question now is, are we up to the challenge? We must accept the fact that we are taking on a huge and daunting task. We cannot and should not ever back down or back away on what we are working toward accomplishing, which is a more civilized, more humane and sustainable society. As wealth, poverty, education and health disparities between blacks and whites grow wider, and the number of blacks, poor whites, and Latino homeless, jobless, and incarcerated increases, there is a host of questions abolitionists need to find answers to and to act upon. I am dedicating my time, energy, and the rest of my life to various efforts that I hope will contribute to social, political and economic change, and most importantly to move other people to take action and help them develop skills, political analysis and personal confidence to truly believe in themselves and the fact that only acting collectively and consciously can we help to bring about the abolition of prisons.

Please try on this idea of abolition if it is new to you. Take some time to dialogue with others and help us live our commitment to justice most authentically. I gained my learning, dedication and confidence from my teachers, namely Monty Neill, Howard Zinn, Paul Alan Smith, Mecke Nagel, Erika Arthur, Lois Ahrens and my student prisoners. Overcoming adversity not only has made me stronger it has made me more hopeful. My interest and dedication to help bring about the abolition of prisons and the Prison Industrial Complex is for real and reflects more than academic curiosity.

Thirteen

AN UBUNTU ETHIC OF PUNISHMENT

Mechthild Nagel

1. Introduction

Philosophers have come belatedly to the prison or penal debate, a matter of a concern for reform-minded United States citizens, policy makers, criminologists, and certainly the millions of people mired in the carceral complex. It was only when it hit a crisis point with mass incarceration in the last twenty years that a few started to pay closer attention. The profession's silence is quite odd given that our first philosopher, Socrates, was jailed before taking the poisonous drink. Plato's *Apology* presages famous and controversial modern defenses in the courtroom (from Fidel Castro, to Nelson Mandela, Steve Biko, and John Africa). Socrates dared the jury to give him a pension rather than punishment for being a gadfly in the market place.

Philosophers today have taken stock of theories of punishment, (that is, retribution, deterrence, and incapacitation; Honderich, 1970) as well as of the repressive prison apparatus (Foucault, 1977). However, how successful have we, as public intellectuals, been in addressing our concerns to a general public? In this chapter, I link *political* analysis with questions about human values by engaging with contemporary *ethical* theories. I focus on Ubuntu, a Southern African ethic (cf. Metz, 2007) and compare it with an ethic of care (Gilligan, 1982).

Engaged Quakers and criminologists have used a pragmatist approach rather than thinking through an ethical paradigm. I don't know of any sustained *philosophical* analyses of restorative or transformative penality—with the exception perhaps of Plato. Taking my cue from Angela Y. Davis's concept of abolitionism, I argue for a transformative model of justice rather than a restorative model. In her critique of the prison industrial complex, Davis engages in "tarrying with the negative," rather than providing a non-ideal account of "abolition democracy."

I turn to an Ubuntu inspired penal ethic to see if it can give us guidance for a novel justice paradigm the world over. Ubuntu is a Southern African concept that refers to shared humanity as in the Nguni saying: *umuntu ngumuntu ngabantu* ("one is only human through other humans").

2. Ubuntu Principles

In his insightful article "Toward an African Moral Theory," Thaddeus Metz proposes a bold secular theory of right action shared by "most friends of *Ubuntu*" (2007, p. 323), meaning Africans. This theory should also have overlapping consensus with Westerners, who are wedded to normative ideals based in justice principles. He outlines six violations such as killing innocent people, rape, deceit, theft, breaking promises, racial discrimination as being universally accepted as egregious, or, using Kant's language "vices" (*Laster*) which have to be countered by perfect duties (for example, dignity, reverence for life, and telling the truth).

Here of course, it is important to note that Kant was not beyond racist sentiments himself (see Eze, 2001; Bernasconi, 2002). On the other hand, sub-Saharan societies would find these six behaviors abhorrent: majoritarian rule; retribution; possessive individualism; greed; nonconformity, failure to marry and procreate, and, especially, disrespecting tradition. These beliefs, attitudes and practices are of course ingrained in much of Western tradition that is wedded to a public patriarchal, capitalist ideology, and a moral code based on individualist rights. Virtues such as generosity, unanimity, cooperation, and sharing that are prized according to an African ethic would be at best imperfect duties according to Kant. Metz then proceeds to lay out six different postulates of an Ubuntu (U) ethic, with the intent to derive a "right action." I mention here the final step: "*U6: An action is right just insofar as it produces harmony and reduces discord; an act is wrong to the extent that it fails to develop community*" (p. 334, his italics). According to Metz, an African moral theory based on right action would be founded in good-will and shared identity to produce harmony. Furthermore, he thinks with his revised and enriched version he would be able to bridge the ethical gap between ego-centric Western and communitarian African thought:

> An action is right just insofar as it promotes shared identity among people grounded on good-will; an act is wrong to the extent that it fails to do so and tends to encourage the opposites of division and ill-will. (p. 338)

This statement seems to enrich a (Western) utilitarian account, yet he admits it is not robust enough to account for deontological restrictions (Ibid.).

I do wonder if it makes sense to *excise* the spiritual component of Ubuntu in the way Metz presented it, to make African moral theory more compatible with Western secular tradition. It is of course a worthy goal to go beyond the enduring racialized questions—whether Africa has a philosophy, or in Hegel's terms, whether it actually has a history—and Metz presents a convincing case that an Ubuntu ethic has great promise in helping to construct a "competitive African moral theory" (p. 341).

What then is "African" about this ethic? Metz focuses on imperfect duties such as generosity, communal fervor, promoting harmony, all of which are tenets of an ethic of care, and a Muslim ethic, amongst others. Certainly, discovering one's humanity through other persons seems to be germane to all indigenous pre-colonial value systems. What may be uniquely "African" about the idea that my humanity inextricably linked with yours, as Desmond Tutu would put it, is that Ubuntu has been (1) characterized as a "manly" virtue (Gade, 2011); and (2) it tends to be limited to humans, separated from their spiritual connections to the crawling ones, the stone people, the wind, the fire, the water, and importantly the earth—to put it in the language of indigenous American peoples. Dirk Louw espouses that African humanism is imbued with deeply religious/spiritual meaning:

> For the Westerner, the maxim "A person is a person through other persons" has no obvious religious connotations. He/she will probably interpret it as nothing but a general appeal to treat others with respect and decency. However, in African tradition this maxim has a deeply religious meaning. The person one is to become "through other persons" is, ultimately, an ancestor. And, by the same token, these "other persons" include ancestors. Ancestors are extended family. Dying is an ultimate homecoming. Not only the living must therefore share with and care for each other, but the living and the dead depend on each other. (Van Niekerk, 1994, p. 2; Ndaba, 1994, pp. 13–14, cited in Louw, 1998.)

Thus, a Westerner may now appreciate the deeper meaning of the famous burial court case of S. M. Otieno, whose body was eventually buried at his ancestral land among the Luos (Western Kenya), even though his widow, a Gikuyu, fought to have his body buried in Nairobi (central Kenya). According to custom and belief, Luos need to be buried among their people so that they will not haunt the living relatives (cf. Onyango, 2002). The Kenyan Court eventually ruled in favor of customary law and ordered the return of Otieno's body to the Luos.

Louw then adds a political element to the African "spirit" of Ubuntu:

> However, although compassion, warmth, understanding, caring, sharing, humanness et cetera are underscored by all the major world views, ideologies and religions of the world, I would nevertheless like to suggest that Ubuntu serves as a distinctly African rationale for these ways of relating to others. The concept of Ubuntu gives a distinctly African meaning to, and a reason or motivation for, a decolonizing attitude towards the other, including and especially the religious other. As such, it adds a crucial African appeal to the call for the decolonization of the religious

> other—an appeal without which this call might well go unheeded by many Africans (cf. also Mphahlele, 1974:36; Ndaba, 1994:18-19). In this, and only in this peculiar sense, Ubuntu is of Africans, by Africans and for Africans. (Ibid., emphasis Louw's)

In a way, Thaddeus Metz's version of Ubuntu principles might better represent the cosmopolitan version of an ethic of strangers proposed by Kwame Anthony Appiah than a genuine indigenous African viewpoint. This is particularly true since Metz explores the idea of harmony at a global level (2010, p. 341). Appiah's version of cosmopolitanism seems to be, prima facie, a compatible theory because it explores tensions between an obligation relationship to strangers beyond walls and borders, that is, a universal concern, and respect for different expressions of living, a particular concern (cf. Appiah, 2006, p. xv).

Our ethical imagination is stretched when we are asked to reflect on the humanity of prisoners, whether they are *génocidaires* of Rwanda housed in a Malian prison, or political prisoners housed on death row in a Pennsylvania state facility. What is it that they deserve? Is it natal alienation, civil death, or a certain modicum of human rights that simply limits their freedom of movement? Our toleration of the other's way of expression gets tested when judging those who are disappeared behind tall walls.

Appiah does not offer assistance about adjudication of where worldviews collide, or punishment has to be meted out. In his early writings (1993), he openly objects to the ideology of Afrocentrism. Even though he was raised in Ghana, he seems more at home with the Western classical liberal tradition than African postcolonial philosophers. In that vein, his praise of universalism writ large then seems indebted to EuroAmerican values, which tend to favor individual human rights over community or cultural particularities; put in another way: rights language trumps cultural difference. Appiah's (2006) reflections on ethical comportment toward strangers also seem to overlap with (Western) feminist care ethic concerns, namely partiality toward one's kin over having responsibility for distant starving children, say, in Africa.

3. Ubuntu and Feminist Considerations

Ubuntu has already been referred to as a "manly" virtue. One of the most fervent criticisms of Ubuntuism comes from feminist scholar Fainos Mangena (2009). He calls attention to a masculinist ethos in Ubuntu, which he finds particularly worrisome in the age of HIV/AIDS, which has had a devastating impact on many African countries. African women are told by community elders to take care of husbands who have HIV/AIDS by extolling the spirit of Ubuntu (or Hunhu, in Shona).

If Ubuntu is not the answer and salvation for "the" African woman, what about an ethic of care that has captured Western feminist's imagination ever since Carol Gilligan (1977) popularized it with her study of differences between girls' and boys' different sense of morality?

The ethic of care developed out of a need to differentiate girls' experiences in their moral socialization from that of boys. Gilligan suggests that boys are tasked to follow an ethic dominated by (public) sphere concerns of impartiality and justice, which is made most plainly in the deontological version of the categorical imperative. Girls on the other hand have a (private) sphere concern for partiality, and they may justify theft of a necessary medication to keep a sick family member alive. Clearly, their justification doesn't meet the basic demands of the categorical imperative (that is, that theft can never be considered a universalizable maxim). One of the criticisms Gilligan incurred was that her study was one of white middle class women. Mangena notes that her ethic of care may be fitting for a Western (white) possessive individualist ethical framework, but it carries very little weight in a society where the community comes first and the needs and the desires of the individual are quite secondary—and especially frowned upon when uttered by a (married) woman. "So, for the Western woman, it is a question of saying: What form should a care-giving ethic take? While for the African woman the question is: What am I expected to do by my culture" (Mangena, 2009, p. 24).

However, following Gilligan, other feminists, notably Nancy Chodorow (1978), have articulated a relational theory of the self that girls are enculturated, if not pressured, to adopt, whereas boys are steered toward an autonomous sense of self. So, women, especially qua mothers and daughters of elderly parents, are summoned to be compassionate in order to meet society's approval in the West.

Such patriarchal expectations seem mirrored in the African concept of Ubuntu where hospitality toward strangers, compassion, magnanimity, and certainly care for the other is part and parcel of expressing of one's humanity. On the other hand, African men's sense of irresponsibility as painted by Fainos Mangena (for example, engaging in risky behavior) mirrors any patriarchal society's *Anspruch* (in the global North as well as South) to individual freedom and autonomous expressions. (I leave aside some of the disturbing conclusions of the author, including a eugenic sounding wish for the disappearance of African patriarchal men due to AIDS, p. 27.)

My criticism of Mangena's ethic mirrors my concern about Metz's version: Mangena's description of an African feminist ethic is clearly based upon the liberal Anglo-American human rights agenda (for example, by suggesting that women should have a public voice and influence policy decisions, whether and under what circumstances they want to be caregivers to men living with HIV/AIDS). Thus, I am unsure what else (maybe virtues? another set of principles?) he brings to a normative discourse. His critical intervention on Ubuntu is however useful to get us to look into the challenge of avoiding a romantic perspective on Ubuntu. Is it descriptive or normative, that is, of aspirational value? The following quote suggests something of both:

> It has been suggested that the transformation of an apartheid South Africa into a democracy is a rediscovery of ubuntu (Maphisa, cited in Loew, 2003). Ubuntu is a given and a task in African societies. It is part and parcel of Africa's cultural heritage. However, it clearly needs to be revitalized in the hearts and minds of some Africans (Koka, 1997; Shutte, 1993; Teffo, 1994). The actions suggested in the literature are part of this renaissance. (Outwater, 2005; emphasis added)

A non-charitable interpretation of the Nguni saying of "a human is only human through other humans" (*umuntu ngumuntu ngabantu*), which encapsulates the Ubuntu spirit, might indicate that it is brotherhood that is celebrated not gender liberationist humanity. After all, as Gade's (2011) catalogue of Ubuntu genealogy shows, one of the early explanations of Ubuntu refers to "manly virtue." Historically, many pre-colonial African societies were not only patrilocal and patrilineal, but their customs certainly had and continue to have patriarchal tendencies with precarious consequences.

Female Genital Circumcision (FGC) is one the most infamous practices mentioned at international forums, because young girls are not able to give consent to such procedures. An engaging African pro-feminist critique of FGC is portrayed in Ousman Sembène's film *Moolaadé* (2004), wherein the protagonist who offers magical protection (*moolaadé*) to uncircumcised girls is punished by her own husband for doing so, being whipped so severely that she could have been killed. Then in a turn of fortune, she returns to the village center quite victoriously with a band of women who defy patriarchal elders and accuse them of a misreading of the Qu'ran—which does not condone FGC.

Can Ubuntu be redeemed for a feminist ethic? One way it certainly can is to postulate that "manly virtue" is a deliberate or unconscious biased misapplication of the concept that seems so foundational to what counts as African philosophy (cf. Ramose, 2003). It may be problematic to venture into ideal theory, yet if one attends to roots of a concept, it seems to me important to provide a corrective to an ideologically convenient retrieval of a concept that demands submission of women to a masculinist ethos. Of course, it is disconcerting that African women philosophers' voices are missing in this debate (cf. Presbey, 1997).

4. Ubuntu and Punishment Theories

This section deals with the engaging ways an Ubuntu ethic could assist in thinking about punishment. I maintain that the most promising aspect of Ubuntu is that it can serve as a powerful antidote to traditional Western punishment theories. Metz outlines that Africans tend to resort to forward-looking rationales for punishment, for spiritual and practical reasons (2007, p. 325). An Ubuntu ethic of punishment favors restitution over revenge. This is what Desmond Tutu strategically deployed in the Truth and Reconciliation Commission (TRC), when he admonished victims and survivors of apartheid violence to forgive as well as excoriated offenders to deliver genuine, credible apologies for their deeds of atrocity and crimes against humanity. It is worth quoting Archbishop Tutu's explanation of Ubuntu in toto, because it shows how he Christianizes the concept to speak to a global audience that may not understand ancestor reverence (as explained in Louw, 1998). He makes the connection with Christian morality by appealing to agape, reciprocity, and shared suffering:

> [Ubuntu] is the essence of being human. It speaks of the fact that my humanity is caught up and is inextricably bound up in yours. I am human because I belong. It speaks about wholeness, it speaks about compassion. A person with *ubuntu* is welcoming, hospitable, warm and generous, willing to share. Such people are open and available to others, willing to be vulnerable, affirming of others, do not feel threatened that others are able and good, for they have a proper self-assurance that comes from knowing that they belong in a greater whole. They know that they are diminished when others are humiliated, diminished when others are oppressed, diminished when others are treated as if they were less than who they are. The quality of *ubuntu* gives people resilience, enabling them to survive and emerge still human despite all efforts to dehumanise them. (1999, pp.34–35)

If it is the case that my humanity is connected to another person (for example, an offender), then I have a bit of cruelty, sadism, lack of love in me as well, and, as such, I can related to the action of the offender/oppressor. Radically put, I (as a victim) am also responsible for the ghastly deed of the oppressor. However, such heightened level of responsibility sits uneasily with a Western philosophical audience, steeped in notions of individual culpability. John Braithwaite claims that asking victims to forgive, or offenders to apologize, is wrong, if not cruel. Forgiveness and apology "are gifts that have no power as gifts when they are demanded" and they only play a role in restorative justice as "emerging values" that might arise out of the process (2011, p. 349). Tutu's overreach then may consist in making these values into "constraining values" that have to be part of any successful restorative process, (that is, ground rules of conduct). Braithwaite, on the other hand, claims that constraining values deal with respectful listening, non-domination, empowerment, equal concern for all stakeholders, and freedom from racist and sexist oppression, appealability, and accountability (Ibid., p. 348). Tutu would, in all likelihood agree to these ground rules, and the TRC Commission mixed indigenous principles with Western rule of law, since the TRC referred those who didn't win amnesty to criminal court. The TRC was the first commission of its kind for letting victims, victims' families and offenders speak, as well as offering psychological counseling to those who were deeply traumatized by recounting past events. However, many critics of the TRC note that it was a

"Truth" commission, rather than one of reconciliation, since, despite Tutu's strenuous efforts, victims often did not sense that justice was served and that offenders apologized in a lighthearted way in order to receive the coveted amnesty. Furthermore, as Tutu (1999) acknowledges, the whole process was undermined by the government's delay of reparations to bona fide victims and victims' families.

Some critics of the TRC proceedings would probably agree with critics of restorative justice, who hold that a fanatical focus on the restorative "process" may actually yield injustice (for the victim and/or her community). In order for restorative processes to work in consort with "doing justice," certain sentencing guidelines have to be met that are shared by the larger community, that is, the rule of law and codification of criminal offenses (Robinson, 2011). "Doing justice" then amounts to "just punishment" of the offender, even if it goes contrary to the wishes of the victim. Hence, the principle of appealability comes to play here, since any consensual agreements arrived at by both parties in a, say, sentencing circle, which includes community members of both offender and victim, can then be appealed by a state actor, for example a district attorney, to the conventional criminal court system. A much-quoted case study from New Zealand illuminates the trouble of interweaving mediation or community justice with criminal courts.

In this case, the victim, Patrick Dale Clotworthy, survived a violent assault, leaving him with a scar that needed cosmetic surgery repair, which the offender was willing to pay for in addition to community service. The Court of Appeal reduced the payment, which then made surgery impossible, and instead argued from the principle of deterrence, interning the defendant for four years. Subsequently, Clotworthy committed suicide, "for reasons unknown" (cf. Braithwaite, 2011, p. 347).

I argue that appealing community justice or sentencing circles' decisions to an adversarial criminal justice system fundamentally violates the ethic of Ubuntu, as the trust between the parties is broken and dissent is the final outcome. The underlying principle of appealability is based on abstract rights, individualism, and retribution that goes against the ideas of compassion (Tutu, 1999), power sharing (Louw, 2002) and interconnectedness with those who are living-dead (the ancestors) and the yet-to-be-born (Ramose, 2003). In precolonial times, African jurisprudence focused on restoring (divine) order in the human community after a crime was committed and a decision had to be made to appease both the living and spiritual realm beings (cf. Achebe, 1958). In some African cultures, it may have involved gift-giving and apologies by both parties (the offending and the aggrieved) with the outcome that future generations of their families could be intermarried and live harmoniously. Such practices of Ubuntu are still used across the South of the Sahel (cf. Nagel, 2007; Murithi, 2005).

The Western rule of law in democratic theory takes a keen interest in human rights, in the abstract rights of the individual. Ubuntu also allows for individuality in balance with concern for the community. This is of particular interest to citizens in the New South Africa, as the following makes clear:

The Ubuntu respect for the *particularities* of the beliefs and practices of others (cf. also Wiredu, 1995), is especially emphasized by a striking, yet (to my mind) lesser-known translation of *umuntu ngumuntu ngabantu*: "A human being is a human being through (*the otherness of*) other human beings" (Van der Merwe, 1996:1, italics added). For post-apartheid South Africans of all colors, creeds, and cultures, Ubuntu dictates that, to be human, we need to recognize the genuine otherness of our fellow citizens (Louw, 1998).

How do we recognize the individual in her particularity? Louw offers playfully this (African) solution:

> This is all somewhat boggling for the Cartesian mind, whose conception of individuality now has to move from solitary to solidarity, from independence to interdependence, from individuality *vis-à-vis* community to individuality *à la* community. (Ibid.)

In other words, individualism cannot trump communalism, and lest there would be a celebration of communal dictate over individual rights and ontology, Ubuntu holds in balance both as co-equal and as such giving rise to a full expression of the diversity of humaneness. So, it may not be the solipsistic Cartesian or Kantian ego that we find reflected in Ubuntu metaphysics, but rather a version of Hegelian intersubjectivity.

Here I will make note of the controversial, yet exciting, findings of Susan Buck-Morss (2000) in her essay, "Hegel and Haiti." The trope of the master-slave dialectic is indebted to Georg Wilhelm Friedrich Hegel's reflections on the Haitian revolution (1791–1804), which was a unique world event in that it freed Haiti both from slavery and colonialism at once. I mention her discovery, since it's well known that Hegel disparaged Africa for being devoid of history and human ingenuity and agency; yet he was sufficiently inspired by the Haitian revolution to make light of it (by erasing the historical event) in the deadly dance of recognition between "master" and "slave" in his masterwork of the *Phenomenology of Spirit*, which he completed in 1806 (see Hegel, 1977).

Given what we know of the normative tenets of an Ubuntu ethic, what would be the ramifications for a postcolonial theory of such an ethic, in particular vis-à-vis the concept of punishment? Is it an ideal theory that is disconnected from social context, much as a Rawlsian theory of justice has been described by feminist theorists (cf. Jaggar, 2009)? The answer is complicated. On the one hand, Desmond Tutu's prophetic fervor and zeal is seductively simple and appealing to the kernel of love in each of us. On the other hand feminists contest such sentiment by noting that men have excused male chauvinist behavior under the cover of Ubuntu in order to pressure women to respond compassionately. Thus, a non-ideal theory of an Ubuntu ethic of punishment would have to stay clear of romanticism and wishful disappearance of racist, ethnocentric, sexist, and homophobic realities in the postcolonial polity. And perhaps we have to say with Braithwaite that some values are aspirational, or emerge out of the restorative justice process. However, here I question, also, the concept of "restorative justice."

In a non-ideal world, the status quo ante is not simply harmonious; the violence of poverty, racism, and sexism all impact our lives, albeit in differentiated ways within the matrix of domination. Abolitionist penal theory tends to frame the "justice project" in terms of transformational considerations (Davis, 2005). How does this work with respect to Ubuntu?

When a personal crime is committed, the community gets together along with the offender (also a troubled term according to transformative justice analysis) and the victim and, of course, the ancestors. The process may involve ritual ceremonies and prayers, and the focus will be on an outcome that will be arrived at through consensual, respectful listening and speaking. Space does not allow for an extensive discussion of comparing Ubuntu ethic with Plato's moral theory of punishment (cf. Mackenzie, 1981). However, let me briefly note that there are interesting similarities that derive from an organic worldview that focuses on the harmony of the polis/community, and even though Plato does not articulate it as such, except through the tri-partite structure of the soul, if one person breaks a law, the entire group/polis will be seen as lawbreakers, and all have to commit to solve the conflict to restore cosmos/order (Murithi, 2006).

Ubuntu-based justice that follows the transformational paradigm (cf. also Davis, 2003) advocates for broader goals of justice, other than adjudicating conflicts, which would include demands for dismantling power structures that favor the elite one percent over the bottom ninety-nine percent in all aspects of society. This indeed might be an ideal worth striving for (peacefully) and would spell the end of punishment.

WORKS CITED

Introduction
Mechthild Nagel and Anthony J. Nocella II

Best, Steve, and Anthony J. Nocella II. (2006) *Igniting a Revolution: Voices in Defense of the Earth*. Oakland, Calif.: AK Press.

CBS News. (2011) "Pregnant Woman Pepper Sprayed at Occupy Seattle" http://www.cbsnews.com/8301-201_162-57325688/pregnant-woman-pepper-sprayed-at-occupy-seattle/ (accessed 3 September 2012).

Churchill, Ward, and Jim V. Wall. (2001a) *The COINTELPRO Papers: Documents from the FBI's Secret War against Dissent in the United States*. Cambridge: South End Press.

———. (2001b) *Agents of Repression: The FBI's Secret Wars against the Black Panther Party and the American Indian Movement*. Cambridge: South End Press.

Davis, Angela Y. (1981) "The Myth of the Black Rapist." In *Women, Race, Class*. New York: Random House.

———. (2007) "The Prison: A Sign of U.S. Democracy?" Paper presented at Cornell University (September).

Foucault, Michel. (1977) *Discipline and Punish*. New York: Random House.

Linebaugh, Peter. (2006).*The London Hanged: Crime And Civil Society In The Eighteenth Century*. Second Edition. New York: Verso.

———, and Marcus Rediker. (2001) *The Many-Headed Hydra: Sailors, Slaves, Commoners, and the Hidden History of the Revolutionary Atlantic*. Boston: Beacon Press.

Merchant, Carolyn. (1977) *The Death of Nature: Women, Ecology, and the Scientific Revolution*. New York: Harper Collins.

Mirkinson, Jeff. (2011) "Press Freedom Index: Occupy Wall Street Journalist Arrests Costs US Dearly in Latest Survey," *Huffington Post*. http://www.huffingtonpost.com/2012/01/25/press-freedom-occupy-wall-streetus-arrests_n_1230825.html (accessed 3 September 2012).

Nocella II, Anthony J. (2012) "Challenging Whiteness in the Animal Advocacy Movement," *Journal for Critical Animal Studies*, 10:1, pp. 142–154.

Pinney, Leah. (2007) "Pepper Spray in the Texas Youth Commission: Research Review and Policy Recommendations" Texas Criminal Justice Coalition-Juvenile Justice Initiative. http://www.njjn.org/ (accessed 3 September 2012).

Sullivan, Amy. (2011) "The Myth of Sharia in America," *Huffington Post*. http://www.huffingtonpost.com/amy-sullivan/sharia-myth-america_b_876965.html (accessed 3 September 2012).

Chapter One
Anthony J. Nocella II

Akram, S. M., and K. R. Johnson. (2002) Race, Civil Rights, and Immigration Law after September 11, 2001: The Targeting of Arabs and Muslims. *New York University Annual Survey of American Law*, 58.
http://www.privacysos.org/sites/all/files /akram.pdf (accessed 3 September 2012).

Balbus, I. (1973) *The Dialects of Legal Repression*. New York, N.Y.: Russell Sage.
Beccaria, C. (2009) *On Crimes and Punishments*. Seattle, Wash.: CreateSpace.
Becker, G. S. (1976) *Economic Approach to Human Behavior*. Chicago, Ill.: University of Chicago Press.
Beirne, P., and N. South, N. (2007). *Issues in Green Criminology: Confronting Harms against Environments, Humanity, and Other Animals*. Portland, Ore.: Willian Publishing.
Bernard, T. J., G. B. Vold, G. B., J. B. Snipes, and A. L. Gerould. (2009) *Vold's Theoretical Criminology*. New York: Oxford University Press.
Bodley, J. H. (2005) *Cultural Anthropology: Tribes, States, and the Global System*. New York: McGraw Hill.
Bourdieu, P. 1977. *Outline of a Theory of Practice*. Cambridge, UK: Cambridge University Press.
Burton-Rose, D., D. Pens, and P. Wright. (1998) *The Celling of America: An Inside Look at the United States Prison Industry*. Monroe, Maine: Common Courage Press.
Buss, A. (1961) *The Psychology of Aggression*. New York: John Wiley and Sons.
Cameron, S. (1988) "The Economics of Crime Deterrence: A Survey of Theory and Evidence," *Kyklos*, 41, pp. 301–332.
Chang, N. (2002) *Silencing Political Dissent*. New York: Seven Stories Press.
Chomsky, N. (2002) *Media Control: The Spectacular Achievements of Propaganda*. New York: Seven Stories Press.
———. (2005) *Chomsky on Anarchism*. Oakland, Calif.: AK Press.
Churchill, W., and J. Vander Wall. (2002a). *The COINTELPRO Papers: Documents from the FBI's Secret War against Dissent in the United States*. Cambridge, Mass.: South End Press.
———. (2002b). *Agents of Repression: The FBI's Secret Wars against the Black Panther Party and the American Indian Movement*. Cambridge, Mass.: South End Press.
Claassen, R., and R. Claassen. (2008). Discipline that Restores: Strategies to Create Respect, Cooperation, and Responsibility in the Classroom. Seattle, Wash.: BookSurge.
Cohen, S. (1980) *Folk Devils and Moral Panics*. New York: Psychology Press.
Cole, J. (2008) The FBI's Plan to "Profile" Muslims. http://www.salon.com /opinion/feature/2008/07/10/muslim_profiling/ (accessed 3 September 2012.
Davenport, C., ed. (2000) *Paths to State Repression: Human Rights Violations and Contentious Politics*. New York: Rowman and Littlefield.
Davis, A. Y. (2003) *Are Prisons Obsolete?* New York: Seven Stories Press.
DeKeseredy, W. S., and B. Perry. (2006) *Advancing Critical Criminology: Theory and Application*. New York: Lexington Books.
Denardo, J. (1985) *Power in Numbers: The Political Strategy of Protest and Rebellion*. Princeton, N.J.: Princeton University Press.
Fernandez, L. A. (2008) *Policing Dissent: Social Control and the Anti-Globalization Movement*. Piscataway, N.J.: Rutgers University Press.

Ferrell, J. (1997) "Against the Law: Anarchist Criminology." In *Thinking Critically about Crime*. Edited by D. MacLean and D. Milovanovic. Collective Press.

Ferrell, J. and S. Clinton. (1995) "Toward a Cultural Criminology." In *Cultural Criminology*. Edited by J. Ferrell and C.R. Sanders. Boston, Mass.: Northeastern University Press.

Fiona, D., G. Chesters, I. Welsh, and A. Tickle. (2004) "Rebels with a Cause, Folk Devils without a Panic: Press Jingoism, Policing Tactics and Anti-Capitalist Protest in London and Prague," *Internet Journal of Criminology*. http://www.internetjournalofcriminology.com/Donson%20et%20al%20%20Folk devils.pdf (accessed 3 September 2012).

Foucault, M. (1975) *Discipline and Punish: The Birth of the Prison*. New York: Vintage Books.

Glick, B. (1989) *War at Home: Covert Action against U.S. Activists and What We Can Do About It*. Cambridge, Mass.: South End Press.

Goffman, E. (1963) *Stigma: Notes on the Management of Spoiled Identity*. New York: Simon and Schuster.

Goldstein, R. J. (1986) "The Limitations of Using Quantitative Data in Studying Human Rights Abuses," *Human Rights Quarterly*, 8:4, pp. 607–627.

Goldstein, R. (1978) *Political Repression in Modern America: 1870 to the Present*. New York: Schenkman.

Goldstein, R. (2001) *Political Repression in Modern America: From 1870 to 1976*. Chicago, Ill.: University of Illinois Press.

Gupta, D., and Y. P. Venieris. (1981) "Introducing New Dimensions in Macro Models: The Socio-Political Environment," *Political Psychology*, 13, pp. 379–406.

Gurr, T. R. (1970) *Why Men Rebel*. Princeton, N.J.: Princeton University Press.

Gurr, T. R. (1969) A Comparative Study of Civil Strife. In *Violence in America*. Edited by H. Graham and T. Gurr. New York: Praeger.

Gramsci, A. (1989) *Selections from the Prison Notebooks*. 10th Edition. New York: International Publishers.

Hartnett, S. J. (2010) *Challenging the Prison-industrial Complex: Activism, Arts, and Educational Alternatives*. Chicago, Ill.: University of Illinois Press.

Henderson, C. W. (1991) "Conditions Affecting the Use of Political Repression," *The Journal of Conflict Resolution*, 35:1, pp. 120–142.

James, J. (1996) *Resisting State Violence: Radicalism, Gender, and Race in United States Culture*. Minneapolis: University of Minnesota Press.

Jones, C. E. (1988) "Political Repression of the Black Panther Party 1966–1971: The Case of Oakland Bay Area," *Journal of Black Studies*, 18:4, pp. 415–435.

Jones, C. E. (1998) *The Black Panther Party Reconsidered*. Baltimore: Black Classic Press.

Kahn, R. (2010) *Critical Pedagogy, Ecoliteracy, and Planetary Crisis: The Ecopedagogy Movement*. New York: Peter Lang Publisher.

King Jr., M. L. (1964) *Why We can't Wait*. New York, NY: Mentor.

Kopkind, A., and F. Lang, F. (1970) "The Face of Repressions," *Current*, 115, pp. 36–38.

Levin, M. (1971) *Political Hysteria: The Democratic Capacity for Repression*. New York: Basic Books.

Lichbach, M. I. (1987) “Deterrence or Escalation? The Puzzle of Aggregate Studies of Repression and Dissent,” *The Journal of Conflict Resolution*, 31, pp. 266–297.

Lynch, M. J., R. J. Michalowski, and B. Groves. (2006) *Primer in Radical Criminology: Critical Perspectives on Crime, Power, and Identity*. Monsey, N.Y.: Criminal Justice Press.

Magnani, L. and H. L. Wray. (2006) *Beyond Prisons: A New Interfaith Paradigm for our Failed Prison System*. Minneapolis, Minn.: Fortress Press.

Marx, K. (1959) *Capital*. Volume 1. Moscow: Foreign Languages Publishing House.

Mathúna, S. M. (2000) Shaka Sankofa Murdered by the State of Texas. *Flame*. 5 (Summer). http://www.fantompowa.net/Flame/shaka_sankofa.htm (accessed 3 September 2012).

Michell, C., M. Stohl, D. Carleton, and G. A. Lopez. (1986a) “State Terrorism: Issues of Conflict and Measurement.” In *Government Violence and Repression*. Edited by M. Stohl and G.A. Lopez. Westport, Conn.: Greenwood. Neufville, J.I.

——— (1986b). “Human Rights Reporting as a Policy Tool: An Examination of the State Department Country Reports,” *Human Rights Quarterly*, 8:4, pp. 681–699.

Millies, Stephen. (2008) “Never Forget Fred Hampton and Mark Clark,” *Workers World* (11 December).

Nocella II, A. J., S. Best, and P.McLaren, P. (2010) *Academic Repression: Reflections from the Academic Industrial Complex*. Oakland, Calif.: AK Press.

Odartey-Wellington, F. (2009) “Racial Profiling and Moral Panic: Operation Thread and the Al-Qaeda Sleeper Cell That Never Was,” *Global Media Journal*, 2: 2, pp. 25–40.

Parenti, M. (1993) *Inventing Reality: The Politics of the News Media*. 2nd Edition. New York: St. Martin’s Press.

Pfohl, S. (1994) *Images of Deviance and Social Control: A Sociological History*. New York: McGraw-Hill.

———. (2009) *Images of Deviance and Social Control: A Sociological History*. 2nd Edition. Long Grove, Ill.: Waveland Press Inc.

Reiter, R. B., M. V. Zunzunegui, and J. Quiroga. (1986) “Guidelines for Field Reporting of Basic Human Rights Violations,” *Human Rights Quarterly*, 8:4, pp. 628–653.

Renzetti, C. M. (2008) *Feminist Criminology*. New York: Routledge.

Rodley, N. S. (1986) “U.N. Action Procedures against ‘Disappearances:’ Summary of Arbitrary Executions, and Torture,” *Human Rights Quarterly*, 8:4, pp. 700–730.

Ross, B., and R. El-Buri. (2008) Obama’s Pastor: God Damn America, United States to Blame for 9/11. http://abcnews.go.com/Blotter/DemocraticDebate/story?id=4443788&page=1 (accessed 3 September 2012).

Schultz, B., and R. Schultz, eds. (1989) *It did Happen Here: Recollections of Political Repression in America*. Los Angeles: University of California Press.

Shane, S. (2008, October 3). Obama and 60s bomber: A Look Into Crossed Paths. New York Times. Retrieved on September 29, 2012 from http://www.nytimes.com/2008/10/04/us/politics/04ayers.html?pagewanted=all&_r=0.

Snyder, D., and C. Tilly. (1972) "Hardship and Collective Violence in France: 1830–1960," *American Sociological Review*, 42, pp. 105–123.
Stockdill, B. C. (2002). Activism *against AIDS: At the Intersections of Sexuality, Race, Gender, and Class*. Boulder, Colo.: Lynne Rienner Publishers.
Stohl, M., and G. A. Lopez. (1984) "Introduction." In *The State as Terrorist*. Edited by M. Stohl and G. A. Lopez. Westport, Conn.: Greenwood.
Justice Policy Institute (2000) "The Punishing Decade: Prison and Jail Estimates at the Millennium." http://www.justicepolicy.org/images/upload/00-05_rep_punishing decade_ac.pdf (accessed 3 September 2012).
Tilly, C. (1978) *From Mobilization to Revolution*. New York: McGraw-Hill.
———. (2003) *The Politics of Collective Violence*. Cambridge, UK: Cambridge University Press.
Tucker, R. C., ed. (1978) *The Marx-Engels Reader*. 2nd Edition. New York: W. W. Norton.
United Farm Workers of America. (1993) Press Release: Statement from the United Farm Workers (24 April).
Van Ness, D., and K. H. Strong. (1997) *Restoring Justice*. Cincinnati, Ohio: Anderson.
Washington, D. (2007) *Great Debaters*. Los Angeles: Metro-Glodwyn-Mayer Inc.
Zehr, H. (1995) *Changing Lenses*. Scottdale, Penn.: Herald Press.

Chapter Two
David Gabbard

Advancement Project (2010). Test, Punish, and Push Out: How Zero Tolerance and High-Stakes Testing Funnel Youth into the School to Prison Pipeline. http://www.journalismcenter.org/resource/k-through-12/how-zero-tolerance-and-high-stakes-testing-funnel-youth-school-prison-pipeline (accessed 3 September).
Alliance for Excellent Education (n.d). About the Crisis http://www.all4ed.org/about_the_crisis (accessed 3 September 2012).
Beard, Charles A. (1913) *An Economic Interpretation of the Constitution of the United States*. New York: Macmillan.
Cayley, D. (2005) *The Rivers North of the Future: The Testament of Ivan Illich*. Toronto: House of Anansi Press.
Center for Labor Market Studies at Northeastern University. (2009) Joblessness and Jailing for High School Dropouts and the High Cost for Taxpayers http://iris.lib.neu.edu/.
Delany, Arthur. (2011) "'I Played By The Rules' —'The Rules Have Changed,'" *Huffington Post*. (23 May 23) http://www.huffingtonpost.com/2011/05/23/long-term-unemployment_n_864873.html (accessed 3 September 2012).
Forbes Magazine. (2010) "No. 15: Groton School, A Profile of One of America's 20 Best Prep Schools," *Forbes Online* (29 April).
http://www.forbes.com/2010/04/29/best-prep-schools-2010-opinions-groton-school.html (accessed 3 September 2012).

Foucault, M. (1977). *Discipline and Punish: The Birth of the Prison*. New York: Vintage.

Gates, Bill. (2010) "TEACH: Government, Business Leaders Thank Their Teachers," U.S. Department of Education (29 September). http://www.ed.gov/blog/2010/09/teach-government-business-leaders-thank-their-teachers/ (accessed 3 September 2012).

Hitchens, Christopher. (2007) *God Is Not Great*. New York: Twelve Books.

Jefferson, T. (1904–5). "A Bill for the More General Diffusion of Knowledge. In The Works of Thomas Jefferson." Federal Edition. New York: G. P. Putnam's Sons.

National Association for the Advancement of Colored People (2011). Misplaced Priorities: Over Incarcerate, Under Educate. (7 April). http://www.naacp.org/pages /misplaced-priorities (accessed 3 September 2012).

National Commission on Excellence in Education. (1983) A Nation at Risk: The Imperative for Educational Reform: A Report to the Nation and the Secretary of Education, United States Department of Education. Washington, D.C.: U.S. GPO.

Obama, Barack. (2011) State of the Union Address. http://www.npr.org/2011/01 01/26/133224933/transcript-obamas-state-of-union-address (accessed 3 September 2012).

Pelaez, Vicky. (2008) "The Prison Industry in the United States: Big Business or a New Form of Slavery?" Global Research Centre for Research on Globalization. http://wwwglobalresearch.ca/index.php?context=va&aid=8289 (accessed 3 September 2012).

Pew Forum on Religion and Public Life. (2010) Can Civilization Survive without God? A Conversation with Christopher and Peter Hitchens. http://www.pewforum.org/Belief-in-God/Can-Civilization-Survive-Without-God-.aspx (accessed 3 September 2012).

Quinn, S. , and C. Hitchens. (2008) "Divine Impulses," *The Washington Post*. http://www.washingtonpost.com/wp-dyn/content/video/2008/01/08/VI20080108 02108.html?hpid=topnews (accessed 3 September 2012).

Rohrlich, Justin. (2011) "Why are Prisoners Building Patriot Missiles?" *Minyanville*. http://www.minyanville.com/businessmarkets/articles/defense-industrial-base-defense-budget-defense/3/7/2011/id/33198 (accessed 3 September 2012).

Scott, Robert E. (2003) "The High Price of 'Free' Trade: NAFTA's Failure Has Cost the United States Jobs across the Nation," Economic Policy Institute (17 November 17). http://www.epi.org/publication/briefingpapers_bp147/ (accessed 3 September 2012).

Shierholz, Heidi, and Kathryn Anne Edwards. (2011) The Class of 2011: Young Workers Face a Dire Labor Market without a Safety Net. Economic Policy Institute. Briefing Paper #306. (20 April) http://www.epi.org/publication/bp306-class-of-2011/ (accessed 3 September 2012).

Chapter Three
Ernesto Aguilar and Melissa Chiprin

Alcindor, Habiba. (2011) "How People of Color Occupy Wall Street," *The Nation* (4 November).http://www.thenation.com/article/164405/how-people-color-occupy-wall-street (accessed 3 September 2012).

Alexander, Michelle. (2010) *The New Jim Crow: Mass Incarceration in the Age of Colorblindness.* New York: The New Press.

Amnesty International USA. (1998) Betraying the Young: Children in the U.S. Justice System http://www.amnesty.org/en/library/asset/AMR51/060/1998/en/f77a7749-d9bc-11dd-af2b-b1f6023af0c5/amr510601998en.html (accessed 3 September 2012).

Bliss, Jesse. (n.d.) The Roots and Wings Project. http://www.Therootsandwingsproject.com.

Boland, Bobbie, and Melody Morton Ninomiya. (2009) *Time Better Spent: Seeking Justice for Women Offenders in the Criminal Justice System.* Paper submitted to Stella Burry Community Services. www.stellaburry.ca/media/uploads/Time_Better _Spent_Report.pdf (accessed 3 September 2012).

Boyd, Graham. (2001) The Drug War is the New Jim Crow. NACLA Report on the Americas, July/August: 6.

Braz, Rose, and Craig Gilmore. (2006) "Joining Forces: Prisons and Environmental Justice in Recent California Organizing," *Radical History Review* (Fall), pp. 93–111.

Burton, A. O. (2010). "They Use it Like Candy—How the Prescription of Psychotropic Drugs to State-Involved Children Violates International Law," *Brooklyn Journal of International Law*, 35, pp. 492-493.

Critical Resistance. (2009) Prisons: New Forms of Environmental Racism. http://www.campusactivism.org/server-new/uploads/CR.enviracism.pdf (accessed 3 September 2012).

Daniels, Ron. (2011) Occupy Wall Street: Black Voices for Economic Justice Must Be Heard. Institute of the Black World. http://ibw21.org/commentary_and_news /vantage-point/occupy-wall-street-black-voices-for-economic-justice-must-be-heard (accessed 3 September 2012).

Davis, Angela Y. (1990). *Women Culture and Politics.* New York: Vintage Books.

———. (2003) *Are Prisons Obsolete?* New York: Seven Stories Press.

DRCNet. (2007) Communities of Color and the Drug War. http://www.drcnet.org /gateway/poc.html (accessed 3 September 2012).

Dunnaville Jr., Clarence M. (2000) "Unequal Justice Under the Law: Racial Inequities in the Justice System," *Virginia Lawyer* (December), pp. 20–25.

Ehrenreich, Barbara. (2011) How America Turned Poverty into a Crime. http://www.salon.com/news/politics/war_room/2011/08/09/america_crime_poverty (accessed 3 September 2012).

Feagin, Joe R. (1999) "Excluding Blacks and Others from Housing: The Foundation of White Racism," *Cityscape: A Journal of Policy Development and Research*, 4:3, pp. 79–91.

Food First. (2010) Democratizing Development: Land, Resources and Markets. http://www.foodfirst.org/en/node/2860 (accessed 3 September 2012).

Hollman, B., and J. Zeidenberg. (2006). *The Dangers of Detention: The Impact of Incarcerating Youth in Detention and Other Secure Facilities.* Washington, D.C.: Justice Policy Institute.

hooks, bell. (2001) *Salvation: Black People and Love.* New York: HarperCollins.

Illingworth, James. (2010) "Slavery and the Origins of the Civil War," *International Socialist Review.* http://www.isreview.org/issues/78/feat-civilwarslavery.shtml (accessed 3 September 2012).

Jarvis, Brooke. (2011) *How Inequality Poisons Society and Equity Benefits Everyone: An Interview with Richard Wilkinson. This Changes Everything: Occupy Wall Street and the 99 Percent Movement.* Edited by Sarah van Gelder. San-Francisco: Berret-Koehler Publishers.

Jackson, George. (1994) *Soledad Brother: The Prison Letters of George Jackson.* New York: Lawrence Hill Books.

Kilmer, Beau, Jonathan P. Caulkins, Brittany M. Bond & Peter H. Reuter. (2010) Reducing Drug Trafficking Revenues and Violence in Mexico: Would Legalizing Marijuana in California Help? Rand Corporation White Paper.

Leadership Conference. (2000) "Consequences of Too Little Justice." In *Justice on Trial.* http://www.civilrights.org/publications/justice-on-trial/consequences.html (accessed 3 September 2012).

Lee, Trymaine. (2012). "Tea Party Groups In Tennessee Demand Textbooks Overlook U.S. Founder's Slave-Owning History," *Huffington Post Black Voices* (23 January). http://www.huffingtonpost.com/2012/01/23/tea-party-tennessee-textbooks-slav ery_n_1224157.html (accessed 3 September 2012).

Marshall, Lucinda, and Kathy Miriam. (2011) About Occupy Patriarchy. http://occupypatriarchy.org/about/ (accessed 3 September 2012).

Massey, Douglas S., and Nancy A. Denton. (1993) *American Apartheid: Segregation and the Making of the Underclass.* Cambridge: Harvard University Press

Mauer, Marc. (1999) *Race to Incarcerate.* New York: New Press.

Most, Jonah. (2011) "Going Hungry For Ethnic Studies," *Truthout.* http://www.truth

National Mental Health Association. (2004) Mental Health Treatment for Youth in the Juvenile Justice System: A Compendium of Promising Practices. Washington, D.C.: NMHA. https://www.nttac.org/views/docs/jabg/mhcurriculum/mh_mht.pdf (accessed 8 September 2012).

Parenti, Christian. (2000) *Lockdown America: Police and Prisons in the Age of Crisis.* New York: Verso.

Patton, Stacey. (2011) "Why Blacks aren't Embracing Occupy Wall Street." *The Washington Post.*

http://www.washingtonpost.com/opinions/why-blacks-arent-embracing-occupy-wall-street/2011/11/16/gIQAwc3FwN_story.html (accessed 3 September 2012).

Peña, Yesilernis L., Christopher Federico, and Jim Sidanius. (2006) "Race and Support for the Criminal Justice System: A Matter of Asymmetry." In *Race and Criminal Justice Attitudes*. Working Paper #181, pp. 1–32. New York: Russell Sage Foundation.

Petit, Becky, and Bruce Western. (2004) "Mass Imprisonment and the Life Course: Race and Class Inequality in U.S. Incarceration," *American Sociological Review* (April), pp. 151–169.

Price, Byron. (2010) "The Motivation behind Black Imprisonment." *Atlanta Post* (7 December). http://atlantapost.com/2010/12/07/the-motivation-behind-black-imprisonment/ (accessed 3 September 2012).

Rau, Ashley, and Kelly Manning. (2007) Youth Perceptions of Law Enforcement Officers: Potential Solutions. Cambridge: Center for Crime and Justice Policy Research.

Rios, Victor. (2011) *Punished: Policing the Lives of Black and Latino Boys: New Perspectives in Crime, Deviance, and Law.* New York: New York University Press.

Sen, Rinku. (2011) "Race and Occupy Wall Street," *The Nation*, 14 (November).: 12

Sheridan, Claire. (2003) "Another White Race: Mexican Americans and the Paradox of Whiteness in Jury Selection," *Law and History Review*, 134 (Spring)

St. George, Donna. (2011) "Texas Students Sent from Classroom to Courtroom," *The Washington Post*, (August 21).

Tomek, Beverly C. (2011) *Colonization and Its Discontents: Emancipation, Emigration and Antislavery in Antebellum Pennsylvania.* New York: New York University Press.

Van Gelder, Sarah, ed. (2011) *This Changes Everything: Occupy Wall Street and the 99 Percent Movement.* San Francisco: Berre-Koehler Publishers.

Wagner, Peter. (2003) The Prison Index: Taking the Pulse of the Crime Control Industry. New York: Western Prison Project and the Prison Policy Initiative.

Ward, Jason Morgan. (2011) *Defending White Democracy: The Making of a Segregationist Movement and the Remaking of Racial Politics, 1936-1965.* Chapel Hill: University of North Carolina Press.

Wilderson Jr., Frank B. (2007) "The Prison Slave as Hegemony's (Silent) Scandal." In *Warfare in the American Homeland: Policing and Prison in a Penal Democracy.* Edited by Joy James. Durham, N.C.: Duke University Press.

Williams, Kristian. (2006) *American Methods Torture and the Logic of Domination.* Boston: South End Press.

Williams, Patricia J. (2000) "Obstacle Illusions: The Cult of Racial Appearance." In *Police Brutality: An Anthology.* Edited by Jill Nelson. New York: W. W. Norton.

Youth Justice Coalition. (2007) "Things You Need To Know if You're Stopped by the Police." *LA Prison Times* (Spring).

http://www.youth4justice.org/dev/wpcotent/uploads/2011/04/ThingsYouNeedToKnowIfYoureStoppedByThePolice.pdf (accessed 3 September 2012).

Chapter Four
Ute Ritz-Deutch

Amnesty International. (2009) Jailed without Justice: Immigration Detention in the USA. www.amnestyusa.org.

Brotherton, D., and P. Kretsedemas, eds. (2008) *Keeping Out the Other: A Critical Introduction to Immigration Enforcement Today*. New York: Columbia University Press.

Bureau of Justice Statistics: http://bjs.ojp.usdoj.gov/.

Center for Constitutional Rights: http://ccrjustice.org/.

Detention Watch Network: www.detentionwatchnetwork.org/aboutdetention.

Fletcher, L., and E. Stover. (2008) Guantánamo and Its Aftermath: United States Detention and Interrogation Practices and their Impact on Former Detainees. Berkeley: University of California Press.

Government Accountability Office. (2008) Alien Detention Standards: Observations on the Adherence to ICE's Medical Standards in Detention Facilities. Testimonies before the Subcommittee of Immigration, Citizenship, Refugees, Border Security and International Law, Committee on the Judiciary, House of Representatives. http://www.gao.gov/.

Greene, J., and S. Patel. (2007) The Immigrant Gold Rush: The Profit Motive Behind Immigrant Detention. Report submitted to the United Nations Special Rapporteur on the Rights of Migrants.

Human Rights Watch. (2009) Forced Apart (By the Numbers): Non-Citizens Deported Mostly for Nonviolent Offenses. http://www.hrw.org/en/reports/2009/04/15/forced-apart-numbers (accessed 3 September 2012).

Human Rights Watch. (2010) United States: Protect Families in Deportation Cases; Inter-American Commission's Ruling Slams United States Law for Violating Rights of Legal Residents. http://www.hrw.org/en/news.

ICE Fact Sheet: Delegation of Immigration Authority Section 287 (g) Immigration and Nationality Act. http://www.ice.gov/news/library/factsheets/287g.htm (accessed 3 September 2012).

Meeropol, R., ed. (2005) *America's Disappeared: Detainees, Secret Imprisonment, and the "War on Terror."* New York: Seven Stories Press.

Migrants, Refugees, and Asylum Seekers. (2010) Report submitted to the United Nations Human Rights Council as part of the Universal Periodic Review.

New York University School of Law Immigrant Rights Clinic, the New York Civil Liberties Union and Families for Freedom. (2011) Justice Derailed: What Raids on New York's Trains and Buses Reveal about Border Patrol's Interior Enforcement Practices. http://www.nyclu.org/publications/report-justice-derailed-what-raids-trains-and-buses-reveal-about-border-patrols-interi (accessed 3 September 2012).

Olshansky, B. (2007) *Democracy Detained: Secret Unconstitutional Practices in the United States War on Terror*. New York: Seven Stories Press.

Office of the Inspector General Special Report. (May 2008) A Review of the FBI's Involvement in and Observations of Detainee Interrogations in Guantanamo Bay, Afghanistan and Iraq. http://www.justice.gov/oig.
Villalón, Roberta. (2010) *Violence against Latina Immigrants: Citizenship, Inequality, and Community*. New York University Press.
Walmsley, R. (2009) World Prison Population List. Eighth Edition. International Centre for Prison Studies. http://www.kcl.ac.uk/depsta/law/news/news_details.php?id=203 (accessed 3 September 2012).

Chapter Five
Ben Carnes

Adams, David Wallace. (1995) *Education for Extinction: American Indians and the Boarding School Experience, 1875-1928*. Lawrence: University Press of Kansas.
Encyclopedia Britannica. (2011) "Indian Reorganization Act," *Encyclopedia Britannica Online*. http://www.britannica.com.
Debo, Angie. (1970) *A History of the Indians of the United States*. Norman: University of Oklahoma Press.
Debo, Angie. (1991) *And Still the Waters Run: The Betrayal of the Five Civilized Tribes*. Princeton, N.J.: Princeton University Press.
Deloria, Jr., Vine & Clifford M. Lytle. (1983) *American Indians, American Justice*. Austin: University of Texas Press.
Denzin, Norman K., Yvonna S. Lincoln, and Linda Tuhiwai Smith. (2008) *Handbook of Critical and Indigenous Methodologies*. Thousand Oaks, Calif.: SAGE.
Johnson, George, D. (2011) *Profiles in Hue*. Bloomington, Ind.: Xlibris Corporation.
Kappler, Charles J. (1904) *Indian Affairs: Laws & Treaties*. Volume 2. Washington, D.C.: Government Printing Office.
Lubowski, Ruben N., Marlow Vesterby, Shawn Bucholtz, Alba Baez, and Michael J. Roberts. (2006) Major Uses of Land in the United States, 2002. Economic Information Bulletin, No. 14, May.
Matthiessen, Peter. (1983) *In the Spirit of Crazy Horse*. New York: Viking Press.
Meriam, Lewis, Ray A. Brown, Henry Roe Cloud et al. (1928) *The Problem of Indian Administration. The Institute for Government Research*. Baltimore, Md.: Johns Hopkins Press.
Meserve, John Bartlett. (1941) "Chief Allen Wright," *Chronicles of Oklahoma*, 19:4. http://digital.library.okstate.edu/Chronicles/v019/v019p314.html (accessed 3 September 2012).
Moquin, Wayne, and Charles Lincoln Van Doren. (1995) *Great Documents in American Indian History*. New York: Da Capo Press.
National Atlas. (N.d.) Map Layer Info: Indian Lands of the United States. http://nationalatlas.gov/mld/indlanp.html (accessed 3 September 2012).

Chapter Six
Liat Ben-Moshe

Appel, L. (2002) Race, Culture and Incarceration. Anarchist Black Cross www.anarchistblackcross.org (accessed 7 October 2008).

Ben-Moshe, L. (2005) "Lame Idea: Disabling Language in the Classroom." In *Building Pedagogical Curb Cuts: Incorporating Disability in the University Classroom and Curriculum.* Edited by L. Ben-Moshe., M. Feldbaum, R. Cory, and K. Sagendorf. Syracuse, N.Y.: Syracuse University Press.

———. (2011a). "The Contested Meaning of 'Community.' Discourses of Deinstitutionalization and Community Living in the Field of Developmental Disability," *Research in Social Science and Disability*, Special issue on disability and community, 6, pp. 241-264.

———. (2011b). *Genealogies of Resistance to Incarceration: Abolition Politics within Deinstitutionalization and Anti-Prison Activism in the U.S.* PhD Dissertation, Syracuse University.

Blatt, B., R. Bogdan, D. Biklen, and S. J. Taylor. (1977) "From Institution to Community: A Conversion Model." In *Educational Programming for the Severely and Profoundly Handicapped.* Edited by E. Sontag, J. Smith, and N. Certo. Reston, Va.: Council for Exceptional Children.

Carey, A. C. (2009) *On the Margins of Citizenship: Intellectual Disability and Civil Rights in Twentieth-Century America.* Philadelphia: Temple University Press.

Conrad, P. (2007).*The Medicalization of Society: On the Transformation of Human Conditions into Treatable Disorders.* Baltimore: Johns Hopkins University Press.

Davis, A. Y. (1998) "Racialized Punishment and Prison Abolition." In *The Angela Y. Davis Reader.* Edited by J. James. Malden, Mass.: Blackwell.

———. (2000) "From the Convict Lease System to the Super-Max Prison." In *States of Confinement: Policing, Detention, and Prisons.* Edited by J. James. New York: St. Martin's Press.

———. (2002) "The Challenge of Prison Abolition: A Conversation," *Social Justice*, 27:3, pp. 212–218.

———. (2005) *Abolition Democracy: Beyond Prisons, Torture, and Empire. Interviews with Angela Y. Davis.* New York: Seven Stories Press.

de Haan, W. (1990). *The Politics of Redress: Crime, Punishment, and Penal Abolition.* Boston: Unwin Hyman.

Du Bois, W. E. B. (1999 [1935]) *Black Reconstruction in America, 1860–1880.* New York: The Free Press.

Gilmore, K. (2000). "Slavery and Prison—Understanding the Connections," *Social Justice*, 27:3, pp. 195–205.

Gottschalk, M. (2006) *The Prison and the Gallows: The Politics of Mass Incarceration in America.* New York: Cambridge University Press.

Hames-Garcia, M. R. (2004) *Fugitive Thought: Prison Movements, Race, and the Meaning of Justice.* Minneapolis: University of Minnesota Press.

James, J., ed. (2005) *The New Abolitionists: (Neo) Slave Narratives and Contemporary Prison Writings*. Albany: State University of New York Press.

Knopp, F. H., (1976) *Instead of Prisons: A Handbook for Abolitionists*. Syracuse, N.Y.: Prison Research Education Action Project.

Lee, Alexander (2008) "Prickly Coalitions: Moving Prison Abolitionism forward." In *Abolition Now! Ten Years of Strategy and Struggle against the Prison Industrial Complex*. Oakland, Calif.: AK Press.

Leung, M. (1999) "The Origins of Restorative Justice," Canadian Forum on Civil Justice. http://cfcj-fcjc.org (accessed 4 July 2008).

Magnani, L. and H. L. Wray. (2006) *Beyond Prisons: A New Interfaith Paradigm for Our Failed Prison System*. Minneapolis, Minn.: Fortress Press.

Mathiesen, Thomas (1974) *The Politics of Abolition*. New York: Halsted Press.

Miller, J. G. (1991) *Last One over the Wall: The Massachusetts Experiment in Closing Reform Schools*. Columbus: Ohio State University Press.

Morris, R. (1989) *Crumbling Walls: Why Prisons Fail*. Oakville, Ontario: Mosaic Press.

———. (1995) *Penal Abolition: The Practical Choice: A Practical Manual on Penal Abolition*. Toronto: Canadian Scholars Press.

Saleh-Hanna, V. (2000) *Penal Abolition: An Ideological and Practical Venture against Criminal (In)Justice and Victimization*. Masters Thesis, School of Criminology, Simon Fraser University, Canada.

Sauve, R. (1988) "Prison Abolition: The Need for Decriminalization," *Journal of Prisoners on Prisons*, 1:1 (Summer), pp. 39-43.

Sudbury, J. (2004) "A World without Prisons: Resisting Militarism, Globalized Punishment, and Empire," *Social Justice*, 31:1/2, pp. 9–30.

———. (2005) *Global Lockdown: Race, Gender, and the Prison-Industrial Complex*. New York: Routledge.

Senger, W. (1988) "Abolition: Good Idea/Bad Approach," *Journal of Prisoners on Prison*, 1:1 (Summer), pp. 45-48.

Szasz, T. S. (1977) *Psychiatric Slavery*. New York: Free Press.

Szasz, T. S. (2002) *Liberation by Oppression: A Comparative Study of Slavery and Psychiatry*. New Brunswick, N.J.: Transaction Publishers.

Taylor, S. J. (1995/96) Thoughts and Impressions on Institutional Closure. In *IMPACT: Feature Issue on Institution Closures*. Edited by M. F. Hayden, K. C. Lakin, and S. Taylor. 9(1), pp. 8–9.

Wolfensberger, W. (1972) *The Principle of Normalization in Human Services*. Toronto: National Institute on Mental Retardation.

Wolfensberger, W. (1974) *The Origin and Nature of Our Institutional Models*. Syracuse, N.Y.: Center on Human Policy Syracuse University Division of Special Education and Rehabilitation.

Zola, I. K. (1991) "The Medicalization of Aging and Disability," *Advances in Medical Sociology*, 2, pp. 299–315.

Chapter Seven
Dennis J. Stevens

Alexander Jr., Rudolph. (2004) "United States Supreme Court and the Civil Commitment of Sex Offenders," *The Prison Journal*, 84:3, pp. 361–378.

American Psychiatric Association. (1999) *Dangerous Sex Offenders: A Task Force Report of the American Psychiatric Association*. Washington, D.C.

Anderson, S. L. (2010) *Rape in Prisons*. Port Townsend, Wash.: Loompanics Unlimited.

Barr, Mary. (2007) Some Facts and Anecdotes of Women Arrested and Imprisoned in the United States. In *Prisons and Punishment. Reconsidering Global Penalty*. Edited by Mechthild Nagel and Seth Nii Asumah. Trenton, N.J.: Africa World Press.

Becker, Howard. (1963) *Outsiders: Studies in the Sociology of Deviance*. New York: Free Press.

Bennett, Hans. (2008) *Organizing to Abolish the Prison Industrial Complex*. http://colorlines.com/archives/2008/07/organizing_to_abolish_the_pris.html (accessed 4 September 2012).

Bonczar, Thomas. (2010a) Table 12. First Entries to Parole Supervision from State Prison, 2006. Washington D.C.: National Corrections Reporting Program, NCRP0612.

———. (2010b) Table 14. State Parole Discharges, 2006. Washington D.C.: National Corrections Reporting Program, 2006. NCRP0614.

Bottoms, Anthony E., Will Hay, and Richard J. Sparks. (1990) "Situational and Social Approaches to the Prevention of Disorder in Long Term Prison," *Prison Journal*, 80:1, pp. 83–85.

Boudreaux Monique, and Wayne D. Lord. (2005) "Combating Child Homicide: Preventive Policing for the New Millennium," *Journal of Interpersonal Violence*, 20:4, pp. 380–387.

Brownmiller, Susan. (1975) *Against Our Will: Men, Women, and Rape*. New York: Simon and Schuster.

Bureau of Justice Statistics. (2002) Recidivism of Sex Offenders Released from Prison in 1994. Washington, D.C.: U.S. Department of Justice. Office of Justice Programs. NCJ 193427. bjs.ojp.usdoj.gov/content/pub/pdf/rsorp94.pdf (accessed 4 September 2012).

———. (2004) Violent Felons in Large Urban Communities: 1990–2002. Washington, D.C.: U.S. Department of Justice.

———. (2008) Parents in Prison and Their Minor Children. 2007.Washington, D.C.: U.S. Department of Justice. Office of Justice Programs. NCJ 222984.

———. (2010a) Felony Sentences in State Courts, 2006 Statistical Tables. NCJ 226846. Washington, DC: U.S. Department of Justice.

———. (2010b) State Court Processing: Violent Felons in Large Urban Communities:2006. NCJ 228944. Washington, DC: U.S. Department of Justice. Office of Justice Programs.

Christakis, Nickolas, and James Fowler. (2009) *Connected: The Surprising Power of Our Social Networks and How They Shape Our Lives*. New York: Little, Brown and Co.

Claridge, T. (2004) *Social Capital and Natural Resource Management*. Master's Thesis, University of Queensland, Brisbane, Australia.

Clemmer, Donald. (1940, 1958) *The Prison Community*. New York: Holt, Rinehart and Winston.

Comfort, Megan. (2007) "Doing Time Together: The 'Secondary Prisonization' of Women with Incarcerated Partners." Paper presented at the annual meeting of the American Society of Criminology, Atlanta Marriott Marquis, Atlanta, Georgia.

D'Amora, David. (1999) "In Defense of the Community: Effective Community-Based Responses to Sex Offenders." Paper presented at training session by Center for the Treatment of Problem Sexual Behavior at Westchester County, N.Y.

De Crespigny, Anthony, and Kenneth R. Minogue. (1976) *Contemporary Political Philosophers*. New York: Routledge.

Eigenberg, Helen, M. (2000) "Correctional Officers' Definitions of Rape in Male Prisons," *Journal of Criminal Justice*, 28:5, pp. 435–449.

Fleisher, Mark, and Jessie Krienert. (2009) *The Myth of Prison Rape: Sexual Culture in American Prisons*. New York:Rowman & Littlefield.

Fortney, Timothy, Jill Levenson, Yolanda Brannon, and Juanita Baker. (2007) "Myths and Facts about Sexual Offenders: Implications for Treatment and Public Policy." Sexual Offender Treatment.org. http://www.sexual-offender-treatment.org/55.html (accessed 4 September 2012).

Foucault, Michel. (1965) *Madness and Civilization: A History of Insanity in the Age of Reason*. New York: Random House.

Gould, Jon, and Stephen D. Mastrofski. (2004) "Suspect Searches: Assessing Police Behavior Under the Constitution," *Criminology and Public Policy*, 3, pp. 316–362.

Grossman, Linda, Brian Martis, and Christopher G. Fichtner (1999) "Are Sex Offenders Treatable? A Research Overview," *Psychiatric Services*, 50:3, pp. 349–361.

Hairston, Creasie Finney. (2001) "Prisoners and Families: Parenting Issues During Incarceration." http://aspe.hhs.gov/hsp/prison2home02/Hairston.htm (accessed 4 September 2012).

Hall, Annette M. (2006) *Sex Offenders: In My Neighborhood?* Reliable Answers.com. http://reliableanswers.com/general/sex_offenders.asp (accessed 4 September 2012).

Hunter, Ronald D. (1994) "Who Guards the Guardians? Managerial Misconduct in Policing" pp. 169–183. In *Police Deviance*. Edited by Thomas Barker and David L. Carter. Cincinnati, OH: Anderson Publishing.

insideprison.com. (2010) *Sex Offending and Sex Offenders: Theories, Factors, and Treatment*. http://www.insideprison.com/Sex-Offending-and-Offenders.asp (accessed 4 September 2012).

Katsavdakis, Kostas, Marsha Weissman, and Allen Rosenthal. (2006) Responding to Sex

Offenders: Research, Reason, and Public Safety. Center of Community Alternatives. www.communityalternatives.org/pdf/responding.pdf (accessed 4 September 2012).

Kendall, Wanda, and Monit Cheung. (2004) "Sexually Violent Predators and Civil Commitment Laws," *Child Sexual Abuse*, 13:2, pp. 41–57.

LaFond, John Q. (2004) Preventing Sexual Violence: How Society Should Cope with Sex Offenders. Washington, D.C.: American Psychological Association.

Langan, Patrick A., Erica L. Schmitt, and Matthew R. Durose. (2003) Recidivism of Sex Offenders Released from Prison in 1994. Washington, D.C.: U.S. Department of Justice, Bureau of Justice Statistics. NCJ 198281.

American Psychology-Law Society (2001) Legal Update: Constitutional Challenge to Sexually Violent Predator Laws Post *Kansas v. Hendricks*. Washington, D.C.: http://www.ap-ls.org/publications/newsletters/spr01.pdf (accessed 4 September 2012).

Melby, Todd. (2006) "Convicted Once, Punished Twice: U.S. Begins to Address the Problem of Prison Rape," *Contemporary Sexuality*, 40:9, pp. 1, 4–6.

Nagel, Mechthild. (2007) "The Role of Prisons in a Socialist Future, or: The Incorrigible Ethos of Incarceration." In *Toward a New Socialism*. Edited by Anatole Anton and Richard Schmitt. Lanham, Md.:Lexington Books.

New York State Division of Criminal Justice Services. (2012) Sexual Offenders by County. http://www.criminaljustice.state.ny.us/nsor/stats_by_county.htm (accessed 4 September 2012).

Petersilia, Joan. (2000) "When Prisoners Return to the Community: Political, Economic, and Social Consequences." *Sentencing and Corrections: Issues in the 21st Century*. National Institute of Justice. http://www.ncjrs.gov/pdffiles1/nij/184253.pdf (accessed 4 September 2012).

Rathbone, Christina. (2005) *A World Apart: Women, Prison, and Life Behind Bars*. New York: Random House.

Ravlich, Anthony, G. (2008) *Freedom from Our Social Prisons: The Rise of Economic, Social, and Cultural Rights*. New York: Lexington Books.

Salzberg, Alana. (2010) Wrongful Convictions. New York City: The Innocence Project. http://www.innocenceproject.org.

Sentencing Law and Policy. (2007) On Severe Sex Offenders Sentencing. http://sentencing.typepad.com/sentencing_law_and_policy/2007/03/on_severe_sex_o.html (accessed 4 September 2012).

Stevens, Dennis J. (1992) "Research Note: The Death Sentence and Inmate Attitudes," *Crime & Delinquency*, 38:2, pp. 272–279.

———. (1995) "The Depth of Imprisonment and Prisonisation: Levels of Security and Prisoners' Anticipation of Future Violence," *The Howard Journal of Criminal Justice*, 33:2, pp. 137–157.

———. (1997a) "Violence Begets Violence: Study Shows that Strict Enforcement of Custody Rules Causes more Disciplinary Problems than it Resolves," *Corrections Compendium: The National Journal for Corrections*, 22:12, pp. 1–3.

———. (1997b) "Prison Regime and Drugs," *Howard Journal of Criminal Justice*, 36:1, pp. 14–27.

———. (1998) The Impact of Time-Served and Regime on Prisoners' Anticipation of Crime: Female Prisonisation Effects," *The Howard Journal of Criminal Justice*, 37:2, pp. 188–205.

———. (2000) "Education: Programming Offenders." *Forum: Correctional Research of Canada*, 12(2), 29-31.

———. (2005) "The History of Prisons: Continental Europe and England." In *The Encyclopedia of Criminology*. Edited by Richard A.Wright and J. Mitchell Miller. New York: Routledge.

———. (2006) *Applied Community Corrections: An Applied Approach*. Upper Saddle River, N.J.: Prentice Hall.

———. (2008) "Forensic Science, Prosecutors, and Wrongful Convictions," *Howard Journal of Criminal Justice*, 47:1, pp. 31–51.

———. (2011a) *Wicked Women: A Journey of Super Predators*. Willmington, Ind.: Iuniverse.

———. (2011b) *Media and Criminal Justice: CSI Effect*. Sudbury, Mass.: Jones and Bartlett.

———. (2012) "Women in Solitary Confinement: Health and Recidivism." In *Modern American Prisons*. Edited by Stephen Richards. Southern Illinois University Press. Forth coming.

———, and Charles Ward. (1997) "College Education and Recidivism: Educating Criminals is Meritorious," *Journal of Correctional Education*, 48:3, pp. 106–111.

Sykes, Gresham. (1966) *Society of Captives*. New York: Athenaeum.

Talvi, Silja, J. A. (2007) *Women Behind Bars*. Emeryville, Calif.: Seal Press.

Von Hirsch, Andrew. (1976) *Doing Justice: The Choice of Punishment*. New York: Hill and Wang.

Wakefield, Hollida. (2006) "The Vilification of Sex Offenders: Do Laws Targeting Sex Offenders Increase Recidivism and Sexual Violence?" *Journal of Sexual Offenders Civil Commitment: Science and Law*, 1, pp. 141–149.

Warden, Rob. (2005) "Illinois Death Penalty Reform: How it Happened, What it Promises," *The Journal of Criminal Law & Criminology*, 95:2, pp. 381–426.

Chapter Eight
Amit Taneja

Burrington, Deborah. (1998) "The Public Square and the Queer Citizen: Towards a New Political Geography," *Polity*, 31:1, pp. 107–131.

Ettelbrick, Paula L. (1989) "Since when is Marriage a Path to Liberation?" *Out/Look: National Gay & Lesbian Quarterly*, 4:1, pp. 21–26.

Farrow, Kenyon (2005). Is Gay Marriage Anti-Black? (personal blog). http://kenyonfar row .com/2005/06/14/is-gay-marriage-anti-black/ (accessed 4 September 2012).

Ford, Jeffry G. (2002) "Healing Homosexuals: A Psychologist's Journey Through the Ex-Gay Movement and the Pseudo-Science of Reparative Therapy," *Journal of Gay and Lesbian Psychotherapy*, 5:3, pp. 69–86.

Frye, Marilyn. (1983) The Politics of Reality. Trumansburg, N.Y.: The Crossing Press.

Gay, Lesbian & Straight Education Network. (2010) The 2009 National School Climate Survey. http://www.glsen.org/binary-data/GLSEN_ATTACHMENTS/file/000/001/1676-2.PDF (accessed 19 December 2010).

Gipson, Laura. (2002) "Poverty, Race and LGBTQ Youth," Poverty and Race Research Action Council Newsletter, 11:2, pp. 3–10.

Grant, Jaime. M. (2010). Outing Age 2010: Public Policy Issues Affecting Lesbian, Gay, Bisexual and Transgender Elders. Washington, D.C.: National Gay and Lesbian Task Force Policy Institute.

Grant, Jaime M., Lisa A. Mottet, and Justin Tanis. (2011) Injustice at Every Turn: A Report of the National Transgender Discrimination Survey. http://transequality.org/PDFs/Executive_Summary.pdf (accessed 4 September 2012).

Grattan, Regina. M. (1999) "It's not just for Religion Anymore: Expanding the Protections of Equal Access Act to Gay, Lesbian, and Bisexual High School Students," George Washington Law Review, 67:3, pp. 577–592.

Greytak, Emily. A., Joseph G. Kosciw, and Elizabeth M. Diaz. (2009) Harsh Realities: The Experiences of Transgender Youth in Our Nation's Schools. http://www.glsen.org/binarydata/GLSEN_ATTACHMENTS/file/000/001/1375-1.pdf (accessed 4 September 2015).

Hamilton, Gillian. (1999) "Property Rights and Transactional Costs in Marriage: Evidence from Prenuptial Contracts," Journal of Economic History, 59, pp. 68–103.

Haywood, Todd A. (2011). "House Approves Penalty for Colleges that Offer Partner Benefits," Michigan Messenger. http://michiganmessenger.com/48816/house-approves-penalty-for-colleges-that-offer-partner-benefits (accessed 4 September 2012).

Krieger, Nancy (1988) "Aids Funding: Competing Needs and the Politics of Priorities," International Journal of Health Services , 18:4, pp. 521–541.

Kurdek, Lawrence A. (2004) "Are Gay and Lesbian Cohabiting Couples really Different from Heterosexual Married Couples?" Journal of Marriage & Family , 66:4, pp. 880–900.

Lev, Ari I. (2004) Transgender Emergence: Therapeutic Guidelines for Working with Gender Variant People and Their Families. Binghamton, New York: Haworth.

McCready, Lance. T. (2003) "Some Challenges Facing Queer Youth Programs in Urban High Schools: Racial Segregation and De-normalizing Whiteness," Journal of Gay & Lesbian Issues in Education, 1:3, pp. 37–51.

Morrison, Linda L., and Jeff L'Heureux. (2001) "Suicide and Gay/Lesbian/Bisexual Youth: Implications for Clinicians," Journal of Adolescence, 24:1, pp. 39–49.

Oswald, Ramona F., Libby B. Blume, and Stephen R. Marks. (2005) Decentering Heteronormativity: A Model for Family Studies. In Sourcebook of Family Theory & Research, pp. 143–165. Edited by Vern L. Bengtson, Alan C. Acock, Katherine R. Allen, Peggey Dilworth-Anderson, and David M. Klein. Thousand Oaks, Calif: Sage Publications.

Puar, Jasbir K., and Amit S. Rai. (2002) "Monster, Terrorist, Fag: The War on Terrorism and the Production of Docile Patriots," Social Text, 20:3, pp. 117–148.

Puar, Jasbir. K. (2005). "On Torture: Abu Ghraib," *Radical History Review*, 93, pp. 13–38.

Ray, Nicholas (2006). Lesbian, Gay, Bisexual & Transgender Youth: An Epidemic of Homelessness. National Gay & Lesbian Task Force. http://www.thetaskforce.org /reports_and_research/homeless_youth (accessed 4 September 2012).

Richter-Montpetit, Melanie. (2007) "Empire, Desire and Violence: A Queer Transnational Feminist Reading of the Prisoner 'Abuse' in Abu Ghraib and the Question of 'Gender Equality,'" *International Feminist Journal of Politics*, 9:1, pp. 38–59.

Turkewitz, Justin (2011). *Palma, AIDS Activists Attack Bloomberg AIDS Funding Cuts.* (personal blog). http://www.housingworks.org/blogs/detail/palma-aids-activists-attack-bloomberg-aids-funding-cuts/ (accessed 4 September 2012).

Ura, Alexa. (2011). "Texas House Votes on Traditional Values Center," *The Daily Horn.* http://www.readthehorn.com/campus/3950/texas_house_votes_on_traditional_values_center (accessed 4 September 2012).

Yoshino, Kenji. (2006). *Covering: The Hidden Assault on Our Civil Rights.* New York: Random House.

Chapter Nine
Amy J. Fitzgerald

Adams, Carol. (1996) "Ecofeminism and the Eating of Animals." In *Ecological Feminist Philosophies*. Edited by K. J. Warren. Bloomington: Indiana University Press.

Adams, William M., and Jon Hutton. (2007) "People, Parks and Poverty: Political Ecology and Biodiversity Conservation," *Conservation and Society*, 5, pp. 147–183.

Beirne, Piers, and Nigel South. (2007) "Approaching Green Criminology." In Beirne and South, *Issues in Green Criminology*.

———, eds. (2007) *Issues in Green Criminology: Confronting Harms against Environments, Humanity, and Other Animals*. Portland, Ore.: Willan.

Birke, Lynda. (2002) "Intimate Familiarities? Feminism and Human-Animal Studies," *Society & Animals*, 10, pp. 429–436.

Boyd, Susan C., Dorothy E. Chunn, and Robert Menzies. (2002) *Toxic Criminology: Environment, Law, and the State in Canada.* Halifax: Fernwood Publishing.

Coad, L., A. Campbell, L. Miles, and K. Humphries. (2008) The Costs and Benefits of Protected Areas for Local Livelihoods: A Review of the Current Literature. Working Paper prepared for The United Nations Environment Programme World Conservation Monitoring Centre (UNEP-WCMC). http://www.unep-wcmc.org/the-costs-and-benefits-of-forest-protected-areas-for-local-livelihoods_473.html (accessed 4 September 2012).

Connell, R., and James Messerschmidt. (2005) "Hegemonic Masculinity: Rethinking the Concept," *Gender and Society*, 19, pp. 829–859.

Dietz, Thomas, Elinor Ostrom, and Paul C. Stern. (2003) "The Struggle to Govern the Commons." *Science*, 302, pp. 1907–1912.

Fitzgerald, Amy. (2005) "The Emergence of the Figure of 'Woman the Hunter': Equality or Complicity in Oppression?" *Women's Studies Quarterly*, 33, pp. 86–104.

———. (2010)"The 'Underdog' as 'Ideal Victim'? The Attribution of Victimhood in the 2007 Pet Food Recall," *International Review of Victimology*, 17, pp. 131–157..

———, and Lori Baralt. (2010) "Constructing Responsibility for the Production of Environmental Harms: The Case of Mercury-Contaminated Fish," *Canadian Journal of Criminology and Criminal Justice*, 52, pp. 341–368.

Foucault, Michel. (1977) *Discipline and Punish: The Birth of the Prison*. Translated by A. Sheridan. Toronto: Random House.

Gaard, Greta. (1997) "Ecofeminism and Wilderness," *Environmental Ethics*, 19, pp. 5–24.

Goldman, Michael, and Rachel A. Schurman. (2000) "Closing the 'Great Divide': New Social Theory on Society and Nature," *Annual Review of Sociology*, 26, pp. 563–584.

Griffen, Susan. (1997) "Ecofeminism and Meaning." In Warren, *Ecofeminism*.

Gruen, Lori. (1997) "Revaluing Nature." In Warren, *Ecofeminism*.

Hardin, Garrett. (1968) "The Tragedy of the Commons," *Science*, 162, pp. 1243–1248.

Heynen, Nik, and Paul Robbins. (2005) "The Neoliberalization of Nature: Governance, Privatization, Enclosure, and Valuation," *Capitalism, Nature, Socialism*, 16, pp. 5–8.

Himley, Matthew. (2008) "Geographies of Environmental Governance: The Nexus of Nature and Neoliberalism," *Geography Compass*, 2, pp. 433–451.

Johnston, Josée. (2006) "Who Cares about the Commons?" In *Nature's Revenge: Reclaiming Sustainability in an Age of Corporate Globalization*. Edited by J. Johnston, M. Gismondi, and J. Goodman. Toronto: University of Toronto Press.

King, David, and William P. Stewart. (1996) "Ecotourism and Commodification: Protecting People and Places," *Biodiversity and Conservation*, 5, pp. 293–305.

King, Roger J. H. (1991) "Environmental Ethics and the Case for Hunting." *Environmental Ethics*, 13, pp. 59–85.

Lane, Pauline. (1998) "Ecofeminism Meets Criminology," *Theoretical Criminology*, 2, pp. 235–248.

Lynch, Michael. (1990) "The Greening of Criminology," *Critical Criminologist*, 2, pp. 1–5.

Messerschmidt, James. (2004) "Varieties of 'Real Men.'" pp. 3–20. In *Men's Lives*. Edited by M. Kimmel and M. Messner. Toronto: Pearson.

Noske, Barbara. (1989) *Humans and Other Animals: Beyond the Boundaries of Anthropology*. London: Pluto Press.

O'Connor, James. (1994) "Is Sustainable Capitalism Possible?" In *Is Capitalism Sustainable? Political Economy and the Politics of Ecology*. Edited by M. O'Connor. New York: The Guilford Press.

Ostrom, Elinor, Larry Schroeder, and Susan Wynne. (1993) *Institutional Incentives and Sustainable Development: Infrastructure Policies in Perspective*. Boulder, Colo.: Westview Press.

Robbins, Paul, and April Luginbuhl. (2005) "The Last Enclosure: Resisting Privatization of Wildlife in the Western United States," *Capitalism, Nature, Socialism*, 16, pp. 45–61.

Salleh, Ariel. (1995) "Nature, Woman, Labor, Capital: Living the Deepest Contradiction," *Capitalism Nature Socialism*, 6:1, 21–39.

Schnaiberg, Alan. (1980) *The Environment: From Surplus to Scarcity*. New York: Oxford University Press.

Shiva, Vandana. (1997) *Biopiracy: The Plunder and Nature and Knowledge*. Cambridge: South End Press.

South, Nigel. (1998) "A Green Field for Criminology," *Theoretical Criminology*, 2, pp. 211–233.

South, Nigel, and Piers Beirne. (2006) Introduction. In *Green Criminology*. Edited by N. South and P. Beirne. Burlington, Vt.: Ashgate.

Spiegel, M. (1996) *The Dreaded Comparison: Race and Animal Slavery*. Philadelphia: New Society Publishers.

Timko, Joleen A., and Terre Satterfield. (2008) "Seeking Social Equity in National Parks: Experiments with Evaluation in Canada and South Africa," *Conservation and Society*, 6, pp. 238–254.

Tombs, Steve, and Paddy Hillyard. (2004) "Towards a Political Economy of Harm: States, Corporations and the Production of Inequality.". In *Beyond Criminology: Taking Harm Seriously*. Edited by P. Hillyard. Black Point, Nova Scotia: Fernwood Publishing.

Warren, Karen, ed. (2007) *Ecofeminism: Women, Culture, Nature*. Indianapolis: Indiana University Press.

West, Paige, James Igoe, and Dan Brockington. (2006) "Parks and Peoples: The Social Impact of Protected Areas," *Annual Review of Anthropology*, 35, pp. 251–277.

White, Rob. (2007) "Green Criminology and the Pursuit of Social and Ecological Justice.". In Beirne and South, *Issues in Green Criminology*.

Wordie, J. R. (1983) "The Chronology of English Enclosure, 1500–1914." *The Economic History Review*, 36, pp. 483–505.

Chapter Ten
Jenna McDavid

Brandt, Allan M. (1978) "Racism and Research: The Case of the Tuskegee Syphilis Study," *Hastings Center Magazine* (December).

Butler, Paul. (2009) *Let's Get Free: A Hip-Hop Theory of Justice*. New York: The New Press.

CR10 Publications Collective. (2008) *Abolition Now!: Ten Years of Strategy and Struggle Against the Prison Industrial Complex*. Oakland: AK Press.

Cuolo, Steve. (2000) "Animal Agribusiness Industry," *The Abolitionist*, 9, pp. 2–4.

Durand, Adam. (2004) *Wegmans Cruelty*. New York: Compassionate Consumers.

Foucault, Michel. (1995) *Discipline and Punish: The Birth of the Prison*. Vintage.

Fouts, Roger. (1997) *Next of Kin*. New York: Avon Books.

Greek, C. Ray. (2000) *Sacred Cows and Golden Geese: The Human Cost of Experiments on Animals*. New York: Continuum.

Hammer, Ida. (2008) "Pets: Exploitation and Affection." *The Vegan Ideal*. http://veganideal.org/content/pets-exploitation-and-affection (accessed 4 September 2012).

Haq, Husna. (2010) "*Sea World* Tragedy: How Common Are Killer Whale Attacks?" *The Christian Science Monitor*. http://www.csmonitor.com/USA/2010/0225/Sea-World-tragedy-How-common-are-killer-whale-attacks (accessed 4 September 2012).

Harlow, Harry F. (1958) "The Nature of Love," *American Psychologist*, 13, pp. 673–685.

Hartman, Kim L. (2010) "Digital Journal Reports: Australian Wool Industry Refuses to End Mulesing Mutilations," *Digital Journal*. http://www.digitaljournal.com /article/298625 (accessed 4 September 2012).

Hyslop, Peggy. (2011) New Impetus for Leg-Hold Trap Ban. *Maryland Community News Online*. http://www.gazette.net/stories/02042011/polinew191441_32536.php (accessed 4 September 2012).

Kemp Smith, N. (1952) *New Studies in the Philosophy of Descartes*. Edited by T. Regan and P. Singer. London: Macmillan.

Mason, Jim. (1980) *Animal Factories: The Mass Production of Animals for Food and how it Affects the Lives of Consumers, Farmers, and the Animals themselves*. New York: Crown.

McEwan, Melissa. (2011) Depressing. (personal blog) Shakesville. http://shakespearessister.blogspot.com/2011/02/depressing.html (accessed 4 September 2012).

Miserandino, Dominick. (2008) "Sacred Cows and Golden Geese… An Interview with Ray Greek." *All Creatures Animal Rights Interviews*. http://www.allcreatures .org/articles/ar-sacredcows.html (accessed 4 September 2012).

Mohr, Noam. (2010) "59 Billion Land and Sea Animals Killed for Food in the U.S. in 2009." Free From Harm. http://freefromharm.org/farm-animal-welfare/59-billion-land-and-sea-animals-killed-for-food-in-the-us-in-2009/ (accessed 4 September 2012).

NOVA (2004) *Dogs and more Dogs*. Los Angeles: PBS.

Popham, Peter. (2000) "How India's Sacred Cows Are Beaten, Abused and Poisoned to Make Leather for High Street Shops." *The Independent*. Retrieved from: http://www.independent.co.uk/news/world/asia/how-indias-sacred-cows-are-beaten-abused-and-poisoned-to-make-leather-for-high-street-shops-724696.html (accessed 4 September 2012).

Regan, Tom. (2004) *Empty Cages: Facing the Challenge of Animal Rights*. Lanham, Md.: Rowman & Littlefield.

———. (1989) The Case for Animal Rights. In *Animal Rights and Human Obligations*. Second Edition. Edited by Tom Regan and Peter Singer. Englewood Cliffs, N.J.: Prentice Hall.

Reinhardt, Viktor. (2009) "The Impossible Housing and Handling Conditions of Monkeys in Research Laboratories."*Animal Welfare Institute*. http://awionline.org/content/impossible-housing-and-handling-conditions-monkeys-research-laboratories (accessed 4 September 2012).
Richman, Joe. (2006) "From the Belgian Congo to the Bronx Zoo." *All Things Considered.* http://www.npr.org/templates/story/story.php?storyId=5787947 (accessed 4 September 2012).
Robinson, Deborah. Circus Facts. http://www.idausa.org/facts/circusfacts.html (accessed 4 September 2012).
Robinson, Jo. (2011) Super Natural Milk. *Eatwild*. http://www.eatwild.com/articles/superhealthy.html (accessed 4 September 2012).
Runkle, Nathan. (2005) "What's Wrong with Dairy?" *The Free Press*. Retrieved from: http://www.freepress.org/journal.php?strFunc=display&strID=317&strJournal=35 (accessed 4 September 2012).
Singer, Peter. (1990) *Animal Liberation*. New York: New York Review of Books.
Solinger, Rickie, et al., eds. (2010) *Interrupted Life: Experiences of Incarcerated Women in the United States*. Los Angeles: University of California Press.
Talvi, Silja J.A. (2007) *Women behind Bars: The Crisis of Women in the U.S. Prison System*. Emeryville: Seal Press.
Whiting, Amy. (2009) "What's Wrong with Zoos?" *Animal Liberation Victoria*. Retrieved from: http://www.alv.org.au/issues/whatswrongwithzoos.php (accessed 4 September 2012).

Chapter Eleven
Mechthild Nagel

Alcoff, Linda Martín. (1997) "Cultural Feminism versus Post-Structuralism: The Identity Crisis in Feminist Theory." In *The Second Wave: A Reader in Feminist Theory*. Edited by Linda J. Nicholson. New York: Routledge.
Allen, Paula Gunn. (1984) "Who Is Your Mother? Red Roots of White Feminism," *Sinister Wisdom* (Winter), pp. 34–46.
Barr, Mary. (2007) "Some Facts and Anecdotes of Women Arrested and Imprisoned in the United States." In Nagel and Asumah, *Prisons and Punishment: Reconsidering Global Penality*.
Barstow, Anne L. (1994) *Witchcraze: A New History of the European Witch Hunts*. San Francisco: Pandora.
Baus, Janet, Dan Hunt, and Reid Williams, dirs. (2006) *Cruel and Unusual*. Alluvial Filmworks.
Bernstein, Nell. (2005) *All Alone in the World: Children of the Incarcerated*. New York: The New Press.
Boudin, Kathy. (2010a) "'Did You See No Potential in Me?' The Story of Women Serving Long Sentences in Prison." In Solinger, *Interrupted Life*.
———. (2010b) "Prison Education." Paper presented at workshop on Prisons. Binghamton University (April).

Butler, Judith. (1993) *Bodies That Matter: On the Discursive Limits of "Sex."* New York: Routledge.

Cohen, Sherrill. (1992) *The Evolution of Women's Asylums since 1500: From Refugees for Ex-Prostitutes to Shelters for Battered Women*. New York: Oxford University Press.

Collins, Patricia Hill. (1990) *Black Feminist Thought: Knowledge, Consciousness, and the Politics of Empowerment*. Boston: Unwin Hyman.

Daniels, Lee, dir. (2009) *Precious*. Lionsgate.

Davis, Angela Y. (2003) *Are Prisons Obsolete?* New York: Open Media.

———. (1998) "From the Prison of Slavery to the Slavery of Prison: Frederick Douglass and the Convict Lease System." In *The Angela Y. Davis Reader*. Edited by Joy James. Malden, Mass.: Blackwell.

———. (1981) *Women, Race, and Class*. New York: Random House.

De Beauvoir, Simone. (1949/1972) *The Second Sex*. Translated by H. M. Parshley. New York: Penguin.

Dewey, Susan, ed. (2010) "Demystifying Sex Work and Sex Workers," *Wagadu*, 8. http://appweb.cortland.edu/ojs/index.php/Wagadu/article/view/568/803 (accessed 4 September 2012).

Dodge, Mara L. (2006) *"Whores and Thieves of the Worst Kind": A Study of Women, Crime, and Prisons, 1835–2000*. DeKalb: Northern Illinois University Press.

Elshtain, Jean Bethke. (1993) *Public Man, Private Woman*. Second Edition. Princeton, N.J.: Princeton University Press.

Feder, Ellen. (2007) *Family Bonds: Genealogies of Race and Gender*. Oxford: Oxford University Press.

Federici, Silvia. (2004) *Caliban and the Witch: Women, The Body, and Primitive Accumulation*. New York: Autonomedia.

Foucault, Michel. (1978) *The History of Sexuality*. Volume 1: *An Introduction*. New York: Pantheon.

———. (1977) *Discipline and Punish*. New York: Pantheon.

Freeman, Jo, ed. (1995) *Women: A Feminist Perspective*. Fifth Edition. Mountain View, Calif.: Mayfield.

Freeman, Jo. (1995) "The Revolution for Women in Law and Public Policy." In Freeman, *Women: A Feminist Perspective*.

Gage, Matilda Joslyn. (1998 [1893]) *Women, Church and State*. Edited by Sally Roesch Wagner. Aberdeen, S.D.: Sky Carrier Press.

García, Ana María, dir. (1982) *La Operación*.

Glass, Ira. (2010) *This American Life*. WBNEZ, Chicago (10 September).

Gaspar de Alba, Alicia, and Georgina Guzmán. (2010) *Making a Killing: Femicide, Free Trade, and La Frontera*. Austin: University of Texas Press.

Gilligan, Carol. (1982) *In a Different Voice: Psychological Theory and Women's Development*. Cambridge, Mass.: Harvard University Press.

Himmelstein, Kathryn, and Hannah Brückner. (2011) "Criminal-Justice and School Sanctions against Nonheterosexual Youth: A National Longitudinal Study," *Pediatrics*, 127:1, pp. 49–57.

Howe, Adrian. (1994) *Punish and Critique: Towards a Feminist Analysis of Penality*. New York: Routledge.

James, Joy, (2005) "Introduction: Democracy and Captivity." In *The New Abolitionists: (Neo)Slave Narratives and Contemporary Prison Writings*. Edited by Joy James. Albany: SUNY Press.

———. (1996) *Resisting State Violence: Radicalism, Gender and Race in U.S. Culture*. St. Paul, Minn.: University of Minnesota Press.

Johnson, Paula. (2002) *Inner Lives: Profiles of African American Women in Prison*. New York: New York University Press.

Kempadoo, Kamala, and Jo Doezema, eds. (1998) *Global Sex Workers: Rights, Resistance, and Redefinition*. New York: Routledge.

Kilroy, Debbie, and Kim Pate. (2011) "Women are the Fastest Growing Prison Population: Why You Should Care," *Journal of Prisoners on Prisons*, 20:1, pp. 94–97.

Kilty, Jennifer M. (2011) "Criminalizing Women—Past and Present," *The Journal of Prisoners on Prisons*, 20:1, pp. 3-16.

Kramer, H., and J. Sprenger. (1971) *Malleus Maleficarum*. Translated by Montague Summers. New York: Dover.

Kristof, Nicholas D., and Sheryl WuDunn. (2009) *Half the Sky: Turning Oppression into Opportunity for Women Worldwide*. New York: Knopf.

Law, Victoria. (2009) *Resistance behind Bars: Struggles of Incarcerated Women*. Oakland, Calif.: PM Press.

LeGates, Marlene. (1995) Feminists before Feminism: Origins and Varieties of Women's Protest in Europe and North America before the Twentieth Century. In Freeman, *Women: A Feminist Perspective*.

MacKinnon, Catherine. (1983) "Feminism, Marxism, Method, and the State: Towards a Feminist Jurisprudence," *Signs*, 8:4, pp. 635–658.

Marshall, Susan E. (1995) Keep Us on the Pedestal: Women against Feminism in Twentieth Century America. In Freeman, *Women: A Feminist Perspective*.

Marston, Cathy. (2011) "Stopping the Real 'Cycle of Violence': A Feminist Critique of Patriarchal Battering and the Criminalization of Women by American Police," *Journal of Prisoners on Prisons*, 20:1, pp. 72–83.

———. (2012) "Justice is a Woman." Unpublished.

Nagel, Mechthild. (2000) "A Week in Court: Chronicling Domestic Violence." *IthacaToday.com* (August).

———. (2007) "Gender, Incarceration and Peacemaking: Lessons from Germany and Mali." In Nagel and Asumah, *Prisons and Punishment*.

———. (2008) "Prisons as Diasporic Sites: Liberatory Voices from the Diaspora of Confinement," *Journal of Social Advocacy and Systems Change*, 1 (March), pp. 1–31.

———. (2008) "Women's Rights behind Walls." In Saleh-Hanna, *Colonial Systems of Control*, pp. 223–244.

———. (2011) "Anti-Black Racism, Gender, and Abolitionist Politics," *Peace Review: A Journal of Social Justice* (July-September), pp. 304–312.

———, and Seth Asumah, eds. (2007) *Prisons and Punishment: Reconsidering Global Penality*. Trenton, N.J.: Africa World Press.

Narayan, Uma. (1997) *Dislocating Cultures: Identities, Traditions, and Third-World Feminism*. New York: Routledge.

Neve, Lisa, and Kim Pate. (2005) "Challenging the Criminalization of Women who Resist." In *Global Lockdown: Race, Gender, and the Prison-Industrial Complex*. Edited by Julia Sudbury. New York: Routledge.

Nicholson, Linda, ed. (1995) *The Second Wave Reader: A Reader in Feminist Theory*. New York: Routledge.

Ochoa, Maria and Barbara Ige, eds. (2007). *Shout Out: Women of Color Respond to Violence*. Emeryville, Calif.: Seal Press.

Paley, Noelle Chaddock. (2010). "Girls in Prisons." Paper presented at Reimagining Girlhood Conference, SUNY Cortland (October).

Pateman, Carole and Charles Mills. (2007) *Contract and Domination*. Cambridge, UK: Polity.

Patterson, Orlando. (1982) *Slavery and Social Death: A Comparative Study*. Cambridge, Mass.: Harvard University Press.

Payne, Allison Ann, and Welch, Kelly. (2010) "Racial Threat and Punitive School Discipline," *Social Problems*, 57:1, pp. 25–48.

Ransdell, Lisa. (1995) "Lesbian Feminism and the Feminist Movement." In Freeman, *Women: A Feminist Perspective*.

Ravoira, Lawanda. (2010) "A Call for Gender Equity for Girls in the Juvenile Justice System." http://web.archive.org/web/20100204224139/http://www.justiceforall girls.org /call.html (accessed 4 September 2012).

Saleh-Hanna, Viviane, ed. (2008) *Colonial Systems of Control: Criminal Justice in Nigeria*. Ottowa: University of Ottowa Press.

Schnyder, Damien. (2009) *First Strike: The Effect of the Prison Regime Upon Public Education and Black Masculinity in Los Angeles County, California*. PhD Dissertation, University of Texas at Austin.

Sheffield, Carole J. (1995) "Sexual Terrorism." In Freeman, *Women: A Feminist Perspective*.

Smith, Andrea. (2005) *Conquest: Sexual Violence and American Indian Genocide*. Boston: South End Press.

Solinger, Rickie, et al., eds. (2010) *Interrupted Life: Experiences of Incarcerated Women in the United States*. Berkeley and Los Angeles: University of California Press.

Stanton, Elizabeth Cady. (2007) "Declaration of Sentiments and Resolutions" in *50 Essays: A Portable Anthology*. Second Edition. Edited by Samuel S. Cohen. Boston: Bedford/St. Martin's.

Sudbury, Julia. (2010) "Marooned Abolitionists. Black Gender Activists in the Anti-Prison Movement in the U.S. and Canada," *Meridians*, 9:1, pp. 1–29.

———, ed. (2005) *Global Lockdown: Race, Gender, and the Prison-Industrial Complex* New York: Routledge.

Sweeny, Megan. (2010) *Reading Is My Window: Books and the Art of Reading in Women's Prisons*. Chapel Hill: University of North Carolina Press.

Takaki, Ronald. (1995) *A Different Mirror: A History of Multicultural America*. New York: Little, Brown.

Weissman, Marsha. (2008) "The School to Prison Pipeline and Criminalizing Youth: Costs, Consequences, and Alternatives," *The Link: Connecting Juvenile Justice and Child Welfare*, 6:4, pp. 6–9, 15–17.

Weitz, Rose. (1995) "What Price Independence? Social Reactions to Lesbians, Spinsters, Widows, and Nuns." In Freeman, *Women: A Feminist Perspective.*

White, Armond. (2009) Pride and Precious. (personal blog) http://hiphopandpolitics.wordpress .com/2009/11/19/armond-white-precious-is-the-most-damaging-film-to-the-black-image-since-birth-of-a-nation/ (accessed 4 September 2012).

Williams, Wendy. (1997) "The Equality Crisis: Some Reflections on Culture, Courts, and Feminism." In Nicholson, *The Second Wave.*

Ybanez, Victoria Lucia. (2007) "The Evolution of Domestic Violence Efforts across Indian Country." In Ochoa and Ige, *Shout Out: Women of Color Respond to Violence.*

Young, Iris M. (1994) "Gender as Seriality: Thinking about Women as a Social Collective," *Signs*, 19:3, pp. 713–738.

Zinn, Howard. (2003) *A People's History of the United States: 1492–Present.* New York: HarperCollins.

Twelve
Tiyo Attallah Salah-El

Farrell, Michael B. (2009) Parole Holds Key to California Prison Overcrowding. *The Christian Science Monitor.* http://www.csmonitor.com/USA/2009/0929/p20s01-usgn.html (accessed 3 September 2012).

Federal Interagency Reentry Council. (2011) http://www.nationalreentryresource center.org/ (accessed 3 September 2012).

Thirteen
Mechthild Nagel

Achebe, Chinua. (1958) *Things Fall Apart.* Oxford: Heinemann.

Appiah, Anthony Kwame. (2006) *Cosmopolitanism: Ethics in a World of Strangers.* New York: Norton.

———. (1993). "Beyond Race: Fallacies of Reactive Afrocentrism," *The Skeptic*, 2:4, pp. 104–107.

Bernasconi, Robert. (2002) "Kant as an Unfamiliar Source of Racism." In *Philosophers on Race.* Edited by T. L. Lott and J. K. Ward. Oxford: Wiley-Blackwell.

Braithwaite, John. (2011) "In Search of Restorative Jurisprudence." In Tonry, *Why Punish? How Much? A Reader on Punishment*

Buck-Morss, Susan. (2000) "Hegel and Haiti," *Critical Inquiry*, 26:4 (Summer), pp. 821–865.

Chodorow, Nancy. (1978) *The Reproduction of Mothering: Psychoanalysis and the Sociology of Gender.* Berkeley: The University of California Press.

Davis, Angela Y. (2005) *Abolition Democracy: Beyond Empire, Prisons, and Torture.* New York: Seven Stories Press.

———. (2003). *Are Prisons Obsolete?* New York: Seven Stories Press.

Eze, Emmanuel Chukwudi. (2001) *Achieving Our Humanity: The Idea of the Postracial Future.* New York: Routledge.

Foucault, Michel. (1977) *Discipline and Punish.* New York: Random House.

Gade, Christian B. N. (2011) "The Historical Development of the Written Discourses on *Ubuntu*," *South African Journal of Philosophy*, 30:3, pp. 303–329.

Gilligan, Carol. (1977) "In a Different Voice: Women's Conceptions of Self and Morality," *Harvard Educational Review*, 47:4, pp. 481–517.

Hegel, Wilhelm Friedrich. (1977) *The Phenomenology of Spirit*. Translated by Arnold Miller and J. N. Findlay. Oxford: Clarendon Press.

Honderich, Ted. (1970) *Punishment: The Supposed Justifications*. New York: Harcourt Brace Jovanovich.

Jaggar, Alison. (2009) "'*L'imagination au pouvoir'*: Comparing John Rawls's Method of Ideal Theory with Iris Marion Young's Method of Critical Theory". In *Dancing with Iris: The Philosophy of Iris Marion Young*. Edited by A. Ferguson and M. Nagel. New York: Oxford University Press.

Louw, Dirk J. (2002) "Power Sharing and the Challenge of Ubuntu Ethics." Paper presented at the Forum for Religious Dialogue Symposium of the Research Institute for Theology and Religion held at the University of South Africa, Pretoria, 26–27 March.

———. (1998). "Ubuntu: An African Assessment of the Religious Other." Paper presented at Symposium: *Paideia,* Philosophy in Africa. http://www.bu.edu/wcp/Papers /Afri/AfriLouw.htm (accessed 4 September 2012).

Mackenzie, Mary Margaret. (1981) *Plato on Punishment*. Berkeley: University of California Press.

Mangena, Fainos. (2009) "The Search for an African Feminist Ethic: A Zimbabwean Perspective," *Journal of International Women's Studies*, 11:2, pp. 18–30.

Metz, Thaddeus. (2010) "Toward an African Moral Theory," *The Journal of Political Philosophy*, 15:3, pp. 321–341.

Murithi, Timothy. (2006) "Practical Peacemaking Wisdom from Africa: Reflections on Ubuntu," *The Journal of Pan African Studies*, 1:4 (June).

Onyango, Peter Ogola. (2002). "A Continuing Study on Sage Philosophy: Emphasis on Jaramogi Ogninga Odinga" (pp. 239-244). *Thought and Practice in African Philosophy*. Nairobi: Konrad Adenauer Stiftung.

Outwater, Anne, Naeema Abrahams, and Jacquelyn C. Campbell. (2005) "Women in South Africa: Intentional Violence and HIV/AIDS: Intersections and Prevention," *Journal of Black Studies*, 35, pp. 135–154.

Presbey, Gail. (1998) "Who Counts as a Sage? Problems in the Further Implementation of Sage Philosophy," Quest: *Philosophical Discussions*, 11:1/2, pp. 53–65.

Ramose, Mogobe B. (2003) "The Philosophy of Ubuntu and Ubuntu as a Philosophy." In *The African Philosophy Reader: A Text with Readings*. Second Edition. Edited by P. H. Coetzee and A. P. J. Roux. New York: Routledge.

Robinson, Paul H. (2011) "The Virtues of Restorative Processes, the Vices of 'Restorative Justice.'" In Tonry, *Why Punish? How Much? A Reader on Punishment*.

Tonry, Michael, ed. (2011) *Why Punish? How Much? A Reader on Punishment*. New York: Oxford University Press.

ABOUT THE AUTHORS

ERNESTO AGUILAR is a journalist who works in radio with the Pacifica Foundation and with the Internet publication, People Of Color Organize, a movement strategy website he founded in 2010.

LIAT BEN-MOSHE is a Postdoctoral fellow at the department of Disability and Human Development at the University of Illinois at Chicago. Her dissertation examined abolitionary demands to close down repressive institutions that house those labeled as criminals, mentally disabled and mentally ill. Her academic interests are in activism, coalition building and intersectionality, Disability Studies, Anarchist Studies, representations of dis/ability and more. Liat has written on such topics as the International Symbol of Access, inclusive pedagogy, academic repression, disability, anti-capitalism and anarchism, queerness and disability, deinstitutionalization and incarceration and the politics of abolition.

BEN CARNES is a full blood of the Chahta (Choctaw) Nation, and has been an activist for Native rights since his teens. A recipient of the 1987 Oklahoma Human Rights Award for advocating for Native prisoners' rights, he has testified before Congressional committees, served as a National spokesperson for Leonard Peltier, and served as a delegate for human rights groups to the United Nations and in Columbia. His writings appear in several online publications.

MELISSA CHIPRIN is a graduate of California State University Long Beach with a BA in Women's Studies. Currently a California journalist and radio producer, she has reported on subjects including juvenile justice, feminism, and activist movements. Chiprin's community involvement has included mentoring at-risk young people and counseling homeless women.

AMY J. FITZGERALD is an Associate Professor of Criminology at the University of Windsor in Ontario, Canada. Her research focuses on the perpetration of harm (criminal and otherwise) by human beings against the environment and non-human animals. She has published articles and books on the coexistence of non-human animal abuse and intimate partner violence, on the sport hunting culture, and on harms produced by the human and "pet" food industries.

DAVID GABBARD is Professor of Educational Foundations at East Carolina University. He has earned national and international recognition for his work in critical educational policy studies and democratic educational theory. His *Knowledge and Power in the the Global Economy* (2000) received a Critic's Choice Award from the American Educational Studies Association in 2001. He has also co-edited *Education as Enforcement* (with E. Wayne

Ross) and *Defending Public Schools* (with Alain Beaulieu, 2004). With Karen Anijar-Appleton, Gabbard co-founded and co-edits *Public Resistance: An Academic Journal to Confront the Lies of the Right*. He currently serves as Program Coordinator for the Marxian Analysis of Society, Schools, and Education Special Interest Group of the American Educational Research Association, and sits on the editorial boards for *The International Journal of Inclusive Democracy* and *The Journal of Critical Education Policy Studies*.

JENNA MCDAVID, currently studying at Columbia University, is a social justice activist and co-founder of Living Opposed to Violence and Exploitation [L.O.V.E.], where she writes extensively and coordinates several projects designed to end oppression, eliminate hierarchies, and empower communities and their members. In addition to the articles written for L.O.V.E., Jenna's essays and op-eds have also been published by Our Hen House, SuperVegan, and the National LGBT Cancer Network. She also runs a prisoner pen pal group, supporting Books Through Bars, Pink and Black, and other programs designed to empower and educate prisoners.

MECHTHILD NAGEL is professor of philosophy at the State University of New York, College at Cortland, Director of the Center for Gender and Intercultural Studies (CGIS), a Senior Visiting Fellow at the Institute for African Development at Cornell University, and DAAD Visiting Professor at Fulda University of Applied Sciences, Germany (2012–2013). She has authored *Masking the Abject* (2002), and co-edited *Race, Class, and Community Identity* (with A. Light, 2000), *The Hydropolitics of Africa* (with M. Kitissou, M. Ndulo, M. Grieco, 2007), *Prisons and Punishment* (with S. N. Asumah, 2007), and *Dancing with Iris* (with Ferguson, 2009). Nagel is also editor-in-chief of the online journal *Wagadu: A Journal of Transnational Women's and Gender Studies* (wagadu.org).

ANTHONY J. NOCELLA II, a social justice educator-activist, is currently Visiting Professor in the Hamline University's School of Education, where he teaches critical urban education and environmental education. Nocella's areas of professional interest are peace and conflict studies, critical criminology, disability studies, queer studies, anarchist studies, and hip-hop studies. He has published more than twelve books and co-founded five academic journals, four book series, and more than ten active political nonprofit organizations.

UTE RITZ-DEUTCH is Adjunct Instructor of History at the State University of New York at Cortland and at Tompkins Cortland Community College. She earned her PhD from SUNY Binghamton, and where she taught courses, including Human Rights and Native American History. Her dissertation examined the conflicts between German immigrants and indigenous peoples in southern Brazil. Her current research centers on human rights, immigrant rights, and indigenous rights. Ritz-Deutch is active in Amnesty International and the Tompkins County Immigrant Rights Coalition in Ithaca, New York; she frequently lectures on human rights and social justice issues.

AMIT TANEJA is a doctoral candidate in Higher Education at Syracuse University. His dissertation focuses on the intersection of race, class, gender, and sexual orientation for LGBT students of color on historically white college campuses. Currently, he also serves as the Director of the Days-Massolo Cultural Education Center at Hamilton College, in Clinton, New York, where he oversees the Race/Ethnicity Programs, the Women's Center, and the LGBTQ Resource Center. He has previously worked in Disability Services, Residence Life, and in LGBT Student Services. Taneja also serves as a consultant and speaker on a range of issues including LGBT inclusion and campus climate, challenges faced by LGBT students of color, Facebook use and implications for higher education professionals, and practicing affirmative action in higher education settings.

TIYO ATTALLAH SALAH-EL is a decorated Korean War Veteran. While serving a life sentence in Pennsylvania, he has earned a BA in African American History and an MA in Political Science. He founded The Coalition for the Abolition of Prisons in 1986, and edits its newsletter. He continues to be involved in prison activist and abolition circles. He has written several articles and self-published his autobiography (2006). His papers, music and photographs are archived at the Special Collections, W.E.B. DuBois Library at the University of Massachusetts, Amherst. A Quaker, Salah-El's interests include helping other prisoners achieve the GED, composing music, and playing jazz saxophone.

DENNIS J. STEVENS currently teaches criminology at the University of North Carolina-Charlotte. He has previously taught at the University of Massachusetts-Boston and Salem State College, has worked at the University of Southern Mississippi as director of its Criminal Justice doctoral program. He holds the PhD from Loyola University of Chicago (1991). A prolific author, Stevens's recent books include *Community Corrections* (2006), *Police Officer Stress* (2008), *Media and Criminal Justice: CSI Effect* (2010), and *Wicked Women: A Journey of Super Predators* (2011). In addition to traditional teaching, Stevens has taught and counseled law enforcement and correctional personnel at law academies such as the North Carolina Justice Academy, and felons at various maximum-security penitentiaries. He has also led group crisis sessions and guided many sexually abused children and their families under the auspices of church-affiliated programs and national organizations.

NAME INDEX

SUBJECT INDEX

VIBS

The **Value Inquiry Book Series** is co-sponsored by:

Adler School of Professional Psychology
American Indian Philosophy Association
American Maritain Association
American Society for Value Inquiry
Association for Process Philosophy of Education
Canadian Society for Philosophical Practice
Center for Bioethics, University of Turku
Center for Professional and Applied Ethics, University of North Carolina at Charlotte
Central European Pragmatist Forum
Centre for Applied Ethics, Hong Kong Baptist University
Centre for Cultural Research, Aarhus University
Centre for Professional Ethics, University of Central Lancashire
Centre for the Study of Philosophy and Religion, University College of Cape Breton
Centro de Estudos em Filosofia Americana, Brazil
College of Education and Allied Professions, Bowling Green State University
College of Liberal Arts, Rochester Institute of Technology
Concerned Philosophers for Peace
Conference of Philosophical Societies
Department of Moral and Social Philosophy, University of Helsinki
Gannon University
Gilson Society
Haitian Studies Association
Ikeda University
Institute of Philosophy of the High Council of Scientific Research, Spain
International Academy of Philosophy of the Principality of Liechtenstein
International Association of Bioethics
International Center for the Arts, Humanities, and Value Inquiry
International Society for Universal Dialogue
Natural Law Society
Philosophical Society of Finland
Philosophy Born of Struggle Association
Philosophy Seminar, University of Mainz
Pragmatism Archive at The Oklahoma State University
R.S. Hartman Institute for Formal and Applied Axiology
Research Institute, Lakeridge Health Corporation
Russian Philosophical Society
Society for Existential Analysis
Society for Iberian and Latin-American Thought
Society for the Philosophic Study of Genocide and the Holocaust
Unit for Research in Cognitive Neuroscience, Autonomous University of Barcelona
Whitehead Research Project
Yves R. Simon Institute

Titles Published

Volumes 1 - 224 see www.rodopi.nl

226. Leonidas Donskis, Editor, *Niccolò Machiavelli: History, Power, and Virtue*. A volume in **Philosophy, Literature, and Politics**

227. Sanya Osha, *Postethnophilosophy*. A volume in **Social Philosophy**

228. Rosa M. Calcaterra, Editor, *New Perspectives on Pragmatism and Analytic Philosophy*. A volume in **Studies in Pragmatism and Values**

229. Danielle Poe, Editor, *Communities of Peace: Confronting Injustice and Creating Justice*. A volume in **Philosophy of Peace**

230. Thorsten Botz-Bornstein, Editor, *The Philosophy of Viagra: Bioethical Responses to the Viagrification of the Modern World*. A volume in **Philosophy of Sex and Love**

231. Carolyn Swanson, *Reburial of Nonexistents: Reconsidering the Meinong-Russell Debate*. A volume in **Central European Value Studies**

232. Adrianne Leigh McEvoy, Editor, *Sex, Love, and Friendship: Studies of the Society for the Philosophy of Sex and Love: 1993–2003*. A volume in **Histories and Addresses of Philosophical Societies**

233. Amihud Gilead, *The Privacy of the Psychical*. A volume in **Philosophy and Psychology**

234. Paul Kriese and Randall E. Osborne, Editors, *Social Justice, Poverty and Race: Normative and Empirical Points of View*. A volume in **Studies in Jurisprudence**

235. Hakam H. Al-Shawi, *Reconstructing Subjects: A Philosophical Critique of Psychotherapy*. A volume in **Philosophy and Psychology**

236. Maurice Hauriou, *Tradition in Social Science*. Translation from French with an Introduction by Christopher Berry Gray. A volume in **Studies in Jurisprudence**

237. Camila Loew, *The Memory of Pain: Women's Testimonies of the Holocaust.*. A volume in **Holocaust and Genocide Studies**

238. Stefano Franchi and Francesco Bianchini, Editors, *The Search for a Theory of Cognition: Early Mechanisms and New Ideas.* A volume in **Cognitive Science**

239. Michael H. Mitias, *Friendship: A Central Moral Value.* A volume in **Ethical Theory and Practice**

240. John Ryder and Radim Šíp, Editors, *Identity and Social Transformation, Central European Pragmatist Forum, Volume Five.* A volume in **Central European Value Studies**

241. William Sweet and Hendrik Hart, *Responses to the Enlightenment: An Exchange on Foundations, Faith, and Community.* A volume in **Philosophy and Religion**

242. Leonidas Donskis and J.D. Mininger, Editors, *Politics Otherwise: Shakespeare as Social and Political Critique.* A volume in **Philosophy, Literature, and Politics**

243. Hugh P. McDonald, *Speculative Evaluations: Essays on a Pluralistic Universe.* A volume in **Studies in Pragmatism and Values.**

244. Dorota Koczanowicz and Wojciech Małecki, Editors, *Shusterman's Pragmatism: Between Literature and Somaesthetics.* A volume in **Central European Value Studies**

245. Harry Lesser, Editor, *Justice for Older People,* A volume in **Values in Bioethics**

246. John G. McGraw, *Personality Disorders and States of Aloneness (Intimacy and Aloneness: A Multi-Volume Study in Philosophical Psychology, Volume Two),* A volume in **Philosophy and Psychology**

247. André Mineau, *SS Thinking and the Holocaust.* A volume in **Holocaust and Genocide Studies**

248. Yuval Lurie, *Wittgenstein on the Human Spirit.* A volume in **Philosophy, Literature, and Politics**

249. Andrew Fitz-Gibbon, *Love as a Guide to Morals*. A volume in **Ethical Theory and Practice**

250. Ronny Miron, *Karl Jaspers: From Selfhood to Being*. A volume in **Studies in Existentialism**

251. Necip Fikri Alican, *Rethinking Plato: A Cartesian Quest for the Real Plato*. A volume in **Philosophy, Literature, and Politics**

252. Leonidas Donskis, Editor, *Yet Another Europe after 1984: Rethinking Milan Kundera and the Idea of Central Europe*. A volume in **Philosophy, Literature, and Politics**

253. Michael Candelaria, *The Revolt of Unreason: Miguel de Unamuno and Antonio Caso on the Crisis of Modernity*. A volume in **Philosophy in Spain**

254. Paul Richard Blum, *Giordano Bruno: An Introduction*. A volume in **Values in Italian Philosophy**

255. Raja Halwani, Carol V. A. Quinn, and Andy Wible, Editors, *Queer Philosophy: Presentations of the Society for Lesbian and Gay Philosophy, 1998-2008*. A volume in **Histories and Addresses of Philosophical Societies**

256. Raymond Angelo Belliotti, *Shakespeare and Philosophy: Lust, Love, and Law*. A volume in **Philosophy, Literature, and Politics**

257. Jim Kanaris, Editor, *Polyphonic Thinking and the Divine*. A volume in **Philosophy and Religion**

258. Michael Krausz, *Oneness and the Displacement of Self: Dialogues on Self-Realization*. A volume in **Interpretation and Translation**

259. Raymond Angelo Belliotti, *Jesus or Nietzsche: How Should We Live Our Lives?* A volume in **Ethical Theory and Practice**

260. Giorgio A. Pinton, *The Conspiracy of the Prince of Macchia & G. B. Vico*. A volume in **Philosophy, Literature, and Politics**

261. Mechthild E. Nagel and Anthony J. Nocella II, Editors, *The End of Prisons: Reflections from the Decarceration Movement*. A volume in **Social Philosophy**

CPSIA information can be obtained at www.ICGtesting.com
Printed in the USA
BVOW031941090413

317743BV00001B/64/P

9 789042 036567